PRAISE FOR *GOING MAINSTREAM*

'With unparalleled insight and urgency, Ebner reveals the dangerous spread of extremist beliefs. This book is a must-read for anyone who wants to understand the terrifying new reality we face'
 – Eliot Higgins, author of *We Are Bellingcat*

'A sober and sobering read that helps disentangle an important though often misunderstood phenomenon'
 – Brendan Daly, *Sunday Business Post*

'A timely and frighteningly revealing book. It should be on the shelves of every Western spy agency working to defeat extremist ideologies'
 – Richard Kerbaj, author of *The Secret History of the Five Eyes*

'A haunting and essential account of how so many people around the world have embraced extreme ideas'
 – Cynthia Miller-Idriss, author of *Hate in the Homeland*

'Piercingly revelatory . . . a tour de force'
 – Carl Miller, author of *The Death of the Gods*

GOING MAINSTREAM

Why extreme ideas are spreading, and what we can do about it

Julia Ebner

ITHAKA

First published in the UK by Ithaka Press
An imprint of Black & White Publishing Group
An imprint of Bonnier Books UK
4th Floor, Victoria House,
Bloomsbury Square,
London, WC1B 4DA

Owned by Bonnier Books
Sveavägen 56, Stockholm, Sweden

Ebook – 978-1-80418-314-4
Paperback – 978-1-80418-378-6

All rights reserved. No part of the publication may be reproduced, stored in a retrieval system, transmitted or circulated in any form or by any means, electronic, mechanical, photocopying, recording or otherwise, without prior permission in writing of the publisher.

A CIP catalogue of this book is available from the British Library.

Typeset by IDSUK (Data Connection) Ltd
Printed and bound by Clays Ltd, Elcograf S.p.A.

1 3 5 7 9 10 8 6 4 2

Copyright © by Julia Ebner 2024

Julia Ebner has asserted their moral right to be identified as the author of this Work in accordance with the Copyright, Designs and Patents Act 1988.

Every reasonable effort has been made to trace copyright holders of material reproduced in this book, but if any have been inadvertently overlooked the publishers would be glad to hear from them.

Ithaka Press is an imprint of Bonnier Books UK
www.bonnierbooks.co.uk

CONTENTS

Preface — vii

Introduction — 1

ON MAINSTREAMING — 13
From *Going Dark* to *Going Mainstream*

CREATING SUBCULTURES — 19
Undercover with Incels

CULTIVATING NETWORKS — 47
Among Climate Change Deniers

BOOSTING ALT-MEDIA — 81
Inside White Lives Matter

PROVOKING BACKLASHES — 115
An Investigation of Transphobia

PERSUADING THE MASSES — 141
Inside the Anti-Vax Networks

WAGING PROXY WARS — 175
Russia's Battle Against Liberalism

WHAT CAN WE DO? — 201
Five Experts, Fifteen Solutions

Acknowledgements — 223
Notes — 225

PREFACE

When I first started researching extremist tendencies in 2015, we lived in a very different world. Back then, most government and security representatives I spoke to agreed with me on the dangers that could stem from political violence and terrorism. But few believed that the radical fringes of society would attain any real political relevance in their lifetime. They could plot attacks and pose a risk to national security, that much was clear. But how would they be able to mobilise masses behind their ideas?

The votes in favour of Brexit and Trump fundamentally changed this assessment. Still, most liberal-progressive policy makers I briefed were convinced that the outcomes of both the EU referendum and the 2016 US election were populist breakthroughs that happened under exceptional circumstances; political accidents that were unlikely to turn into a wider pattern. We would return to the old normal soon. But over the last few years, I have been able to observe – often in real-time from within radical movements – some of the most obscure ideas and extreme conspiracy myths making their way into popular consciousness.

The mainstreaming of these ideas has been fed by and in turn feeds a wider erosion of the political middle ground in recent decades. Confronted with heightened demand for drastic change, political parties have needed to reinvent themselves. In the UK and the US, the Tories and Republicans have eschewed caution in favour of populist nationalism, which has likewise been a rising force in the Australian Liberals. The dynamics in these English-speaking countries echo those in nations like Hungary, Poland and Austria, where parties that originally represented mainstream conservatism have gradually embraced radically illiberal, ultra-nationalist ideas. In other countries, centrist parties have responded to rising competition from the far-right by forming coalitions with the more extreme players. The election victories of the neo-fascist parties Sweden Democrats and Brothers of Italy in 2022 demonstrate the outright success of the radical right. By October 2023, the far-right German Alternative for Germany (AfD) and the Austrian Freedom Party are topping the polls. With both the U.S. elections and the EU elections being on the agenda for 2024, there is one question in particular that has become increasingly urgent: How precisely have the most radical fringes managed to conquer the political middle and influence once-centrist parties?[1]

The people I encountered in the field while researching this book were not all from the traditional far-right. Many of them came from left-wing or even apolitical backgrounds, some were just concerned citizens and parents. Historically, in Europe and North America, extremist movements have been defined by specific tactics, ideological traits, and hierarchical structures. But today we are faced with a new reality. Extremists hold blurred ideologies, form surprising coalitions and use loose post-organisational structures. This has made them less predictable than ever before.

In all my investigations for this book, I discovered a clear pattern to the mainstreaming process of radical ideas. Whether we look at incels, White Lives Matter activists or QAnon, these movements all started off as *fringe subcultures* that had little impact on the wider public discourse. It was when they began to create *powerful international networks* and managed to build their own *alternative media ecosystems* that they started to become influential. They gradually changed public attitudes and fuelled *a hostile societal backlash* against progressive movements. As the 'Overton Window', the window of acceptable discourse, moved in their favour, this paved the way for the *mass adoption of extreme ideas*. The last stage is characterised by violent escalations of liberal versus illiberal visions of the future, what I will call *proxy culture wars*.

As extreme voices grow louder in parliaments, street protests and online debates, our society is becoming increasingly fractured. We are seeing a rise of hyperpolarised communities along the dividing lines of racial justice, gender equality, queer rights, climate activism and vaccine acceptance. But today's polarisation is not just the product of competing ideologies. These conflicts are deeply entrenched in people's identities.[2] Opposing groups hold differing views not simply of the world, but of themselves.

Powerful identity dynamics are the main thread that runs through radicalised communities. Movements create a sense of exclusivity, which evokes a strong feeling of belonging. Sometimes, a group member's personal identity might become equivalent with their group identity. This phenomenon is called 'identity fusion',[3] and it can be triggered in extremist groups when members get into fights with political opponents, or when they perceive themselves as having their rights suppressed by the government. A fused identity based on powerful bonding experiences and a perceived existential threat from an outside enemy may be enough to lead to violence.[4]

Disasters, wars and uncertainty present unique opportunities to extreme movements. The constant crisis mode the world has been operating in over the last few years has given the far-right access to an audience that was previously beyond their reach. Since the outbreak of the pandemic, radical activists have exploited Covid-related grievances. Russian aggression in Ukraine has galvanised Europe's political fringes. Economic crisis – soaring inflation, house prices and energy costs – has added yet more variables to the unsolved equation of discontent.

The psychological side effects of these shared calamities have been deliberately weaponised. Some of the most effective groups have played on all these events and more to create hybrid philosophies. A growing coalition has emerged between a range of activists: climate change deniers, anti-vaxxers, anti-LGBTQ campaigners, anti-feminists, pro-Russia sympathisers, and white nationalists. Individuals mobilise based on their shared anti-elite discourse, a rhetoric of 'freedom' and divisive culture war arguments. Their lowest common denominator is a fundamental distrust in 'the establishment'.

Some of the world's most popular media personalities have begun to amplify extremist ideas. US podcast host Joe Rogan, who reaches an average of 11 million listeners per episode, has aired anti-vaccine conspiracy myths originating in some of the most radical corners on the Internet,[5] while television host Tucker Carlson has endorsed QAnon and the 'Great Replacement' myth. US rap star Kanye West, now called Ye, has shared anti-Semitic tropes with his 30 million followers and Big Brother celebrity Andrew Tate has gained billions of views on his violence-condoning misogynist TikTok videos.

The result of disinformation is often targeted hate and doxxing. The result of hate and doxxing is often physical violence. And disinformation and terrorism are closely intertwined: there have been over 50 criminal cases in the US where perpetrators of violent acts, threats of violence or allegations of assault quoted Trump as having inspired their offences.[6]

The wider effects on public discourse have been chilling. Many politicians, journalists, artists and activists have started to self-censor, some have even withdrawn from their vocation, in order to avoid hateful backlash. In theory, the enemies of progressive liberalism campaign in the name of free speech. In practice, they destroy open debate and suffocate those who hold different views. In theory, radically regressive movements quote their rights to justify provocative campaigns. In practice, they seek to undo the most fundamental human rights milestones: achieving legal, moral, and political equality of opportunity for people independent of their race, religion, gender and sexual orientation. In theory they say they want to protect their democratic rights. In practice, they destroy all trust in democracy.

The Edelman Trust Barometer 2022 found that society trust in politics, the media and science are at a historic low in the UK and many other liberal democratic countries. In the UK, US and Germany, less than half of the population trusts the country's institutions. According to the worldwide survey, concern about fake news is at an all-time high. Distrust is now the default emotion.[7] Who benefits from this severe crisis of confidence? The two winners share an interest in destabilising liberal democracies: foreign state actors and extreme movements.

In retrospect, Brexit and Trump were only the beginning of a new era. They set powerful precedents for a new communication strategy. One that is based on exacerbating societal tensions through strategic provocation, triggering powerful emotional reactions from potential voters as well as opponents, and undermining belief in institutions.

The peak of the pandemic may have ended some time ago, but it continues to leave a trace on our identities. The disruption of our normal lives and months in isolation have left deep traumata in our societies. Rising uncertainty, complexity and information overload in the news cycle left many of us with the very human urge to see patterns in what was happening in the world, a phenomenon psychologists call 'apophenia'. Ever since, extreme communities have been thriving.

'Sometimes I believe in as many as six impossible things before breakfast,' Lewis Carroll wrote in *Alice in Wonderland*. On a typical morning, before my first coffee, I come across six incredible conspiracy myths on the social media feeds of my avatar accounts. Sometimes they are as extreme as Covid vaccines having been designed by global reptilian elites, or transgender people being a gateway to transhumanism. Other times they are milder versions of infodemic mutations. Some memes and ideas die away over time without much impact. But on occasion, I have seen them spread to the mainstream, gain traction among millions of people, impact elections and incite violence. This book is about why this is happening, and how we can stop it.

Julia Ebner, London 2023

INTRODUCTION

Kevin: When are we storming Capitol Hill because I'm in.
Tony: Multiple Capitol buildings will be heated tomorrow, not just DC.

After months of election fraud allegations by former US President Donald Trump, in the first days of 2021 the conversations in the encrypted 4Deep News channel are loaded with emotion. In the pro-Trump chat group on the gaming app Discord, thousands of online activists are getting ready to take their anger to the real world. They compare hotels and travel arrangements, as if anticipating a holiday: 'Trump hotel has the best taco salads and chocolate chip cookies,' Kevin comments. Janet's travel costs have even been sponsored by the group.

Most self-declared patriots arrive in DC on January 5, the day before the US Capitol is stormed. For many activists from the chat group this is the first time they meet each other in real life. There is a sense of solidarity and invincibility among the passionate Trump fans, the 'deplorables'. Anything seems possible.

Jane: My whole hotel is full of Trump supporters. It's amazing!
Kevin: My hotel is a party
Jenn: Omg paradise hotel! Our hotel is full of patriots too

How many of them actually believe that the US election had been rigged? How many of them just want to feel part of something, to gather in person after the isolation of Covid? And how many just want to test the limits of the political establishment? It is hard to say.

Less than 24 hours later, members of the neo-fascist, misogynist movement Proud Boys are seen marching to the Capitol, promising: 'We're taking our country back.'[8] 'We fight like hell,' Trump is about to tell his supporters on the Ellipse. 'And if you don't fight like hell, you're not going to have a country anymore.' While Congress is certifying Joe Biden's victory in the 2020 presidential election, the crowd at the 'Stop the Steal' rally is growing. 'Fight for Trump! Fight For Trump! Fight for Trump,' the protesters chant, echoing his calls for battle.

'Fuck you traitors,' a man dressed in an army shirt with a red hat, sunglasses and a scruffy beard screams at police officers as they move through the crowds. 'You pieces of shit!' He turns to the camera of the Young Patriot Society's livestream: 'We won't use force. We won't use *lethal* force. We will use this force. God's force.' The man flexes his biceps. 'Look how scared they are. Look how many of us there are. We can easily take this place.' He sounds almost delirious: 'Fuck our job, fuck our homes, fuck everything else. We're gonna make a stand. Cause if we don't make a stand now we're gonna lose it all. We're gonna lose it all. Let 'em shoot us. Let 'em shoot us!'[9]

Lori: I'm at the Capitol
Lori: So I'm storming the Capitol
Tony: Motherfuckers, do it

At 12.53 p.m. the crowd is starting to march towards the police barriers. The Capitol police officers are massively outnumbered by thousands of Stop the Steal, QAnon, Kekistan and Confederate flags. People are beginning to break through the police patrol line. Some climb over the fences, cheered on by the rest.

Footage from the body cameras of the Capitol police shows the battle's frontline, with its exchanges of mace and baton blows.[10] The police are losing ground. Flags can be seen waving and jubilant cries heard as the first rioters reach the west steps to the Capitol. 'Fuck you, bitches,' one of them hisses. In the background the mob chants 'U-S-A!'[11]

It is 1.45 p.m. when a police officer declares that they have been attacked from multiple sides on the upper west deck and asks Military Personnel Divisions (MPD) to join them for reinforcement. 'Cruiser 50. We've lost the line. We've lost the line. All MPD, pull back!'[12] It is too late. More and more rioters are breaching the gates. They break the windows of the Capitol building with sticks and climb inside. Inside they kick the doors open and protestors stream in. 'This is our house,' they chant, as they flow past reception and towards the Senate Chamber. 'U-S-A. U-S-A. U-S-A.'

The Secret Service begins to evacuate former Vice President Mike Pence. One floor below him, rioters call to hang him and Nancy Pelosi, as they mill around in search of the Senate chamber.

Meanwhile, on the Internet the 4Deep News and God Emperor Trump chat groups are lighting up. Members at home watch the protesters' livestreams, euphoric. The line between banter and incitement to violence becomes very thin.

Lori:	Inside Capitol.
Will:	We have taken the Capitol?
Susan:	Welp the capitol has been breached and we are at war
Tony:	I thought they were going to catch Pelosi
Susan:	She ran so fucking fast
Kevin:	She gets the rope first

'Where are you Nancy?,' the rioters shout. They pound on every door, trying to find her. She has escaped just in time, but just a few metres away from the mob her staff hide under tables, barricaded in a conference room. As they hear the rioters breaking through the outer door of their hiding place, they fear for their lives.

Sam: ANOTHER DOOR JUST GOT OPENED TO THE CAPITOL

Rioters have breached the Capitol's eastern side door as well and are spreading throughout the building. Inside, Members of the House of Representatives are warned 'Folks have entered the Rotunda and are coming this way.' They are told to be ready to use gas masks and hide under their chairs. Democratic Congressman Eric Swalwell sends a text to his wife: 'I love you and the babies. Please hug them for me.'[13]

At the east door of the Rotunda the corridors are rammed. Amid tear gas, blows are exchanged, as both sides refuse to back down. It gets more and more chaotic by the minute. A man in a MAGA hat shouts 'We need fresh people!' A woman is screaming 'Stop it!'

Lori: There were dudes that got tear gassed, rinsed out their eyes, and went right back inside the Capitol haha.
Sam: Nice work

Officers and rioters in the frontlines now fear they could be crushed, squeezed to death by the sheer weight of the crowd. 'You see me. You go home. Go home,' one rioter shouts at a policeman who is screaming in pain.[14]

Several police officers who were on duty on 6 January 2021 came out of the Capitol deeply traumatised. Harry Dunn was one of them. He later told the BBC that he thought he was going to die. To him, the massive mob looked like zombies.

* * *

Watching events at the Capitol unfolding in real time via the hundreds of iPhone cameras livestreaming to libertarian social media platform Parler, a few people in the far-right Discord channels are not happy with the scenes they are seeing. But they seem to be in the minority.

> Cathy: Y'all are in favor of whats happening in the US Capitol?

Inside the Capitol building a rioter confronts an officer: 'Back off!' The officer looks intimidated but doesn't move. Some of the protesters who have made their way inside are scared too: 'We're trying to make a point but I don't wanna fight these guys', one says into the camera.[15]

Those who think things haven't gone far enough yet start to change their minds now. Rioters are smashing the windows of a locked door that leads to the Speaker's Lobby in front of the House chamber. They have spotted James McGovern, the House Rules Committee Chairman, trying to leave the House floor. 'Break it down, break it down!' the crowd encourages a rioter who smashes the glass of the door using a baton. Then another shouts 'He's got a gun.' A police officer is pointing a gun at the door. A woman ignores the warning. She jumps forward and climbs up on the door to get through the broken window. Then a shot is fired and Ashli Babbitt collapses on the floor, barely moving. Blood leaks from her mouth. She has been hit in the shoulder.[16]

'Move!' a voice is shouting. 'She needs fucking help!' Several police officers kneel next to the dying woman, trying to stop the bleeding. But Ashli Babbitt will only live for a few more hours. The officers carry her down the stairs, as the eyewitnesses and livestream watchers begin to grasp the severity of the situation. The ravaged floors of the Capitol are strewn with a mix of scattered documents, glass, rubbish and broken furniture. 'Murder the media' is written on one of its doors.

Ashli Babbitt passes away the same evening in Washington Hospital Center. She was a 35-year-old military veteran and QAnon believer from the San Diego area. Babbitt used to be a Barack Obama voter before registering as libertarian and then becoming a devoted Trump supporter and conspiracy theorist. QAnon followers believe that 'The Storm' is the day when Trump will expose the 'paedophile cabal of global elites' and restore America's true greatness. 'Nothing will stop us,' Babbitt had tweeted the day before. 'They can try and try and try but the storm is here and it is descending upon DC in less than 24 hours . . . dark to light!'

Emotions are running high in the far-right Discord groups. Babbitt is portrayed as a martyr who was unjustly killed. 'Justice for Ashli Babbitt' many users write. 'That building needs to be burned down,' Sam announces. Shortly after Ashli Babbitt's death Trump tweets: 'These are the things and events that happen when a sacred landslide election victory is so unceremoniously & viciously stripped away from the great patriots who have been badly & unfairly treated for so long. Go home with love & in peace. Remember this day forever!'

Some users in 4Deep News understand that the Capitol riots were wrong. But others immediately integrate the events into their wider conspiracy myths. In their minds, the riots were an inside plot orchestrated by the FBI, or a false-flag stunt led by Antifa to set them up for police prosecution and public scrutiny. Even members of the Discord channel notice the inconsistency here. One notes: 'You say "we just stormed the capitol" but you've also said you think it's antifa in trump gear?'

* * *

The events of January 6 show how extreme ideas have gone mainstream. The Americans who were arrested in connection with the Capitol insurrection were not your typical far-right extremist mob. An analysis by researchers at the Chicago Project on Security and Threats found that of the 716 individuals charged with illegally entering the Capitol grounds on January 6 2021, 90 per cent had no obvious affiliation to the far-right militias or right-wing extremist groups such as Proud Boys, Oath Keepers, Three Percenters or Aryan Brotherhood.[17]

'It's a broader mass movement with violence at its core,' Robert Pape, who led the research project, noted. The mob was dominated by business owners and white-collar professionals such as doctors, lawyers, engineers and CEOs. Only 7 per cent of the arrested were unemployed.[18] Babbit was by far not the only woman who participated in the Capitol siege. A year after the January 6 events, 102 women had been arrested for related crimes. Female rioters came from 28 US States and were on average 44 years old, five years older than their male counterparts.[19]

Despite the 'mainstream' profile of the rioters, the willingness to engage in violence was high. Thirty per cent of those arrested were charged with actual or threatened physical violence.[20] What drives someone to risk losing everything, especially when you have a decent job and loving family to return home to?

Guy Reffitt was one of the rioters who was willing to resort to violence. Guy was found guilty of five charges, including obstruction of justice and unlawful possession and transportation of firearms with the intent to use them.[21] In live footage from the riots, the 48-year-old Texan man wore a helmet and what appeared to be a bulletproof vest. His own son Jackson Reffitt reported him to the FBI. Several weeks before the Capitol Insurrection Jackson called domestic security and told them he was worried because his father was talking about doing 'something big'.[22] During the riots Jackson confirmed to the FBI that his father was among the mob storming the Capitol.

When Jackson's dad returned home, he warned the family: 'If you're a traitor, you get shot.' So the 19-year-old went into hiding. 'I took it as a threat personally,' Jackson explained. His mother called him 'the Gestapo'. 'I don't want to be afraid for my life, and I don't think I will be, because I know that I have so many people backing me,' Jackson said.[23] He was still in disbelief about his own father's transition. 'He used to be one of the best dads ever. He made me the man I am today. He taught me to be honest, not to steal, all that cliché stuff. I believe he brought me up to do what I did.'[24]

The insurrection of January 6 did not come out of nowhere. It was the culmination of weeks, months or even years of deepening anti-democratic resentment in far-right, pro-Trump and conspiracy theory networks. Many self-declared patriots voiced radical dreams of taking over the Capitol as early as 2019: 'They'll slice my face and my eye just before I behead the state DNC chairman on top of the state capitol building,' Jonny posted into the group God Emperor Trump on Discord. His account got deleted soon afterwards. 'Storm the fucking capitol building,' Sam told his Discord friends on 3 December 2020. 'Well it's probably better to take every capitol not just DC,' Martin commented on Christmas Eve 2020.

In the days following the riots, the atmosphere stayed tense.

Tim: How are we holding them accountable? They have walked all over our rights, stolen our elections, and

> then laughed in our faces while they set up the storming of the capitol building.
>
> Kevin: The entire capitol bldg should be blown up right now
> Tim: We need to let everyone know they need to head to their Capitol and from there leaders will take charge.
> Sam: You should already be planning the trip to your Capitol. We all should . . . I am gathering ppl as we speak.
> Tim: We start by taking every capitol . . . we declare our states conservative and all others must leave.

Many users agreed. Some even called for a civil war:

> Kevin: War!!! War!!!War!! No more talk we take it back I'll be leaving for my capitol tonight hope you all choose to stand as well
> Sam: Go to war!
> Tim: Imminent war
> Susan: Time for war
> Tony: Civil war!

Leading political scientists have asked whether the US might be at the brink of a civil war. Barbara Walter – one of the world's top experts on civil war who has studied the wars in Myanmar, Northern Ireland, Rwanda, Sri Lanka, Syria, and Yugoslavia – found that the US showed all the signs that lead up to violent conflict.[25] In a follow-up study to the Capitol insurrection, the research team at the Chicago Project on Security and Threats asked a nationally representative sample of Americans if they endorsed the use of force to restore Trump to the White House. Nine per cent expressed insurrectionist sentiments and supported the use of political violence. This would equal 23 million people in the US.[26]

From the Storming of the Bastille in 1789 to the takeover of the Winter Palace in St Petersburg in 1917, violent uprisings against government institutions are characteristic of revolution. But unlike the Bastille and the Winter Palace, where people were fighting to overthrow dictatorships, the mob of January 6 was trying to remove a democratically elected government. Bob, a far-right military veteran who still works on military bases, wrote in the closed group: 'The next time people storm the Capitol it will be hundreds of thousands of people not a few idiots.'

Bob is probably right about one thing: the extreme ideas that drove the insurrection will outlive the Trump era. 'When will people learn that it wasn't about Trump?' Serenity commented. 'Trump started a movement and he was the face of it. The movement isn't going anywhere.'

Seeing pictures of a topless, tattooed man wearing a furry horned headdress amid the rioters, one could easily mistake the insurrectionists for a bunch of absurd trolls who accidentally went one step too far. But when we look closely, it becomes all too obvious that we have to take conspiracy myths such as the Great Replacement and QAnon seriously: surveys show that they were the two key ideological backbones among Americans who are willing to use violent force.[27]

The US is not the only Western democracy at risk of violent revolution and civil war. Both ideas have gained millions of followers across North America, the UK, Europe, and Australia over the past few years. A few months before the Capitol Insurrection, a mix of far-right extremists, QAnon-inspired conspiracy theorists and 'Reichsbürgers' (sovereign citizens who deny the legitimacy of the modern German state and believe in the pre-World War I borders of the German Empire) had attempted to storm the German Reichstag. Almost a year after the US Capitol riots, anti-vaxxers waving QAnon and pro-Trump flags tried to storm New Zealand's parliament.[28] In December 2022 the German police launched its largest anti-terror operation in modern history, preventing a far-right plot to violently overthrow the state. The terror network included a former MP of the far-right populist party Alternative for Germany (AfD), a 72-year-old aristocrat and former elite soldiers.[29]

Back in the US, the violent legacy of the Capitol riot has lived on. On 28 October 2022 Paul Pelosi went to bed in his San Francisco home with no idea what was about to happen. In the middle of the night a man appeared in front of him, armed with a hammer. 'Where is Nancy?' the intruder asked repeatedly, an echo of the Capitol rioters' chants. But Paul Pelosi's wife was in Washington DC, accompanied by her security guard. The alleged attacker David DePape said in court he believed there was 'evil in Washington'. He wanted to tie up Paul Pelosi and wait until his wife returned, but instead got into a fight with the 82-year-old man, hitting him on the head with the hammer and seriously injuring him – Pelosi later had to undergo surgery to repair his fractured skull and serious injuries to his right arm and hands.

DePape called his attack a 'suicide mission' with the goal of kidnapping and torturing Nancy Pelosi. He had wanted to break her kneecaps, so she would have to go to parliament in a wheelchair. Other politicians had featured on his 'hit list' too.[30] DePape turned out to be a QAnon adherent who believed in election fraud narratives, underground child trafficking networks run by the elites and deadly Covid vaccines.

Extreme ideas have conquered the mainstream and they are not confined to the US. How did liberal democratic societies end up here? Why have they become increasingly volatile? What are the human drivers that make anyone potentially prone to radicalisation and polarisation? And what can be done to prevent our democracies from falling apart?

ON MAINSTREAMING

I am Claire Lafeuille. I am a French-British citizen journalist and mother of two toddlers. Before becoming self-employed, I studied marketing and worked in fashion. My social media handles show that I'm passionate about free speech and my website focuses on controversial topics such as race, religion, gender and climate change. Where do I stand? I don't give away too much at first sight, but if you look closely you will understand that I am opposed to Black Lives Matter, climate change action and Covid vaccines.

I am Alex Williamson. I am an unemployed white American man who is fed up with feminism. I'm in my late twenties and unhappily single. I have been looking for a girlfriend, or at least a sexual partner, for over ten years. My two brothers are both married and I'm desperately trying to understand what I'm doing wrong. In lockdown I put on an additional 20kg and started playing video games again, just like when I was a teenager. That's when I joined the misogynist incel community. I have no interest in politics really. All I want is distraction from my frustrations with women, and an antidote to my fear of rejection.

I am Maria Petrova, but you can call me Mary. I am a philosophy student from Bavaria with Russian heritage. My friends and I have taken a strong pro-Russia stance in the Ukraine war. I no longer trust the German media or the government that claims to represent me. I lost a few friends over Ukraine-related debates. But luckily German QAnon and anti-vaxxer groups on

Telegram have filled my social vacuum. Not a day passes when I don't chat to them or join them for a local protest.

I am Julia Ebner. This *is* me. I am an Austrian researcher at the London-based Institute for Strategic Dialogue and the Centre for the Study of Social Cohesion at Oxford University, and as part of my work I create aliases to infiltrate movements that I wouldn't be able to join using my real identity. I have always been fascinated by how radical subcultures gain influence and power. Over the last few years, I have consulted for the United Nations, NATO, the World Bank, and various European and American security services. My research tells me that the coming decade will bring one major threat: the mainstreaming of extreme ideas.

Going undercover takes time, effort and imagination. First, you have to build a story around your avatar identity. The story is not just about who you are today, but also how you got there and who you want to be in the future. Then you have to internalise that story to appear credible and stay in character. And finally, empathy is needed to start engaging with people who hold radically opposed views to yours.

I believe in science, detest racism, and define myself as a feminist. But for this book I met with anti-feminists, racists, climate change deniers and conspiracy theorists. Using undercover identities I was 'recruited' into networks of white supremacists, joined the women-hating incel community and interviewed members of the international conspiracy movement QAnon. I wanted to see what the radical fringe looks like today, because it is their ideas that are slowly taking over the middle ground. What are extremists' mainstreaming tactics? Who is most susceptible to their extreme ideas and why? How have they hijacked the debate?

Over the course of the last decade, I have watched many obscure, initially insignificant movements grow into potent agents of political, societal and cultural change. Who would have thought that QAnon would one day attract millions of people worldwide, find political representation and sway the outcomes of national elections? When I first joined them in 2017, they counted no more than a few thousand members, mostly based in the US. Likewise, youth-centred white identity movements such as White Lives Matter and the misogynist subculture of 'the manosphere' were still in their infancy. Today they are influencing politics, changing cultural codes and reframing our language. Their campaigns have helped to make words like 'feminism', 'diversity' and 'globalism' more controversial, while they have hijacked terms like 'freedom', 'democracy' and 'human rights' to fit their own purposes.

As a society we have a relatively good understanding of what the radicalisation process looks like. There have been many books about how vulnerable individuals get caught up in violent extremist and terrorist movements. But what happens when we all become vulnerable and ready for radical change, in times of crisis? Since I started working in the field of counter-terrorism in 2015, we have seen an acceleration of precisely the political and societal changes that terrorists seek to create. We have witnessed liberal democracies tearing themselves apart along various axes, social progress going into reverse, and democracy itself being delegitimised.

How many of you reading this book have lost a friend or fallen out with a family member over Brexit? How many have had debates over vaccines? Feminism? Climate change? Transgender rights? The Ukraine war? Studies show that most people have had heated arguments with friends or family over at least one of these topics. More than one in twelve Britons have stopped speaking to a friend because of a Brexit-related dispute. Almost a quarter have had emotional debates with family members. Five per cent have experienced threats of physical violence from strangers.[31] Brexit was one example of a binary debate that was bound inextricably to identity conflicts between two opposed groups: you did not just choose to leave or stay in the EU, you were a Leaver or a Remainer. It seemed as though there was no middle ground.

We are in a decade of mainstreamed radicalism and hyper-polarisation. The 2020s thus far have already been marked by rapidly widening divisions along the frontiers of racial justice, gender equality, queer rights, climate change action, and vaccine acceptance. Across the world, Black Lives Matter protests have been met with racist violence from White Lives Matter activists. Anti-feminists have launched intimidation campaigns against women, and queer rights activists have been attacked by anti-LGBTQ campaigners. In 2021, a member of the violent misogynist incel community shot dead five people in Plymouth, while a terror attack in 2022 at an LGBTQ club in Bratislava killed two people.[32] The UK saw a 56 per cent increase in hate crimes against transgender people between 2021 and 2022, and an 800 per cent increase in the past decade.[33] Climate change deniers have launched disinformation campaigns against environmental movements, and anti-vax conspiracy theorists have staged assaults on scientific institutions. A Covid denier linked to QAnon fatally shot a petrol station cashier in Germany after an argument about a face mask, and a Californian QAnon adherent killed his two young children because he believed they would turn into lizards.[34]

Extreme ideas are no longer confined to dark corners of the Internet or secret meet-ups. They echo through parliaments and are heard at mass street protests. What they all have in common is a feeling of powerlessness and disenfranchisement. We can observe how deep frustration with the status quo translates into toxic anti-democracy activities such as the US Capitol riots and attempts to storm the German Reichstag and New Zealand parliament.

Violent assaults on local politicians and journalists have recently hit record highs in many Western countries. The near-deadly attack on Paul Pelosi is just one example of the violence that politicians and their families are exposed to.[35] The past few years have brought an accumulation of far-right-inspired assassinations of local politicians who stood up for refugees, feminism and LGBTQ rights: anti-Brexit Labour MP Jo Cox, the Polish mayor of Gdansk, Paweł Adamowicz, and mayor of the German city of Kassel, Walter Lübcke.

Meanwhile, radical online subcultures have inspired gamified terrorist attacks against minorities with the goal of sparking global war. The Christchurch shooter who murdered over 50 people in his attack at two mosques in New Zealand in 2019 was the first terrorist to make his hateful attack appear like a video game. He livestreamed the assault from a first-person shooter angle and used gaming vocabulary in his manifesto. As intended by the attacker, his shooting set off an online competition to receive higher 'scores', in other words to kill more people, and was followed by a series of lethal far-right copycat attacks that also used gamification.

My last book, *Going Dark*, used a series of field reports to trace pathways of radicalisation towards violence and terrorism. But terrorists are just the most acute examples of the wider conflicts of their time. Here, I will investigate identity battles that are raging closer to home and how our everyday lives are now influenced by fringe beliefs. To do this, I want to speak directly to the people who are at the forefront of the increasingly hostile culture wars. My avatars Claire, Alex and Mary, along with my real self, will meet a range of radical activists from across the globe, from the UK and US to the furthest reaches of the Dark Net.

I am convinced that we have to pay attention to the human sides of all activists, no matter how bizarre or counter-factual their ideas. Of course, it's not easy to calmly listen when someone tells you the inhabitants of Buckingham Palace are reptiles who drink the blood of children to stay young. Researching this book, I sometimes wasn't sure if I should laugh or cry. I often felt repulsed when listening to hateful rants from incels or white supremacists. One man told me he wanted to take revenge on women by raping and murdering them, another one said he would like to see all Jews dead. But even the most disturbing individuals I encountered have stories that are worth listening to. Understanding the identity crises that lie behind extreme ideologies is crucial, particularly when political opponents increasingly fail to treat each other as fellow human beings.

Ultimately, what worries me most in my undercover work is not the increase in terrorism and hate crimes. Less obvious but even more chilling are the long-term effects on the pillars of democracy. Looking at cases of mass radicalisation, I repeatedly ask myself what we can expect from the future: less trust in key democratic institutions? More tribalistic elections? A higher willingness to give up on universal human rights to protect our in-group? With the challenges of global pandemics, the resumption of war in Europe and spiralling technological change, we need to prepare our democratic institutions for a seismic shift in our identities. Otherwise, we are looking at an escalation of ongoing identity conflicts towards violence, terrorism and war.

CREATING SUBCULTURES

In the beginning was a deviant subculture.

My heart races as I slam my laptop shut and tuck it away in the back of my wardrobe. Hidden behind my socks, I wouldn't have to look at it for at least a few hours. I try to forget the menacing photos of me and a graveyard that an anonymous person on Twitter has just sent me. Not that this is unusual. It's just the latest in a series of threatening messages I have received after speaking publicly about the rise of anti-feminism.

For women in public-facing professions in the 2020s there is no escape from online harassment. A 2021 UN survey of 901 female journalists from 125 countries found that almost three quarters of the respondents experienced online abuse of some sort. One quarter received sexual threats and death threats. Other frequent incidents include leaked private data, harassment of the victims' families and targeted hacking attacks.[36]

Over the past decade, anti-feminist hate has gone mainstream. I want to understand why. The best starting place is one of the most radical subcultures on the Internet: incels. Short for Involuntary Celibates, the term incel was originally coined in the late 1990s by a young woman called Alana, who created it as a self-help forum for lonely people who were unable to find love or intimacy. But over the years, major parts of the incel community have radicalised towards violent misogyny. Today their online forums have some tens of thousands of members worldwide and are the wellspring for many of the misogynist slurs and conspiracy myths found in hate campaigns against female activists, influencers and political leaders.

I am about to join the incels on their two biggest forums Incels.is and Incels.net, as well as in more intimate groups on the encrypted messaging apps Telegram and Discord. To join any incel community you first have to understand their dos and don'ts. Although most groups were founded with the intention of giving a home to people who felt they didn't fit into society, their forums have ironically become some of the most exclusive places you can find online.

Rule 1: Most misogynists don't want to speak to women. I think it's best to log on with a male account.

> Hi, I am Alex. I'm in my mid-twenties and spent the last 10 years looking for a girlfriend. I just want a normal girl, not even having high expectations at this point. Still no success, no matter what I do. I have two older brothers who are better looking than me and happily married by now. I gained 20kg during the lockdowns in 2020 and 2021 and have given up all hope of finding a romantic or sexual partner.

I am right to have chosen a male identity. As I learned later, women are 'banned on sight, no exceptions' There have been several attempts to legitimise female incels, so-called 'femcels', but the forum hosts are generally against admitting women. Gay and transgender people are not welcome.

Rule 2: You have to be a romance nihilist. As part of my application, I have to indicate whether Alex is 'bluepilled', 'redpilled' or 'blackpilled':

> *Bluepill* is the belief that couple matching is based on personal compatibility and genetic flaws are redeemable, if

you are kind and respectful towards women. Genetic flaws in men would include being short, having an asymmetrical face, feminine features, a disappearing hairline or oversized ears . . .

Redpill is the theory that people universally follow naturally predetermined laws: all women go for the most 'alpha' men (aggressive, dominant, physically strong, influential, wealthy, powerful etc.). The only way to compensate for poor genes is by becoming an alpha.

Blackpill is the idea that socially acquired status does not outweigh biological status and women can only be truly attracted to men with superior genes.

I select 'blackpilled', which for the moderators is the only correct answer. 'Welcome. This is a forum for people who have trouble finding a significant other.'

If you are not 'unpopular' enough, you are most likely not going to be accepted. For example, a man who writes that he only gets interest from women who are overweight and much older than him is immediately called out as a 'fakecel'. A true incel never gets any matches or sexual interest from anyone, according to the moderators. Most incels in the group claim they have already tried getting a haircut and buying some fashionable clothes, but that it didn't help.

Rule 3: You have to despise women, especially feminists. You also have to despise yourself. To the question 'Why are you guys incels?' the standard response is: 'Because of the feminist yoke, and poor genetics.'

'Anything that doesn't involve females is good,' writes Steve from Finland. The incels I encounter use profile taglines such as 'General of the Incels War', 'Breast Cancer Enthusiast' or

'Nuke This Gay Earth'. I decide to go for 'anti-Alpha male looking for blackpilled distraction'. Like many incels, the character I created suffers from deeply ingrained fears of rejection, humiliation and loss of status.

The incel community has been growing rapidly over the last few years,[37] and it is much more diverse than I had expected, attracting men of widely differing demographic, ethnic and religious backgrounds.[38] They also have varying educational levels. Steve, for example, has a Master's degree in accounting. Others are truck drivers or work in supermarkets stacking shelves. Many incels are in their late twenties, unemployed and still living with their parents. Some are frustrated with their job prospects: 'College degrees are mostly worthless, this current economy is hopeless.' Others are convinced their appearance is responsible for their failure to find work. A rare note of professional optimism comes from the truckers: 'The best career opportunity I can think of for a short and ugly man is a trucker. Trucking is an unintentional refuge from heightism and lookism.'

While their demographics vary, a lack of social skills and self-confidence are common characteristics of most incels. One writes: 'I have trouble understanding human emotion and social cues but I don't really care. I enjoy wasting my time playing video games and taking online IQ tests.' The forum hosts admit that 'some incels also struggle with mental illnesses, disabilities and other health conditions'.

* * *

'Rate me and give me tips,' Allan writes, sharing a picture of his face. He gets the following replies:
'0.'
'It's over.'
'Get your ptosis fixed. Makes you look extremely low IQ.'

'Bro I don't even know at this point.'

Incel culture is marked by a pathological focus on 'lookism': prejudice and discrimination based on physical appearance. Lookism.net and Looksmax.org are forums where some incels introduce themselves with openings such as 'I'm a rapist' or 'Hi, I'm an autistic psychopath.' Members can post pictures here and get rated by others on a scale of 0 to 10. They then receive detailed tips on how to improve their appearance.

Have you ever asked yourself what a masculine-shaped head or seductive male eyes should ideally look like? I haven't. But according to incels, there are very clear male beauty standards: wide cheek bones, hunter eyes, thick eyebrows, a square chin, a symmetric nose, rugged jawline and a lean body. Handsome boys with high ratings are called 'Chads', attractive girls are referred to as 'Stacys'.

One of the community's 101 teachings is the 80/20 rule: the hypothesis that '80 per cent of the most attractive women go for 20 per cent of the genetically superior men'. This idea has inspired a strong culture of 'looksmaxxing', essentially a quest for visual self-improvement that stretches from 'softmaxxing' to 'hardmaxxing'. Softmaxxing includes changes in style, haircuts, grooming, skin products and workouts. Incels claim that most women engage in softmaxxing from their teenage years by applying make-up, wearing favourable clothing and introducing hair and skin routines in their lives. Some incels go shockingly far in their attempts to climb up the 'looksladder' and ascend from a low sexual score to a higher rating. Hardmaxxing may involve taking anabolic steroids, or undergoing plastic surgery including jaw fillers, chin augmentation, rhinoplasty and cheekbone surgeries as well as penis stretching, skull implants, nostril shrinking and ear size reduction. To be honest, until I discovered the world of incels I didn't even know all these surgeries existed.

It's not just about looks, though. Of course, incels' problems go much deeper: 'It's the constant rejection I've faced that is really discouraging,' writes one user. 'This is why whenever I try and message someone new, my hands shake so bad that I drop my phone or go all over on the keyboard. At least with the looksmaxxing I can somewhat counteract my emotional/ mental state a little bit.' Some incels feel so uncomfortable with their looks that they claim to not have left the house in years.

After spending some time in the looksmaxxing forums, it is hard not to start feeling insecure. I can watch users getting less and less happy with themselves. The criticism is relentless, and even when you fulfil all criteria, some forum members still find a reason to give you a low rating. One fairly good-looking man who shares his profile picture gets the following reply: 'I think you look decent, but it looks like you have a high trust face even with chad features. Maybe it's the lack of hunter eyes but I see the pain in your eyes and you look uncomfortable.'

Their beliefs might be extreme, but incels aren't just inventing this stuff. Studies show that lookism is real and there may be universal principles of attractiveness. People who are considered physically less appealing according to contemporary beauty standards are discriminated against in many day-to-day situations.[39] Research shows that people who are perceived as less pretty get paid less and are less likely to get a job.[40] They are more likely to be convicted in court than people who are seen as good-looking. The more attractive the criminal, the lower the sentence and vice versa.[41]

Some incels don't think it's worth trying to improve their appearance. Allan is one of the users who has given up on looksmaxxing. He is in his mid-twenties and feels that his body is a prison from which there is no escape. 'Makes me sick our ancestors didn't do eugenics,' he writes in a closed incels thread. 'Women with good genetics and good family lines of genes should have been forced to become breeders having like 8 children. Women with health problems and/or bad family lines genetically should have had their tubes tied.' He also believes that unhealthy babies 'should have been eliminated'.

It is not unusual for incels to become so depressed, lonely and hopeless that they turn to suicide as a solution. 'I really feel like I should just kill myself,' Allan types. 'One of my biggest fantasies in life is killing myself and then watching my family as a ghost and being vindicated by the fact that my death meant absolutely nothing to them and I was nothing other than a liability. I actually want to see how their lives would be better if I was dead.' In incel language he is someone who has decided to LDAR (Lay Down and Rot).

I read Allan's comment and sit back, trying to think of something to cheer him up. But before I can reply the comments from other users start rolling in, sending shivers down my spine. 'A Practical Guide to Suicide', 'Making Peace with Dying', 'How to Hang Yourself', 'Painless Drowning' and 'Two Knot and Bag Method' are all suggestions fellow incels send to Allan, encouraging him to go ahead and commit suicide.

Despair is widespread in the forum, but for other users it comes with a hefty dose of rage. As one user called Steve says, 'I would only kill myself after getting revenge on society.' Wherever I look, hatred of feminism and women is pervasive. Women are seen as robot-like creatures, as 'femoids' ('foids' for short), who can only be tamed with violence. Some users refer to them as 'toilets' or 'holes'. The objectification of women strips them of their humanity and makes them more legitimate targets for violence. Steve writes: 'Low SMV [sexual market value] males don't have any other way of using power than murder or rape. That's the only true ascension. Strip a foid from its power with violent force. Then society will care.'

Both Allan and Steve are convinced that men are the victims of an increasingly female dominated society. Allan writes:

'Women have lives that are 10x better.' Steve agrees: 'It won't be long until the next generations see how bad unattractive men get it.' They blame feminists and powerful women for their own unhappiness. 'The lies of feminism made you an incel, they deserve only retaliation!' The incels incite each other to more and more radical views. But the longer I observe them the clearer it is that their misogyny and violent fantasies stem from self-loathing and self-pity.

* * *

On 12 August 2021, the 22-year-old British apprentice crane operator Jake Davison shot dead five people, including his own mother and a three-year-old girl, in Plymouth before killing himself. It was Britain's worst mass shooting in more than a decade. Investigations found that Davison was inspired by incel ideology and referenced 'inceldom' and 'blackpilling' in videos that he uploaded to YouTube under the alias 'Professor Waffle'. He was also a Trump fan and a supporter of the UK Libertarian party.

Deeply misogynist conversations of the kind I witnessed online have given rise to a spate of incel-inspired hate crimes and terror attacks in recent years. But ideology is never the only driver of violence. Terrorism usually happens when radical ideas meet personal grievances. Davison was filled with hatred for his mother, and in extension all 'single mums'. The fear that he had missed out on sexual and romantic experiences all his life had turned into deep resentment. He first blamed himself: 'I'm still a virgin, fat, ugly, whatever you want to call it,' he said in one YouTube video. Then he re-directed his hatred at women. In one of his last online exchanges with a female teenager he wrote that 'women are arrogant and entitled beyond belief'.

Like so many others, Jake Davison was a deeply lonely man who went on incel forums to find a new family of virtual friends.

But, of course, incels could never fill that vacuum. Extremist forums create an illusion of intimate bonds and evoke kinship feelings between their members. But unlike real friendships, these relationships hardly ever progress from temporary, anonymous and uncommitted interactions to something more sustained and tangible. Instead of finding a stable form of love and belonging, users end up spending their late nights and weekends surrounded by other nihilists, which accelerates existing mental health struggles like depression and anxiety. You can observe this downward spiral in incel chat rooms. 'Now I'm so beaten down, and defeated by fucking life,' Davison said in one of his last YouTube videos. 'That drive I once had has gone'. His self-loathing had transformed into hatred of others, channelling his loss of perspective into one last act of rebellion.

The Plymouth shooting was just the latest in a years-long series of incel-inspired attacks, some thwarted and some successful. Multiple related arrests in Scotland and England preceded the attack.[42] In 2018, the young Canadian Alek Minassian killed ten people and injured sixteen others by ramming (mostly female) pedestrians in a busy street in Toronto. He was radicalised in online incel forums and wanted to impress fellow users with a high death count. Minassian told his psychologist that he felt 'very happy and excited' that people were talking about what he had done. He wanted to reach a world record. If he killed 100 people, he claimed, he would feature at the top of an online leader board of mass killers that he admired.[43]

The most popular incels hero is the misogynist terrorist Elliot Rodger, the inspiration for many more recent attackers. 'Go ER' is still used as an insider code to call for violent terrorist attacks, in reference to the initials of Elliot Rodger. Rodger carried out a series of attacks in 2014, killing six people in Isla Vista, California. He was 22 years old and a virgin. He had never kissed a girl and felt tortured by the thought of rejection. 'Girls gave their affection and sex and love to other men but never to me,' he said in a YouTube video before launching his attack.[44] 'All I've ever wanted is to love you and to be loved by you. (. . .) If I can't have you, girls, I will destroy you.' He laughed out loud before continuing: 'You denied me a happy life, and in turn I will deny all of you life. It's only fair.' His manifesto reveals a similar autobiography to Jake Davison's: a divorced family, a fundamental lack of trust in the world and a constant feeling of personal failure.

Male supremacy is often overlooked in discussions of far-right terrorists: from the Norwegian anti-Muslim extremist Anders Breivik to the German attackers behind the shootings in Halle and Hanau in 2019.[45] In his manifesto, Breivik accused feminists of waging 'war against boys', oppressing women and causing low birth rates among whites. Meanwhile, the Hanau attacker used incel references in his manifesto, and on the day of the attack the Halle shooter listened to a song that has been dubbed the incel anthem. The lyrics include lines such as: 'Hoes suck my dick while I run over pedestrians' and 'ride my dick, I cum inside while I do a homicide'.[46] To my shock, the song by Toby Green under the pseudonym Egg White is still available on Soundcloud, despite glorifying terrorism.

Within the incel community, Egg White is an 'incelebrity'. Toby adopted his pseudonym in reference to the nickname his school bullies gave him, making fun of the shape of his head: 'Eggman'. Egg White's most popular video from 2015 called 'Take the Black Pill' is still live on YouTube with over 600,000 views. In it, he tells his fellow incel viewers that they are probably 'f*cked for life' because 'women have their sights on genetically superior males'. Commenters beneath the video have glorified him as 'the BIGGEST pioneer of the blackpill' and 'a prophet'. According to the incel's Wikipedia page 'Incel.wiki', many incels wanted to nominate Egg White as their official leader – but he declined.

Misogyny and far-right racist ideologies are connected via white male victimhood narratives. When anti-feminist conspiracy myths meet severe mental illness they can spill over into even more outlandish belief systems, such as politicised Satanism. In 2020, the eighteen-year-old teenager Danyal Hussein stabbed to death two sisters in north London in what he believed was a demonic pact with Lucifuge Rofocale, head of government in Hell. In a handwritten contract, Hussein promised to 'perform a minimum of six sacrifices every six months for as long as I am free and physically capable'. The idea was that he should 'sacrifice only women' in order to become 'more attractive to women romantically'.[47]

Incel-inspired terrorism has effectively publicised misogynist online communities. The aftermath of the Plymouth attack illustrated this. A web traffic analysis by *The Times* and the Centre for Countering Digital Hate (CCDH) showed that the number of UK visits to the three largest incel forums increased more than fivefold between March and November 2021. In just nine months web traffic to these websites grew from 114,420 monthly visits to 638,505 in November.[48]

Terrorism is the tip of a largely invisible iceberg, one that recent events have added to. A recent study by the Centre for Countering Digital Hate revealed that rape fantasies are being shared every 29 minutes in incel forums.[49] More than half of incels furthermore supported paedophilia and the sexualisation of minors.[50] Toxic narratives about women, feminism and progressive gender roles are not limited to radical forums. Researchers have used linguistic analysis to show that incels and users on mainstream pornography websites speak the same language of misogyny.[51] For example, dehumanising women by describing them as *animals, beasts, creatures* or *femoids* appears in both incels and porn forums. An underlying idea found in both communities is that men are entitled to sexual services by women who are degraded and given the status of objects or animals. Women who do not comply with patriarchal standards or who highlight their sexual freedoms are targeted with hate. A similar parallel can be observed between incels and prostitution forums. Men who buy women's sex tend to be abusive towards women who refuse their requests or set boundaries for themselves. Both incels and prostitution clients punish women who say 'no'.

During the pandemic, male supremacist movements gained ground online and expanded their reach to Europe.[52] A steep rise in sexualised threats and violence against female journalists, authors, politicians and activists has resulted, and femicides have increased globally over the past few years.[53] Today, male violence is a leading cause of premature death among women. Most femicide victims are killed by their former or current partners, with separation being a key trigger. During the lockdowns there was a sharp increase in domestic violence, but the number of femicides in the UK fell. It then dramatically increased again in 2021 when the lockdowns were eased. According to the Counting Dead Women project, 141 women were killed by a male suspect in 2021.[54]

A 2022 trend on TikTok saw male users mocking female killings and voicing their fantasies of murdering women on first dates.[55] This was not the only time war cries against women went viral on TikTok. Andrew Tate is an example of toxic masculinity that has made it to the mainstream. The American-British ex-kickboxer and *Big Brother* participant who was raised in Luton has posted deeply misogynist videos on TikTok that have attracted more than 11.6 billion views. In his videos the influencer is seen posing with symbols of masculinity such as cars, weapons and cigars. According to him, women belong at home, can't drive and are a man's property. Violence against women who cheat or disobey is normalised: he advocates hitting and choking them. 'It's bang out the machete, boom in her face and grip her by the neck. Shut up bitch,' he said in one of his videos. He claims to date primarily women aged 18 to 19 years old because he can still 'make an imprint on them'. Rape victims, he says, should 'bear responsibility' for attacks against them.

There is no doubt that misogynist social media campaigns have an impact on the attitudes and behaviour of the youngest generations. Teachers in the UK have reported recent upticks in outspoken rape denial and rape apologism among their students.[56] Reactionary ideas have made their way back into politics and mainstream discourse, threatening to undo what women's rights activists have achieved over the past century. Researchers at the Institute for Research on Male Supremacism noted: 'Although misogynist incels use more extreme dehumanising language and glorification of violence, their belief systems and ideologies are developed from and supported by the cultural and societal contexts in which they live.'[57] Misogyny does not exist in a vacuum.[58]

* * *

I grew up as a millennial woman. Our generation were told women could achieve everything that men could, and that we'd be equals provided with the same rights and opportunities. When I first arrived in the UK from Austria my belief in gender equality only grew. As a professional in my twenties I felt empowered. I was taken seriously by journalists, academics and policy makers who questioned neither my gender nor my age. My home country seemed hidebound and hierarchical by contrast. I thought of the UK as a bastion of women's rights.

But misogyny and sexism were just round the corner. Two years into my first job at a think tank researching jihadist terrorism, the English Defence League founder Tommy Robinson stormed my office to intimidate me. He claimed I had offended him by associating him with 'white supremacy' in a piece I had written for the *Guardian*. Online, highly sexualised threats, death wishes and gender-based insults rained down from his followers. Every time I looked at my phone a new message popped up through social media – something along the lines of 'Let's teach this useless slut a lesson' or 'Someone should make that woman have babies, so she adds some value to this world.'

The abuse was awful, but I had also walked into a different power struggle. To my dismay, my male boss asked me to apologise to Robinson. Unbeknownst to me the think tank had a big fanbase on the far-right side of the political spectrum. Upsetting a prominent figure like Robinson was a conflict of interest. Unsurprisingly, I did not feel that it would be right to apologise. A few days later, I was fired for refusing to follow my chief executive's orders. Meanwhile the threats continued, and my security situation became so bad that I had to move out of my flat.

Sexist insults were piling up in my inbox and now I found myself without a job or home. I went to Japan for several weeks to escape the situation and regroup. But even in a traditional Ryokan on the other side of the world I couldn't escape the constant inflow of humiliating and dehumanising comments. On the contrary, the time difference meant I received threatening messages in the middle of the night. Ironically, despite no one knowing I was hiding out in Kyoto, many of them used Japanese anime and manga characters in hyper-sexualised contexts. The misogynist alt-right has a tradition of hijacking and instrumentalising Japanese pop culture in their communications. I logged out of my social media channels only to log on again a few hours later to see how the hate storm was evolving. When your reputation and maybe even your safety is at stake, it is hard to just switch off.

When I returned to the UK, I spoke to other women who had experienced misogyny as a side effect of their work. Many asked themselves similar questions: Should I quit doing research into controversial topics? What if I refrained from voicing my political opinions, would I be better off? And even: Would it just be smarter to stop upsetting men? Should I just leave certain spaces to them? Those questions underlie today's fierce battle between feminists and anti-feminists, but even away from front-line activism a surprising number of people would answer them with a clear 'Yes.' In a 2020 study, the UK-based organisation Hope not Hate found that fifty per cent of men between 16 and 24 years of age believe feminism has indeed 'gone too far'.[59]

Incel forums are only one fraction of the wider so-called Manosphere, a mosaic of anti-feminist online subcultures. The Manosphere also hosts the PickUp Artists (PUAs), who try to manipulate women into having sex with them, the Men's Rights Movement (MRM) which campaigns against laws that are seen as unfair towards men (such as child custody and marital property distribution), and Men Going Their Own Way (MGTOW) who try to avoid any contact with women at all cost.

The popular Canadian psychologist Jordan Peterson has given modern-day anti-feminism a quasi-academic legitimacy. 'The idea that women were oppressed throughout history is an appalling theory,' he has said, and feminists have 'an unconscious wish for brutal male domination'. He has almost 4 million followers on YouTube and has sold more than 5 million copies of his book *Twelve Rules for Life*. An establishment figure, he is a University of Toronto professor and has had several book contracts with Penguin Random House. But in 2019, the clinical psychologist's fall from grace started. He had developed an addiction to benzodiazepines, suffered from severe anxiety, became suicidal and was diagnosed with schizophrenia among other disorders.

Peterson's fans may now be more hesitant to take advice about happiness from someone whose mental health seems tenuous – and whose eccentric advice includes telling his followers to go on an all-beef diet. But his mainstream success has lastingly emboldened the misogynist Manosphere. It turbo-boosted anti-feminism, taking it from a socially awkward subculture to a global mass movement.

If Peterson appeals especially to young white men, it would nonetheless be wrong to assume that anti-feminists are exclusively male. The Tumblr page 'Women Against Feminism' was created in 2013 and hosts posts from women who take a stance against feminism. There are even female influences within the Manosphere: the Trad Wives (Traditional Wives) community is a global network of tens of thousands of female anti-feminists. The female anti-feminist subreddits /RedPillWomen and /RedPillWives have close to 75,000 members.[60]

The conservative American talk show host Rush Limbaugh was another influencer for anti-feminism. He first popularised the slur 'feminazi' to denounce 'a specific type of feminist' in the 1990s.[61] In recent years, the term has been adopted internationally by the wider alt-right who use it in their battle cries against women's rights activists.

The past decade has seen a visible rise in public discussion of feminism: #MeToo campaigns, alongside women demanding higher salaries, climbing up to executive ranks and conquering traditionally male-only spaces such as STEM and finance. Women have even started to occupy more leading roles in Hollywood movies and award-winning novels. But there has been a backlash against feminism that occurred in parallel and with very negative results. One in three men now believe feminism does more harm than good, according to a 2022 global study.[62]

Today feminism is not as powerful or prevalent as anti-feminists appear to suggest. It is not the default attitude or policy. It has not managed to stamp out misogynistic attitudes, violence against women, economic inequality and the gender pay gap. And it has not succeeded in eliminating the lack of female representation in public and private sector leadership or the severe healthcare and data bias that favours men. A US-based Pew Research survey released in 2021 found that 42 per cent of women still experience gender discrimination at work and one in four women earns less than a man who is doing the same job.[63] Even as the number of women in high-ranking positions is increasing, trust in female leaders is falling.[64] Likewise, gendered harassment, defamation and disinformation campaigns against women in powerful and public-facing positions are on the rise.[65]

* * *

Whenever I watch viral campaigns against female MPs and journalists unfold, I see echoes of the hate campaign I experienced, and can spot language and memes from the Internet's misogynist fringes. Coordinated misogyny has made its way into public discourse. Incel terminology and visuals are now being picked up by average social media users.

Targeted online intimidation campaigns against women were first pioneered by male 4chan users during the #Gamergate controversy in 2014. In a concerted effort to push back against feminist influences in the video game industry, male gaming fans and online trolls launched attacks on female game developers such as Zoë Quinn and gaming journalists such as Anita Sarkeesian. Many of the victims received rape and death threats. Some were 'doxxed', having their private details including addresses and phone numbers leaked online.[66]

Hate towards women usually starts with misogynist tropes but is then combined with other (real or invented) identity layers such as race, religion, sexual orientation, social class, age, or disabilities. Traditional hate campaigns often make use of cheap mock-ups,[67] such as fake porn photographs or memes that misattribute quotes to a woman. Much of the hateful content online is user-generated and crowdsourced, even if it ends up being weaponised in a coordinated campaign. Random users with little or no connection to the harassment victim might design memes, manipulate pictures or distort quotes. It doesn't require much technical skill to crop out a head in pornographic images or insert quotes into a picture.

Over the last few years, online and offline abuse of women in public-facing professions has spiralled out of control in many countries, including the UK, US and Germany.[68] The effects of mainstreamed misogyny are chilling. Many women in journalism, politics and activism have started to censor themselves or have withdrawn from their vocation altogether. Gender-specific harassment targeting women's careers and reputations effectively constitutes a new glass ceiling.

Whether in the British Houses of Parliament, the German Bundestag or US Congress – incidents of misogyny, sexual harassment and intimidation have been reported as pervasive problems.[69] In many countries both the scale and the nature of hate directed at women is more severe when compared with their male counterparts. Prominent female politicians such as Heidi Allen of the Liberal Democrats and Nicky Morgan of the Conservative Party bowed out of the 2019 general election in the UK over 'horrific abuse'.[70] During the 2021 German elections, frontrunner Annalena Baerbock became the victim of ten times more targeted disinformation than her two male competitors for the office of chancellor.[71] Meanwhile, the Austrian Green Party chairwoman Sigi Maurer sued a Viennese off-licence owner after receiving a series of sexist hate messages from him via Facebook Messenger. The same man later murdered his former girlfriend and now faces a life-long prison sentence. In April 2022, the female politician was attacked in a restaurant located in the heart of Vienna by an anti-lockdown proponent who first verbally insulted her and then threw a glass at her.[72] She was lucky not to be injured.

The murder of British Labour MP Jo Cox in 2016 was a wake-up call in the UK. In the lead-up to the Brexit referendum, female politicians found themselves at the centre of sexist harassment campaigns – Jess Phillips MP reportedly received 600 rape threats overnight via Twitter. Jo Cox was targeted with similar messages and her security was increased, but tragically, not long after, she was shot and stabbed to death in her own constituency. Just a few years earlier, US Congress member Gabrielle Giffords was nearly killed by a man who believed that women shouldn't be in power.[73] Both Gifford and Cox were symbols of feminism and female political power.

Threats to women don't just come from 'lone wolf' outsiders, they can appear from within powerful institutions. The kidnapping, rape and murder of Sarah Everard by serving Metropolitan Police officer Wayne Couzens exposed a wider problem of aggressive sexism in the police. It demonstrated how institutionalised violent misogyny is.[74] Couzens had been sharing sexist WhatsApp messages with police colleagues prior to his attack. But the content was dismissed as a kind of 'boys will be boys' banter and harmless everyday sexism. Female ex-police officers reported insidious misogyny and toxic 'canteen culture' within the Met Police that tends to go unchallenged.[75] Everard's murder prompted a series of investigations of misogyny and sexist misconduct within the police forces. The deadly stabbing of the two sisters Bibaa Henry and Nicole Smallman in 2020 was found to not have been investigated properly by the police and instead the 'missing person' reports were cancelled. In 2021, two police officers were dismissed and jailed for taking and sharing pictures of the dead bodies of Henry and Smallman in a private WhatsApp group.[76]

Despite all the evidence linking extreme violence and sexism, most countries have not created the legal frameworks to prosecute violent misogyny as a form of extremism. Canada is one of the few countries that has added violent misogyny to the list of terrorism threats; but former UK Prime Minister Boris Johnson made clear that he did not support making it a hate crime.[77] One of the key problems remains that investigations of online threats and abuse often lead nowhere, especially when perpetrators use anonymous accounts. The NGO HateAid has warned that EU citizens are losing trust in their countries' institutions to protect them from hate crimes and that there are excessively strict requirements for reporting online abuse 'that will hardly ever be met by users'.[78] Research found that victims rarely bring civil law actions against hate speech and might be deterred by the costs and responsibilities of litigation.[79]

* * *

Meanwhile, the old glass ceiling may be cracked but it is far from broken. Female subordination and work – both domestic labour and paid jobs – are intimately linked. Today, fewer than seven per cent of couples based in Britain split the domestic workload equally.[80] Even in relationships where the woman is working, she spends on average 1.5 hours per day more on household activities, child care and grocery shopping.[81] On a global scale, women do almost three times as much care work as men and contribute 60 per cent more unpaid labour.[82] This pay gap drives economic inequality: a study found that the 'motherhood penalty' makes up for 80 per cent of the gender pay gap.[83] The pandemic made things worse. Globally, more than 2 million mothers quit their jobs over the course of 2020, many of them due to the increased childcare burden.[84] As Simone de Beauvoir famously argued. 'What makes the lot of the wife-servant ungratifying is the division of labor that dooms her wholly to the general and inessential.'[85]

The idea that women can have careers is a relatively recent one. Before 1977 German women had to ask for their husband's permission to be allowed to work outside home – in over a dozen countries the restriction still exists today.[86] Deeply ingrained gender roles still play a huge role in work and family life, a fact that many anti-feminists deny. In his YouTube video 'Career versus Motherhood', Jordan Peterson says 'The idea that most nineteen-year-old women are fed with, which is that their career will be the primary purpose of their life, is a lie.' But Peterson has it the wrong way round. The real lie is the notion that working mothers will receive adequate societal support, such as access to affordable childcare.

Stereotypes lead to unrealistic expectations of women and men. Whether you look at health care provisions, parental leave schemes, corporate firms' incentive structures or the education system: the mother's responsibility as the primary, perhaps even exclusive, child carer is largely unquestioned. This puts enormous pressure on women, while men lose out too. Research shows that 80 per cent of fathers say they would do anything to spend more time with their children. And when they do, gender pay equality gets a boost. One study by the Swedish government revealed that for every month of paternity leave the father takes, the mother's future annual salary can increase by almost 7 per cent.[87]

Childrearing and reproduction are increasingly contested areas of women's rights. On 24 June 2022, the US Supreme Court overturned *Roe v. Wade*, the 1973 law that constitutionally protects pregnant women's rights to opt for an abortion. Thirteen US states had 'trigger bans' in place that would prohibit abortion within 30 days after the Supreme Court's overturning of *Roe v. Wade*.[88] Women were begging staff in abortion clinics to help them, offering stashed-away money in return for abortion pills.

It seemed surreal that longstanding women's rights could be taken away so easily.

And yet, the destruction of the legal, political and societal progress feminists have achieved in the last decades is not a freak event, but the outcome of protracted cultural warfare which is increasingly waged online. Self-declared 'pro-life' activists tend to emphasise that life begins at conception. Yet research shows that anti-choice attitudes are more about controlling women than about wanting to 'save lives'. A 2019 Supermajority/PerryUndem survey found that people who were against abortion also tended to hold hostile views towards the #MeToo movement and were more likely to believe that men make better political leaders than women.[89] Most incels celebrated the *Roe v. Wade* reversal as a pushback against feminists.

In recent years, many liberal democratic countries have suffered setbacks for women's rights. In Poland, women have died of septic shock because doctors refused to perform lifesaving abortions as long as the foetus was still alive.[90] In Hungary, the policies passed by the ultra-nationalist Fidesz Party of Prime Minister Victor Orbán in recent years reflect archaic gender perceptions, such as the idea that women's roles should be limited to doing housework and bearing and raising children.[91] Even in countries that saw the introduction of the Commonwealth Sex Discrimination Act, sexism and gender-based discrimination have not been eroded. Sixty per cent of young women in Australia say they have experienced gender inequality.[92] The NGO 'Pregnant Then Screwed' campaigns to show how women in the UK still get sacked for being pregnant, miss promotions for having had a baby and are forced to stay at home due to unaffordable childcare costs.[93]

The *Roe v. Wade* ruling shows that women's rights are 'never guaranteed', UK MPs warned.[94] If elected to power, populist parties across Europe could pass ultraconservative laws that repeal protected women's rights. In Germany, the *Alternative für Deutschland* wants to elevate barriers for abortions, increase incentives for families to have more children and discourage all family models that conflict with the traditional family unit.[95]

The idea that feminism has gone too far is a century-old concern. It dates back to at least the 1900s when men opposed the feminist demands for women's suffrage, vocational freedom, education as well as martial and property rights. The pro-family movement of the late nineteenth century and the antisuffragists of the early twentieth century are prominent examples of early anti-feminism. Today's women-hating online communities have co-opted these old and unoriginal ideas and repackaged them using visually appealing memes, internet culture references and slick campaigns to make them seem new and radical. Jordan Peterson's success is based on the same tactic of rehashing ancient reactionary tropes that have been used to hold women back for centuries. But he does it in a way that makes his rhetoric seem fresh and provocative. This has given rise to a new trend for rationalising old patriarchal structures and legitimising anti-feminist criticism.

* * *

To Pauline Harmange, it is clear that feminism has not gone far enough. Pauline looks every bit the French feminist. The 26-year-old blogger, writer and activist is wearing timeless round glasses and she sports a short pixie cut, her unshaven armpits an expression of her politics. Pauline has been politically active on social media since she was fifteen years old. When she doesn't write she volunteers with *L'Échappée*, 'The Escapee', a charity that fights against sexual violence. She has borne witness to the stories of many young women who have been raped, abused, harassed or oppressed by men, and she isn't alone: in the UK, a 2021 YouGov study found that four fifths of all women between 18 and 24 have been sexually harassed.[96]

'Contrary to the claims of anti-feminists and men's rights activists, our society is far from being feminist,' Pauline explains. But that's not a view shared by everyone. Privilege is largely invisible to those who have it, as has been shown by the American sociologist Michael Kimmel.[97] In the US, only 28 per cent of the workforce in Science, Technology, Engineering or Mathematics (STEM) are women.[98] A 2020 study of US students pursuing a university degree in STEM found that white men are largely unaware of the impact that gender and race have on their career opportunities.[99] Just over a quarter of university professors in the UK are women, according to the Higher Education Statistics Agency (HESA). Of over 22,000 professors nationwide only 35 are Black women.[100] A UK study using professor reviews posted by 14 million students on the online website RateMyProfessors.com revealed massive sexist bias against female academics.[101]

To many anti-feminists, a focus on female victimhood seems unfair. They feel men are being systematically demonised, and look for evidence that men are in fact oppressed by women, citing everything from the expectation they will pay on dates to men losing their lives in warfare or more commonly dying from preventable diseases. And they're not entirely wrong: high suicide rates, homelessness, and lack of support for male abuse victims are some of the biggest issues that men as a group struggle with. The reasons for these discrepancies are complex and multi-layered – but not according to the anti-feminists, who see male problems as the result of female advancement; who believe, as Pauline puts it, that 'the implementation of feminist beliefs in society has made things worse for men'.

Men are victims too, she acknowledges. But not of feminism or of women. 'They are victims of a society that expects them to suffer without teaching them to express their emotions. That again is not the fault of feminism but a failure of the patriarchal system. Anti-feminists completely misinterpret the role and goals of feminism,' she tells me. 'The current pain men experience is not because of feminist demands but because of men's prior socialisation.' She thinks the fearful reaction of anti-feminists has a more straightforward source: 'They are not used to seeing their privileges put under scrutiny.'

Pauline knows all about how this 'pain' is being expressed socially. 'I've received thousands of insults regarding my appearance,' she tells me. 'I've been photoshopped as Hitler multiple times, and I've received death threats from all around the world. The most original was a vocal message sent to me on Instagram by a Spanish man who said in a polite tone: 'Hello Pauline. I hope that you will die and if I come across you, you will see what I mean.'[102]

Her conclusion is that misogyny justifies misandry. In 2020 her book *I Hate Men* (*Moi, les hommes, je déteste*) caused a massive controversy in France. It was an explicit plea for the dislike and mistrust of men. 'Women should have the right to hate men,' she tells me in French. The book was originally published by non-profit micro publisher Monstrograph, which only printed 400 copies. They seemed mostly destined for Pauline's friends and followers. But within days it became clear that she had hit a nerve with her treatise. On the day of its release an advisor to France's ministry on gender equality, Ralph Zurmély, called for a ban of the book on the grounds of its gender-based incitement to hate. Though the ministry subsequently distanced itself from Zurmély, who later left his job, there was extensive media coverage and public attention. *I Hate Men* turned into an international bestseller and sold tens of thousands of copies.

Harmange's ideas are controversial, and they are not shared by all feminists, many of whom reject misandry. She explains why, in her view, misogyny and misandry are not comparable. 'Misogyny is used by those in privileged positions to benefit further from the oppressed.' In contrast to misogyny, she believes that misandry is a defence mechanism to protect yourself from misogynist and oppressive men.

Pauline argues for stronger sorority between women to compete with the high degree of fraternity that men display. There could be a female version of Men Going Their Own Way. 'We can actively choose to prioritise women in the literature we read, the films we watch, even in daily relationships.' One of the problems of feminism, Pauline acknowledges however, is that it tends to be too exclusive. Feminist circles often only accept women who are already feminist and part of an intellectual elite. 'The reactionaries on the other side use this vacuum to promote anti-feminism.'

The expectations imposed on women by society also make it hard to live a life without men, Pauline acknowledges. For the majority of heterosexual women, a successful life is defined by entering a marriage with a man and having children with him. 'It is because of this prior socialisation towards male-dominated norms that we need the female emancipation movement to be all the more radical and break out of old patterns,' she concludes. Not an easy task.

Anti-feminists think that modern-day feminism is shaped by 'a huge denial of the way biology and the human psyche work'. To highlight alleged biological differences between the sexes they cite research that shows men are more conscientious than women, which supposedly explains why more men are in higher-ranking positions and earn more. However, many academic studies actually found that women score higher on conscientiousness.[103]

The psychological differences between men and women are complicated and controversial, and academics argue that the difference between gender personalities is more similar to the difference between North Dakota and South Dakota than the difference between Venus and Mars.[104] Besides, even if social hierarchies between men and women had an evolutionary basis, that wouldn't make them fair or desirable.

The anti-feminists' obsession with biological determinism ignores the role of society in shaping gendered behaviour. Pauline Harmange points out that people who deviate from their assigned roles are punished: we denigrate men who show supposedly feminine emotions and character traits. She adds, 'Being perceived as masculine without a certain element of toxicity is almost impossible due to today's gender norms.'

I think about the incels' narrow, rigid image of the aggressive, bread-winning 'alpha', and their obsessions with defining women by their sexual appeal and reproductive potential. I can hear the voice of Jordan Peterson saying that a society run as a patriarchy makes sense. If ideas about gender roles don't become more flexible, the appeal of men's rights ideology will only grow.

* * *

Why are femicide rates rising and women's reproductive rights under threat? How have we reached a point where receiving rape and death threats is the norm for women in the public eye? Radical subcultures achieve societal impact by tapping into widespread grievances while offering a sense of community and agency, and leveraging social media to have a disproportionate impact on politics. And that is exactly what anti-feminism has done.

Misogyny may be the oldest form of prejudice and hatred. Even with the rise of women's rights movements in the nineteenth century and feminist movements in the twentieth century, it never truly went away. Instead, it remained dormant in sub-cultures that woke up over the last decade.

#Gamergate in 2014, Donald Trump's election victory in 2016 and the *Roe v. Wade* repeal in 2022 were all steps in a journey that has taken Western women's dignity backwards. They were victories for extremists who have been working on bringing back forms of male supremacy.

The Manosphere consistently reduces women to their 'sexual market value' and their 'breeding functions'. Today, official policies and mainstream discourse are echoing their backward gender perceptions. Fifty years after the right to abortion was constitutionally protected in the US, women have lost the freedom to decide over their own bodies again. A hundred years after Nancy Astor was elected the first female MP in Westminster, women candidates are standing down before elections over new waves of misogynist abuse. Why could nobody prevent the reversal of some of the most significant milestones in the history of women's rights?

The answer lies in the so-called Breitbart doctrine. 'Politics is downstream from culture,' the prominent conservative journalist and *Breitbart News* founder Andrew Breitbart famously said. The Manosphere movement offers its members not just a political philosophy but also a culture in which they can immerse themselves. Its insider vocabulary, memes and references have cross-pollinated other online subcultures such as the gaming, anime and porn communities.

The reach of the misogynist fringe has expanded far beyond lonely sex-deprived men. Its global influence shows how subcultures can increasingly find social acceptance and political representation. But it doesn't end there: once radicalised, individuals don't confine themselves to one ideology. For many, misogyny is just the start of a slide into far-right extremism.

CULTIVATING NETWORKS

For those with deviant beliefs, it used to be difficult to find likeminded people. By their nature, fringe movements exist outside the establishment. But today it has never been easier for outsiders to connect with each other and gain traction. Climate change scepticism is an example of how activists have built powerful global networks to bring their radical ideas to mainstream audiences. Their members span business, politics and civil society and have given rise to ecosystems of alternative science and biased journalism. They have created their own establishment.

Since first appearing as the figurehead of the #FridaysForFuture movement, the environmental activist Greta Thunberg has repeatedly found herself the target of harassment. It comes and goes in waves. There are entire online databases dedicated to memes that make fun of Greta's Asperger's syndrome or link her to absurd conspiracy theories. Another activist who has been on the receiving end of smear campaigns by right-wing outlets and climate change deniers is Carola Rackete. She is in her early 30s and passionate about Antarctica, biodiversity and the climate. Carola is also one of the world's most famous ship captains. She is best known for her sea rescue activism. In 2019, she made international headlines when she was arrested for docking the rescue ship *Sea-Watch 3*, which was carrying 40 refugees of over fifteen nationalities, in the Italian port of Lampedusa. In a controversial decree, Italy's former interior minister Matteo Salvini had just closed the country's ports to migrant rescue ships a few days earlier. At the same time, dozens of migrants were drowning in the Mediterranean.[105]

Carola could have taken the *Sea-Watch 3* elsewhere, but Lampedusa was the closest safe harbour and the passengers, including pregnant women and children, were exhausted. As the situation on board worsened, some of the migrants had already started self-harming and Carola was afraid it would lead to suicides.[106] Her ship collided with a police boat that tried to block her way to the pier. Salvini called Carola's sea manoeuvre an act of war and had her arrested.[107] Eventually the court ruled that the young activist had acted to protect her passengers' safety and had not broken the law.[108] She was released from house arrest.

In total, Carola spent six months as a sea rescue captain. But she has spent years working in environmental research and activism. She has been a navigation officer on scientific expeditions in the polar regions for the Alfred Wegner Institute for Polar and Maritime Research since 2011 and has travelled to the Antarctic eight times. She only started becoming active as an environmentalist when she saw the effects of global warming with her own eyes. 'When I was in high school other students founded a Greenpeace offshoot but I was not interested.' Her first trip as a navigation officer was during the summer of 2011 to the North Pole. 'I had a clear image in my head of what it would look like and that it would be hard to get there. But it was much easier than I had imagined because there was so little ice there.'

She spoke with explorers and scientists who had been going there for twenty years and had observed the ice caps melting. 'When I realised how little ice there is in the central Arctic I understood that climate change was no longer just a topic for the future, it's already happening.' Today Carola is constantly on the move. Her Twitter location says 'migrating'. When I speak to her she is in Finland working on a restoration project. 'Driving through Finland you don't see a single intact forest, almost everything is plantation,' she says. Ninety-six per cent of the Finnish woods below the Arctic Circle are no longer primary forest with native tree species, but have been turned into forestry territory. Half of the Finnish moorlands have been destroyed, with peatlands burnt or drained to plant forests.

The problem is much bigger than climate however, according to Carola. When she studied conservation she realised how intertwined economic growth and the environment are. 'There is no way to save frogs or people within a system that causes social injustice,' she tells me. 'The separation of GDP and ecological destruction is not possible. So we need to change the way our economic system works. There needs to be a redistribution of power, resources and political participation.'

Carola has observed a shift in ecological problems. Alternative energies are just one example. The Russian aggression war in Ukraine has accelerated Europe's investments in alternative energy to reduce its dependency on Russian fossil fuels. However, many alternative energy sources bring their own challenges for the environment. The lithium for batteries needs to be produced and disposed somewhere, causing ecological damage in countries like Bolivia, Chile and the Deep Sea. This is why we need something like the Green New Deal, Carola concludes. 'But without the economic growth dimension. The oil industry and the Global North will need to take responsibility for the ecological damage done and make compensation payments for their environmental debt.'

Carola believes that radical change will be needed. It was 1988, the year Carola was born, when the first scientifically backed climate warnings were made in front of the US Senate. The former NASA scientist James Hansen said in a congressional hearing that he could declare 'with 99 per cent confidence' that the sharp rise in temperatures was human-made.[109] 'Whether you look at CO2 emissions, deforestation or overfishing – not much has changed in the past 30 years.' For Carola the best realistic scenario would be that Global North votes progressive social democratic and green parties into power and enters a phase of 'just transition'. Globally networked movements like Fridays for Future and Extinction Rebellion could help to drive this forward. The mainstreaming process also works for radically progressive ideas. But progress in the climate debate is likely to go hand in hand with an escalation of the global 'culture wars'. 'I'm afraid we'll see more societal polarisation in the future, as the power structures are finally starting to move,' Carola says.

* * *

It's easy to dismiss online abuse against figures like Carola or Greta as the product of vicious individuals lashing out, but the sinister campaigns against them haven't arisen spontaneously. They are internationally coordinated, and underwritten by vested interests. Investigations at the Institute for Strategic Dialogue found that attempts to discredit and ridicule the environmentalist movement have been linked to the organisations the Heartland Institute and the Committee for a Constructive Tomorrow (CFACT), which are working to undermine trust in climate science and have historic ties to the fossil fuel industry.[110]

Since the early 2000s, a powerful network has been built up to systematically cast doubt on established climate science consensus. In the first decade of the 2000s, anonymous billionaires donated 120 million dollars via Donors Trust to over 100 bogus think tanks and political advocacy groups working to discredit the science behind climate change.[111] During that timeframe, the income of anti-climate science organisations, including think tanks, industry lobbying groups and activist associations, totalled roughly 900 million dollars.[112] Influential advocacy organisations include the American Enterprise Institute, Freedom Works, Americans for Prosperity, The Heritage Foundation and Cato Institute. The network structures and dissuasion tactics employed by climate science sceptics resemble those used by the tobacco industry to discredit research on the links between smoking and lung cancer. It is the same old techniques that have enabled organisations sponsored by traditional industries to run campaigns against Greta Thunberg and Carola Rackete. They are influential enough to lower public concern and delay or block government action. Their messages resonate especially well with those audiences that are most afraid of having to compromise their lifestyles and privileges: wealthy white men.

Social media has allowed climate change sceptics to team up internationally and have a disproportionate impact on the public discourse. A 2022 report by the ISD exposed the online networks driving disinformation and harassment campaigns during the COP26 in 2021. A diverse network of 50 Twitter accounts driving the directions of the climate change debate were found to seed and spread narratives that oppose climate action. Accounts included influencers from anti-science and conspiracy myth communities, right-wing conservatives, ultra-libertarians and business entities from the entire Anglosphere. During COP26 there was a high interconnection and opportunistic collaboration between these sub-communities, as they found common ground in their opposition to climate action.[113]

Campaigns against climate action are boosted by right-wing news outlets such as Fox News in the US and Sky News Australia, which are part of Rupert Murdoch's media empire. Both channels have given a platform to world-leading climate change sceptics such as Norwegian Per Strandberg, Canadian nuclear energy advocate Patrick Moore and UK-based ultra-libertarian Richard Delingpole. Common tactics used to argue against climate action include the use of deny, deceive and delay narratives. The argument that we should wait for new technologies or the idea that climate action brings more negative effects than positives are examples of the 'delay' tactic. The 'deceive' tactic would include misleading audiences about the climate crisis or climate action taken ('green-washing').[114]

Another popular tactic among climate change sceptics is the opportunistic hijacking of other anti-science and conspiracy myth movements. For example, the beginning of the pandemic saw the emergence of the 'Great Reset' conspiracy myth, which suggests that global elites have the dark secret agenda of establishing a tyrannical world government.[115] The idea spread rapidly in 2020 after Klaus Schwab, the executive chairman of the World Economic Forum, and HRH the Prince of Wales announced a new initiative to use the Covid pandemic as an opportunity 'to reflect, reimagine, and reset our world'.[116] It didn't take long until climate change deniers jumped on the bandwagon and added elements to the conspiracy myth that would fit their own narrative, namely that climate change is an invention by the 'global elites'. This idea has also been picked up by white nationalists who skilfully tie the 'Great Reset' to their idea of a 'Great Replacement'.

Right-wing media commentators such as Tucker Carlson, Ben Shapiro and Glenn Beck were instrumental in spreading the idea of a 'Great Reset' to mainstream audiences. Another influencer who amplified the idea was the American political scientist Jerome R. Corsi, previously known for spreading other conspiracy myths such as the 'birther' claim that Barack Obama was born in Kenya and therefore unfit for US presidency, as well as 9/11-related conspiracy myths. Like Jordan Peterson, Corsi is an example of someone spreading dangerous ideas using the platforms of the establishment. His climate science denying book *THE TRUTH about Energy, Global Warming and Climate Change* was released by leading American publishing house Simon & Schuster.

Adapting Covid-related language to climate issues has allowed deniers to tap into widespread anxieties and frustrations triggered by the pandemic and redirect them towards climate action. The term 'climate lockdown' was first picked up by Steve Milloy, director of the Heartland Institute, in April 2020. Quoting a *Guardian* article that challenged the idea of returning to the old normal, he warned his followers on Twitter that 'climate bedwetters hope to translate the #coronavirus lockdown into a climate lockdown'. It didn't take long for the narrative to be amplified across the climate change sceptic network of influencers and commentators. Within a week, mentions of the term on social media rose from a few dozen to a few thousand. Soon after, Fox News commentator Laura Ingraham and Breitbart wrote about it. The conspiracy idea of a looming 'climate lockdown' was then discussed on Fox News a few months later, reaching millions of people.[117]

* * *

On a warm June day Sam Knights and I meet on the terrace of the café Caravan in Fitzrovia. Sam is an actor, writer and environmental activist. He is also the co-founder of Extinction Rebellion's London offshoot. The 22-year-old grew up in Warwickshire and moved to London in 2017 after graduating from Cambridge University in English literature. He took jobs in call centres and searched for a meaning to his existence.

He was never particularly interested in the environment until he read the 2018 United Nations report on global warming. 'Like many others, I woke up,' he tells me. Sam started digging deeper into studies on climate change and scientific assessments. 'Before that I thought the climate crisis was about polar bears on icebergs.' It was only after speaking to experts and engaging with the literature that he understood it was about human beings and about equality, freedom and justice. 'I had a breakdown and felt guilty that I'd been ignoring the issue for so long.' There was no excuse anymore, he wanted to get involved in campaigning for environmental action. At that point Extinction Rebellion was a tiny movement of around a dozen people, mainly based in Bristol and Stroud.

Today Extinction Rebellion is a decentralised mass movement with chapters in 78 countries and tens of thousands of followers worldwide. It uses non-violent civil disobedience to attempt to halt mass extinction and minimise the risk of social collapse. Extinction Rebellion protesters have glued themselves to government buildings and disrupted traffic to try and force policymakers to take action. In Pakistan, they marched through the capital, in Austria they blocked roads and in Chile they lay down in the middle of a street. In the UK they shut down iconic locations in central London for ten days and glued themselves to the entrance of the London Stock Exchange.[118]

In autumn 2018, before they became a global movement, Sam called Extinction Rebellion's founders and told them: 'If you ever want to come to London, you can have my living room as a meeting space.' A week later ten people knocked on his door and wanted to organise a protest in London. This became the Declaration of Rebellion protest, which attracted a thousand people to Parliament Square in November 2018. Sam will always remember the goosebumps on his skin when he walked up the stairs from the Tube. 'It felt like we'd captured the moment and were tapping into an energy that needed a form to express itself.'

Week after week they called new protests and the numbers kept growing. A month later they staged a protest with 6,000 people that shut down six bridges in the centre of London. Extinction Rebellion's biggest achievement was when the UK became the first country to announce a climate emergency. It was seen as the culmination of their efforts. They had managed to establish a movement with which to take on the powerful networks of the fossil fuel lobby and their political agents.

Sam Knights' climate activism has not come without personal sacrifices. In the beginning the sudden international media attention took Extinction Rebellion activists by surprise. 'The level of hatred is immense, and you are absolutely aware of that.' They didn't yet have good systems of communication in place and were not equipped to deal with the high levels of interest they received. For a long time, Sam still used his personal email account. He was getting death threats directly to his private inbox every single day, often from people radically opposed to climate action. 'The people who would message us were not the people who were held up in road blocks,' he tells me. 'They were climate change deniers with too much time on their hands.'

In February 2019, Sam got arrested for gluing himself to the door of a hotel where a fossil fuel conference was happening. In his trial, which lasted for eight months, he was accused of aggravated trespass and criminal damage. Instead of getting a lawyer Sam represented himself in court. 'There is one advantage of not having a lawyer,' he tells me. It allowed him to put forward arguments to the judge that someone with a legal background wouldn't have been allowed to present. He was able to talk at length about the human rights abuses and criminal acts committed by fossil fuel companies. Against this backdrop he was able to argue that his act was meant to prevent greater harm from happening. In the end he was found not guilty on all counts.

Extinction Rebellion's provocative campaigns are meant to raise awareness both among politicians and the general public, provoking behavioural change and policy reforms. Peaceful civil disobedience has a long tradition in civil rights movements. To Sam it is an important tactic that the environmental movement had ignored for too long. 'If you look back in history, no one approved of the suffragettes. It's only afterwards that people look back at these actions and say they were probably necessary in the context of their time.'

But it takes bravery in the present. Many have criticised Extinction Rebellion for their transgressive tactics. Some fellow environmentalists were concerned that they could be putting off sympathisers with their disruption of business as usual. Sam is very aware of the divisiveness of the movement's tactics: 'It struck me that the magnitude of the crisis needs radical tactics to hold power to account.' Like Sam, most activists embrace the risk of getting into trouble. 'You go in knowing there is a high chance you get arrested.' One thing he didn't anticipate, however, was the effect his activism would have on his friends, his family and his career. Sam lost the biggest acting role that he had been offered in his life, a lead role in a BBC 1 drama, because an insurance company wouldn't cover him.

The activists' appetite for risk also depends on the country. 'You can't have the same tactics in Ghana as in the UK,' Sam says. You might be putting your life in danger in some places. Even in Europe, some activists were afraid to anger the governments and face strong clampdowns. In Poland, Extinction Rebellion figured out quickly that they were not able to replicate the tactics used in more liberal democracies. In the UK, Extinction Rebellion was categorised as a domestic extremism organisation by the Home Office and the Metropolitan Police. The movement was put on the national security threat list alongside jihadists and neo-Nazis. Sam got banned from the 2019 Labour Party Conference, despite being a member.

Sam himself is sceptical about the most radical voices within Extinction Rebellion. 'Some of the people in our movement have allowed their egos to run away with them. Those who get most attention in the media and on social media are often those with the most divisive voices and the least thought-through tactics,' he tells me. Extinction Rebellion co-founder Roger Hallam was disowned by the movement after downplaying the Holocaust as 'just another fuckery in human history'.[119]

Some activists want to take civil disobedience to the extreme. As a result, the movement has splintered over disagreements in how far they should go. In October 2019, activists of the young wing of Extinction Rebellion glued themselves to the roof of an underground train at Canning Town tube station during morning rush hour. Their radical disruption sparked public outrage and condemnation, as it targeted a station in a historically poor working-class district of east London. Video footage shows furious commuters trying to drag Extinction Rebellion activists off the Tube.[120] This stunt was planned by a tiny fraction of the movement and opposed by the overwhelming majority, Sam tells me. Yet, it went ahead because in a decentralised movement activists are empowered to take individual action.

In the beginning Extinction Rebellion's calls for direct action came from a place of privilege. By favouring tactics that would lead to arrests, for example, they inevitably became a predominantly white, middle- and upper-class movement. 'Movements have always had a problem with white liberal environmentalism which puts off marginalised groups,' Sam explains. 'In the wake of the Black Lives Matter protests the environmentalist movement has been forced to reckon with its own history of racialised violence and racism.' As seen at the People's Assembly Against Austerity protests in June 2021, Extinction Rebellion and Black Lives Matter are now seen marching side by side. They find common ground in their opposition to the police and in their calls for radical system changes.

Sam ends our conversation with a rather gloomy outlook. 'Intellectually, I'm very pessimistic,' he says. The networks of those endorsing climate change denial and advocating inaction are too strong. Much of the impact of movements such as

Extinction Rebellion and Fridays for Future has been undermined by the campaigns of activists who oppose climate action and enjoy ample support by influential right-wing political parties, powerful private sector businesses and wealthy conservative foundations. 'We are on the way to slipping further into right-wing authoritarian responses to the climate debate. And even if some governments stick to their weak climate targets, we'll still end up with unimaginable tragedy.'

* * *

Matt Ridley does not believe in that tragedy. Matt was an elected member of the British House of Lords, sitting for the Conservatives. Today he holds lectures and publishes opinion pieces based on his book *The Rational Optimist*, claiming that 'climate change can be good for us'.[121] When I speak to him over the phone in 2021, he complains that Extinction Rebellion 'tells a bunch of lies'.

'I am a climate lukewarmer,' he says of himself. He believes recent global warming is real and probably man-made. But he doesn't think we need to worry about it. The scale is overplayed, according to him, and the statistics cited by thousands of scientists are flawed. He calls it climate change alarmism.

Matt didn't want to become a scientist himself. 'I did a PhD in Biology at Oxford University but realised I enjoyed writing about science more than doing science,' he tells me. So he became a science editor at the *Economist* and spent 35 years as a commentator on science and technology. In 2013, he joined the House of Lords.

'I have contrarian instincts. Whenever I see conventional wisdom I like to poke it,' he admits. 'But I'm not a contrarian for the sake of it.' He goes on to blame the media for polarising the public: the *Telegraph* has gone more to the right, the *Guardian* has gone more to the left. 'It has almost become a necessity to take a radical stance in order to survive in journalism. If you want to get heard in a more crowded field, it tends to work to say something somewhat extreme.'

The libertarian, pro-Brexit politician and journalist describes himself as a passionate naturalist and bird watcher. Although he has participated in conservation projects in India and Pakistan, he doesn't think that species extinction is getting worse. His climate science scepticism started in the 1990s. He remembers that his conversion moment was the publication of the Hockey Stick, which has been dubbed 'the most controversial chart in science'.[122]

The Hockey Stick is a graph that was first published by climate scientist Michael Mann and two other researchers in 1999. It was an attempt to reconstruct earth surface temperatures over the past two millennia based on climate proxies such as tree rings, lake sediments, ice cores and corals. The chart, which shows that temperatures are now rising dramatically and faster than ever before, resembles a hockey stick: first there is a long period of relatively minor variations in global temperatures ('the shaft') and then a sudden surge occurs ('the blade').

Right after the chart's publication, both Mann and his research methods and data sources came under fire. They were accused of trying to hide temperature declines and filtering for datasets that gave upticks. However, later publications using more extensive and accurate data sets and enhanced methods reconfirmed Mann's initial findings. The climate science consensus remained unchanged: average global temperatures are rising at unprecedented speed. But this made no impact on Matt's scepticism.

Another 'hugely important moment' for Matt was the 'Climategate' controversy in 2010. Just a month before the Copenhagen Climate Change Conference was to be held in December 2009, the Climate Research Unit (CRU) at the

University of East Anglia was hacked. In a sophisticated attack, thousands of emails and documents were obtained by the hackers. Climate science deniers such as James Delingpole, an English journalist who is now executive editor of the far-right *Breitbart*, immediately popularised the term 'Climategate'. They wrongly accused climate scientists of manipulating data and being involved in a global conspiracy on global warming.

Eight different bodies, including the House of Commons Science and Technology Committee, the US Department of Commerce and the National Science Foundation, investigated the allegations. None of them found evidence of scientific misconduct.[123] It appeared that the hacking and misrepresentation of obtained emails was a globally coordinated smear campaign executed by climate sceptics and backed by their allies in the oil and gas industry with the aim of sabotaging the Copenhagen Summit.

Matt became sceptical over the years. Not about the greenhouse effect and the increasing CO2 levels: 'That is real,' he admits. Not about the human causes behind it: 'That is real – most likely.' But about whether or not the feedback loops built into the models are justified. Positive feedback loops in climate change are dynamics that have been shown to speed up global warming, leading to rapidly escalating effects. The melting ice caps are a powerful example, as they lead to the release of large amounts of methane and carbon held within the permafrost, which in turn exacerbates the greenhouse gas effect. Likewise, the heating of the Amazon could transform the rainforest into savannah, meaning that it would release carbon instead of absorbing it. 'Without those feedback loops,' Matt reasons, 'climate change is going to be a moderate, slow and diminishing effect, giving us at most 1.5 or 2 degrees over a century.'

Over the phone Matt sounds outraged when discussing a 2015 World Health Organization (WHO) statement that described climate change as the greatest threat to human health in the 21st century. 'That's just insulting to all the people in Africa dying from Malaria and HIV, or other people dying of smoking,' he tells me.

Matt is known for his stance against renewable energies. 'The measures we take could do us more harm than good,' he tells me. He doesn't believe in the value of switching to electric cars or using low-energy light bulbs. He is against building wind farms, which according to him are 'unreliable, expensive and require enormous quantities of either land or sea'. But there is a backstory to his opposition to renewables: he benefits from coal mining on his family's land in Northumberland; a financial interest that has prompted many critics to label him as a lobbyist for the coal industry.

This might explain his defensiveness over the phone: 'I hope I didn't get myself into trouble,' he says at the end of our call. He also tells me that he has never been less successful in convincing people to join him on his side of the debate than with climate change-related topics. But he sees potential for the debate to become more dangerous: 'I think there will be a major collision between the green politicians and the less green electorates. This will open up an opportunity for a Farage-like populist to campaign against the climate change obsession in the years to come. I do see a pretty stark polarisation coming in the close future.'

Matt's views are much more mainstream than most climate deniers. In fact, they are so mainstream that many climate change deniers who think global warming is imaginary get annoyed with him. Yet, this type of 'lukewarming' can act as the thin end of the wedge for more extreme climate science scepticism and the discrediting of environmental activism. The networks of climate deniers and lukewarmers are strongly inter-connected. And outright disbelief is more common than you may think: a 2021 poll found that one in fifteen Conservative MPs believe climate change is a 'myth'.[124]

While conservative parties such as the UK Tories and the German Christian Union parties (CSU/CDU) have frequently promoted inaction on the climate, far-right populist parties go further and use denial narratives in their communications campaigns. From leading Alternative for Germany (AfD) politicians to former presidents Donald Trump and Brazil's Jair Bolsonaro, a range of far-right populist politicians have exploited the polarised climate card for their election campaigns.[125]

The German parliamentary elections of 2021 were defined by debate on climate change. Never before had climate policy featured so highly on the agenda. Surveys found that climate policy played the biggest role in voting decisions for 43 per cent of the population.[126] The AfD's climate-sceptic social media posts performed significantly better than those of other parties in favour of climate action. Their anti-climate action tweets received up to 237 per cent more shares than the tweets of green and centrist parties.[127] The demonisation of climate change activists was a key tactic among far-right campaigners, with words such as 'eco extremists', 'climate hysterics' and 'green terrorists' in common use. The tactics observed in Germany were akin to those previously seen in the context of US, UK, Polish and Australian anti-climate action campaigns.

The *Guardian*'s environment editor Damian Carrington categorised climate science deniers into four different groups: the shill, the grifter, the egomaniac and the ideological fool. Shills are paid by private industry to lobby against climate action by casting doubt on the science behind it, while grifters make a living by writing click-bait pieces for right-wing and conservative media outlets. Egomaniacs want to revive their career and rise to prominence by making outrageous statements, whereas the ideological fools are blinded by their libertarian beliefs and worry that global environmental regulations would be disastrous for the world.[128] Even if the motivations that drive them and the stories they tell differ, climate change deniers often share financial stakes in the fossil fuel industry, political backing by right-wing parties and alternative information ecosystems.

* * *

Globally, the US is the second biggest hotbed for climate change denial, ranked right after Indonesia. The situation in Indonesia is special though: the country has seen a strong surge in natural disasters over the past decades.[129] Although most people believe in climate change, many don't think it is man-made. This is in part because of widespread Islamic teachings that view natural disasters as a sign of the End of Times.[130]

The climate change sceptic I speak to next is the ultimate example of how the climate change denial movement has popularised itself via the effective use of social media, political mouthpieces and industry funding. Indeed, he was among the first online influencers to make the term 'climate lockdown' go viral.[131] Marc Morano is a world-famous figure who has been called 'King of the skeptics'[132] by his supporters and been listed as one of the top five 'criminals against humanity, against planet Earth itself' by his opponents.[133] *Rolling Stone* Magazine called him 'the Matt Drudge of climate denial'.

After reading Marc's controversial books *The Politically Incorrect Guide to Climate Change* and *Green Fraud* I decide to speak to him directly to find out more about his motivations. In his early 50s, he has a friendly voice and a strong American accent. Often dressed in a light grey suit, he favours extravagant ties. You can make up your mind which category of climate change denier he best fits into.

To Marc, global warming is a non-problem. 'It has become a new religion,' he says. He likens science on climate change to 'magic' and 'fairy tales', rejects hottest year claims, rebuts news of mass extinction and rising sea levels and ridicules the term climate crisis. Instead, he presents the climate emergency as 'a pretext for the progressive left to achieve its goals'. The Green Deal? 'A ten-year plan to control human behaviour, fight white supremacy and redistribute wealth, a threat to liberty and sovereignty.' He skilfully connects different radical ideas and gives them an overarching explanation that supports his belief in the fabrication of global warming.

On the topic of global ocean levels Marc argues that they 'have been rising for the past 20,000 years and this has not accelerated'. But NASA data shows that sea-level rise is a major effect of climate change. The global average sea level rose from -0.5mm in 1993 to 103mm in 2022.[134] Studies took into consideration longer-term influences such as the change of total volume of sea water and movements of ground and ocean bottom that result in changes to the size and shape of the ocean basins, as well as dynamic factors such as winds, atmospheric pressures, ocean currents, and waves. Data clearly indicates that the sea-level rate of increase almost doubled for 1993 to 2009, relative to 1900 to 2009.[135] A 2019 study tripled previous estimates of global vulnerability to sea-level rise and coastal flooding.[136]

Marc has no scientific experience in the field of climate change. But he has travelled the globe and been to climate change summits. To the 2016 Marrakesh UN climate change summit he brought a cardboard cut-out of Donald Trump, the UN Paris climate agreement and a paper shredder. In a deliberately provocative stunt, he shredded the UN Paris agreement with Trump there and was escorted out by security officers.

Earlier in his career Marc served as the communications director for US Senator James Inhofe who is known for his infamous quote that 'global warming is the greatest hoax ever perpetrated on the American people'.[137] As part of his anti-environmentalist efforts, Marc then started the website ClimateDepot.com, a project of the conservative US think tank CFACT. Climate scientists are his top targets.

Marc doesn't like being labelled a climate change denier because it reminds him of the word 'Holocaust denier'. He prefers climate sceptic or contrarian. Though he can be brash ('We should kick scientists when they're down. They deserve to be publicly flogged,' he wrote in one of his blog posts), his background in communications has also equipped him with the tools needed to come up with a subtler framing of his convictions when needed. 'I care about the environment,' he tells me in an insistent voice. 'I care about the future of my children and their children.' His rhetorical prowess, along with his rejection of arguments that advocate making changes to Western white middle-class lifestyles has turned him into a fairly mainstream figure, popular with conservative and libertarian Republicans in the US. On Twitter Marc has around 25,000 followers and his books are bestsellers, at least according to his bio.

The longer we speak, the more passionate Marc's voice gets. 'A lot of people think the big oil industry funds me, which is not the case,' he tells me angrily. He denies being a spokesman for the fossil fuel companies. 'We have nothing to do with them,' he shouts into the phone. Yet, there's no question that the people Morano works for have vested interests: investigations have found that his previous boss Senator Inhofe received hundreds of thousands of dollars in donations from the oil and gas sector, more than any other senator in the 2001–2002 election cycle.[138] His current employer CFACT also obtained funding from ExxonMobil, Chevron and foundations associated with the oil and aluminium investors of the Mellon family.

Marc tells me that he was a Republican environmentalist and journalist when he was younger. He always loved going out in the woods, loved camping, fishing, hiking. He admits that initially he started writing sceptical pieces about climate change because there was a vacuum that he could fill. 'There were so few people on the critical side of environmentalist reporting that I found my niche just there.'

According to him, deforestation is not a problem. If you use more trees, this will signal to the market the need to plant more trees. Let's quickly factcheck this statement. Of course, trees can be replanted. But anyone who has ever planted a tree knows that regrowth takes time, more time than rapid deforestation allows. Planting new trees also cannot offset all negative effects caused by deforestation. Cutting down and consuming trees means that stored carbon is released, and that the forest's wider ecology and biodiversity are impacted. Changes to the soil and landscape, such as erosion, can result. Tree-planting schemes as used by big firms looking to show they are environmentally conscious often constitute little more than 'greenwashing'.

Marc Morano styles himself as a contrarian. The first two chapters in his *Politically Incorrect Guide to Climate Change* read like a CV in which he showcases the various negative titles the media has awarded him. 'I don't mind if you smear me too,' he tells me. Whenever the media points out the factual flaws in his arguments, he uses their criticism to fuel his narrative that they are biased and corrupt, along with academia and the United Nations.

'Why do people no longer trust scientific institutions and political leaders?' His voice is enthusiastic now. 'First I want to thank Al Gore. Having a partisan political figure who lobbies for the climate meant that immediately half of the population was gonna be sceptical. In terms of PR it was a disaster.' Building on this gift to climate sceptics, as he frames it, Marc created a war room to counter climate change claims put forward by Democrats, the media and the United Nations.

'The greatest loss we've experienced since Trump took office in 2016 is that we don't have debate anymore,' Marc tells me.

He complains about the rise of 'cancel culture' in reaction to Donald Trump's presidency and how the media has shut down any contrarian views on climate change. His frustration appears to be representative of other climate change sceptics I encountered. As climate change deniers are no longer invited to debates, they have resorted to other methods of counterspeech. They organise international meet-ups behind closed doors or in restricted online chat rooms to exchange ideas and conduct mainstreaming campaigns.

* * *

On a full-day train ride through rural Germany's misty November landscape, I prepare for the climate change denial conference I am about to attend: the 14th International Climate and Energy Conference 2021. The two-day conference is organised annually by the European Institute for Climate and Energy (EIKE) and hosts the world's most prominent climate science deniers.

Generous donations from oil and fossil fuel companies aside, I never understood why anyone would oppose protecting the environment. After all, saving our habitat and that of our children seems positive, even in the extremely unlikely event that climate change turned out to be a big hoax. Imagine there was no climate change after all, but we'd spent decades making our oceans cleaner, our land greener, and our energy consumption more sustainable and less dependent on megalomaniac autocrats. Wouldn't it still have been a good investment? That's not how deniers see it, though. 'It's not our climate that's endangered but our freedom' is one of their mottos.

I want to find out how influential the trans-national and cross-ideological networks of climate science deniers have become. EIKE is based in Germany and was founded in 2007 by Dr Holger Thuß, a German historian and former politician of the far-right Alternative for Germany. It is more of a lobbying network than a scientific institute and has created a wide political support network across Europe and North America.[139] I get off the train in Gera, a small town in the Eastern German state Thuringia known for its neo-Nazi music scene.

Three doormen at the entrance check my ID and vaccination passport. My conference registration is under the name Christiane Ebbner. I wanted to avoid using my real name; if the organisers knew who I was they would almost certainly cancel my ticket. But with Covid checks in place I need to show official documents to enter. My assumed name had to be close enough to my real identity that my vaccination passport would be accepted. I had opted for a compromise: Christiane is my actual middle name and Ebbner could just be a typo. 'Thank you,' one of them says, handing me back my documents and waving me in. I hesitate for a few seconds. 'Should I wear my mask?' He smiles, as if this is a ridiculous question. 'Not really.'

When I climb up the stairs I understand why. Nobody is wearing a mask here, although at the moment Germany has a nation-wide policy of wearing medical-grade masks in public places. I should have known: since the beginning of the pandemic EIKE has been spreading doubts about the seriousness of Covid.[140]

The venue is spacious and the tables are elegantly set for dinner. EIKE is clearly not short of money. The conference is co-sponsored by the Heartland Institute, the same fossil fuel industry-funded[141] conservative US think tank whose director coined the term 'climate lockdown' and which has been linked to co-ordinated smear campaigns against environmentalists. As I look around, I immediately realise that I stick out as an outsider. The roughly 250 conference participants are predominantly old white men in suits. I walk by the only young woman, who must be in her early twenties and is nervously speaking into a camera.

'What a pretty ribbon you're wearing in your hair,' a male voice behind me says. I turn round. 'May I kidnap you for a little media interview?'

The man, who is acting authoritatively enough to be one of the organisers, smiles a friendly smile.

'Umm,' I demur. 'You mean now?'

'Yes, we need to show that this is actually a completely legitimate event, it's important for participants to share their experiences.'

'But I just arrived,' I say. 'Can I sleep on it?' Desperately searching for reasons not to give an interview from a climate science denier conference I improvise: 'I have a bit of an eye infection and I won't look good in front of a camera right now.'

'Of course, but I'll follow up on that tomorrow.'

'Germany, that educated and scientific nation, believes this nonsense [referring to the climate crisis] every day anew,' Michael Limburg, EIKE's vice president and AfD politician, opens the conference. He is an electro-technician who wanted to complete his PhD in Physics and Geosciences at Leipzig University, though his dissertation was declined and described as scientifically unsound in 2010.[142] Michael Limburg does not entirely deny climate change, but believes humans can adapt to rising temperatures by installing air conditioning everywhere.[143]

As well as drinks and finger food, there are copies of the far-right newspapers *Epoch Times* and *Junge Freiheit* on offer. I take a copy of the *Epoch Times* and sit down at the back of the room.

'Are you a journalist?' a man next to me asks out of the blue.

I feel a stab of anxiety. Did I look suspicious? 'No' I reply a little too quickly.

'What do you do then?' he asks, now seemingly out of interest.

'I work in marketing and study zoology on the side, but more as a hobby.'

He looks at me. 'I specialise in polar bears,' I add. This caught his interest. The climate change denier community claims that polar bear populations are hitting record highs. 'We have more polar bears now than ever before,' one participant tells me at the conference.

This is incorrect. In fact, data on polar bear populations is insufficient, as the habitat of polar bears is vast and hard to monitor. There are just a couple of regions where the exact numbers are well known: in Canada, for example, it looks as if polar bear populations are stable, but no one really knows whether the bears they are counting come from – they may have migrated from other regions where sea ice is melting. Overall, the population is very vulnerable to the effects of global warming.[144]

Research shows that our planet has lost half of its wildlife in the past 40 years.[145] A peer-reviewed study found that 'nearly half of the 177 mammal species surveyed lost more than 80 per cent of their distribution between 1900 and 2015'.[146] The World Wide Fund for Nature (WWF) does not list polar bears as one of the most critically threatened species but as a vulnerable animal. There are other animals that are much more immediately endangered as a result of climate change, such as the Amur leopard, black rhino and the Bornean orangutan. Also endangered are the blue whale, bluefin tuna and many other animals.[147] But polar bears with their apparently stable populations are a typical starting point for climate 'contrarians' to deny the mass extinction of species.

The speakers at the conference are highly international. Some join in person, others via Skype from the US, Canada and Australia. I am witnessing the global reach of climate denial networks with my own eyes. Among the people who have travelled across the Atlantic to join the international meet-up is James Taylor, the president of the Heartland Institute.

James Taylor would run any campaign if the price was right. In December 2019, two German undercover journalists posed as PR agents who claimed that their clients in the automotive and energy sectors wanted James to run campaigns for them in exchange for large sums of money. He immediately shared his toolbox of climate disinformation tactics with them and explained how clients can make 'donations' completely anonymously, via a controversial service called Donors Trust, even if they give large sums to the organisation. This is how the Heartland Institute receives a large part of its investment.[148] Taylor revealed that their yearly budget is around 6 million dollars.

Between 2016 and 2020 the institute worked closely with the Trump administration.[149] He believes that 'the Democrats are going to be wiped out in the next election' and is bullish about his success. 'In the US we are winning,' he announces at the beginning of his speech. 'Approximately half of Americans don't buy into the so-called climate crisis.' Like most things said at the conference, this is incorrect. A 2020 survey found that 21 per cent of the US population believe that the climate is not changing or that humans are not responsible for the changes.[150] Twenty-one per cent is still a lot. It's not half the population, but contrary to liberals' common assumptions, climate change denial is not a fringe phenomenon.

James is convinced that the 'climate realists' haven't yet been successful enough with their narrative in Europe, where a higher percentage of the population believes in man-made climate change. If it wasn't for organisations like EIKE, 'truth would be lost entirely', he concludes. 'Truth' for James lies far from the scientific consensus. He is not just denying future threats related to the climate crisis but also the destructive effects on lives and livelihoods that communities have already experienced as a result of global warming. A significant part of The United Nations Climate Change Conference COP27 held in Sharm el-Sheikh in 2022 was devoted to the creation of a global 'loss and damage' fund for affected communities. Climate change is no longer an evidence-based concept of the future, it is already happening in front of our eyes. And it is likely to get much worse.

Researchers who are part of a group of more than 14,000 scientists declared in July 2021 that we are not just in a climate crisis but have entered the state of a worldwide climate emergency. According to them, several environmental tipping points are now imminent. In an academic article for *BioScience*, scientists warned of vital signs that indicate the health of the planet is seriously threatened: from deforestation, glacier thickness, and greenhouse gas emissions to sea ice extent – out of 31 signs they found that 18 hit record highs or lows. They also noted an 'unprecedented surge' in climate-related disasters such as devastating floodings in South America, Southeast Asia and Europe, record-shattering heatwaves and wildfires in Australia and the US, and destructive cyclones in Africa and South Asia.[151]

As James Taylor was speaking, around 120 world leaders and thousands of delegates wrapped up the COP26 in Glasgow.[152]

'Those folks are hypocrites,' is Taylor's assessment of Glasgow. He argues that COP26 has turned into the largest carbon dioxide super spreader event in world history, as Joe Biden arrived in Edinburgh on Air Force 1 and activists flew in from all over the world. 'This is nothing more than greenwashing and hypocrisy.'

While this is a valid point to make, the climate science denier camp has systematically used this type of finger-pointing as a targeted attack on the climate activist community. The attack on Joe Biden follows a long history of 'carbon-shaming' climate activists such as Al Gore, Leonardo Di Caprio, Prince Harry, Barack Obama and Greta Thunberg. *The Daily Caller*, a news outlet founded by the conservative Fox News commentator Tucker Carlson, suggested that Gore's home consumed 34 times more energy than the average US household. Over the last decade *The Daily Caller* has received 3.5 million dollars in funding from the Koch Family Foundations and the Charles

Koch Institute. According to Greenpeace, the Koch brothers spent 15 million dollars on financing 90 groups that attacked climate science and policy between 1997 and 2018.[153]

'Carbon shaming' is a shared tactic of the networks that work against green activism, and has been successfully passed from one organisation to the next. The success of carbon shaming against individuals lies in directing attention away from the companies emitting the biggest share of greenhouse gases. An analysis by the Climate Accountability Institute found that 20 fossil fuel companies can be linked to over a third of all carbon emissions.[154] Compared to that, the emissions of activists are negligible.

When climate activists' behaviour can't be used against them, the anti-climate science lobby instead resorts to attacking their character. Large networks of online trolls have sought to discredit and attack Greta Thunberg based on her autism diagnosis and age. EIKE vice president Michael Limburg called Greta Thunberg 'retarded'[155] and said her parents should be punished.[156] Meanwhile, former Brazilian President Jair Bolsonaro called Greta Thunberg a 'little brat' and Donald Trump said she had an 'anger management problem'.[157]

Climate activists are trying various tactics to push back on the deniers, including demonstrating outside the conference. 'The Fridays for Future protests outside the conference building were ridiculously small,' a conference participant says to me before embarking on a rant against environmental activists. I resist the temptation to point to the fact that EIKE did not announce the location of the conference until the last minute. The exact venue was never made public, just communicated to conference participants via email.

Even though I see white hair wherever I look at the conference, the climate change denier networks understand that they need to appeal to young voices too. According to an Avaaz survey, seventy-five per cent of young people aged 16 to 25 across the world feel the future is frightening. Almost four in ten young people hesitate to have children themselves due to concerns over the climate crisis.[158] The data shows that the debate about taking action on climate change is a generational dispute. But the climate change denier networks have stepped up their game to tap into youth culture and reach younger audiences.

Over the past few years, the old structures of the climate science denial lobby have been revolutionised to cater to the next generations. The predominantly older male community understood that they needed to tap into the power of social media, and began to scout young YouTube influencers. If Greta Thunberg is the star of the Fridays for Future movement, the 21-year-old German influencer Naomi Seibt is the climate change deniers' answer to her. The girl with long blonde hair and rigorously applied make-up was originally a local activist in Germany before rising to fame internationally. She became interested in politics as a young teenager after attending events with her mother who is a lawyer with a history of representing far-right populist politicians of the Alternative for Germany (AfD). Two years later, when Seibt was sixteen years old, she participated in an AfD writing competition and published her nationalist poem 'Sometimes I Keep Silent' on the far-right blog Philosophia Perennis.[159] In 2019, she joined the youth wing of the AfD party and began her YouTube activism to campaign against migration, feminism and climate action.[160]

Today, Seibt strikes out at climate activism, Covid vaccines and abortion rights, reaching an audience of hundreds of thousands globally.[161] She owes her success largely to wider conservative and right-wing support networks, which have been pushing her content over the past few years. The white nationalist movement Generation Identity and the far-right populist AfD have promoted her work, while the Heartland Institute has sponsored her activism since 2020, when Seibt appeared at the Conservative Political

Action Conference, the US's largest annual conservative gathering.[162] The effect of the right's networked propaganda machinery is impressive: Naomi Seibt has become one of the most influential young climate sceptics today. The German teenager has been dubbed 'anti-Greta' for pitting her audiences against Greta Thunberg: 'Who do you believe more?'

The inevitable question here is: why would US institutions such as the Heartland Institute invest money in strengthening climate change denial in Germany? Because Germany has taken a lead role internationally in driving climate action, including the reduction of greenhouse gas emissions and the shift to alternative energy sources. As such, the country is seen as strategically important in fighting climate policies.[163] It's become a key battleground in the debate.

* * *

I hold back at the EIKE conference dinner, trying to decide where to sit. Eventually I opt for the youngest-looking table, made up of men in their twenties and early thirties. Big mistake. Could I have anticipated meeting sympathisers of the extreme right at a climate change denier conference? Probably. But of the roughly 200 people who are there I have managed to sit next to a white nationalist. I will call him Tom.

As I put down my plate next to his, Tom announces 'I was kicked out of my student association just because I said Germany should stay white.' While conversations about migrants and non-white minority communities dominate the table, I keep my eyes down and try to focus on my food. These are not good opening topics for me, and I am seriously worried about being recognised. The German Identitarian scene knows me too well from previous undercover investigations in their circles. This conference was not supposed to be about white nationalism. But there is a bigger overlap between the climate change denier scene and white nationalist circles than I had anticipated. A 2020 study by the Oxford Internet Institute found that support for far-right populist parties was strongly linked to scepticism on climate issues and opposition to climate-friendly policies.[164]

The conversation finally moves on from race to criticising climate activists. 'I'm wearing a suit to distinguish myself from these green lefties,' one of the young men proudly proclaims and laughs. I look down at my own black blazer, now glad about my choice of clothing, and try to choke down the big chunk of meat on my plate. At the buffet I automatically headed to the vegetables, before thinking better of it. I didn't want to look like a green lefty vegetarian.

'Do you work in the climate field?' I ask the white nationalist next to me.

'No, I'm just here with some of my friends.' He points to the other side of the table. One of the young men is an EIKE organiser. Moritz tells us that they very intentionally selected Gera as the setting for the conference. 'The circumstances in Thuringia are – let's say – special. We have enough connections here to be able to do this. Usually, conferences of this size wouldn't take place anymore, especially not in a public building like this. But well, it helps to have friends in government.' The AfD has just triumphed in the regional Thuringia Election 2021, where it became the second strongest party after the radical left party The Left.[165]

The rest of the evening's conversation is more or less as I'd expected, mainly bashing climate prediction models and downplaying CO_2 emissions and rising sea levels. 'Weather predictions become more difficult and less accurate the further you go into the future,' the man to my left says. 'Why do scientists think they can predict the temperatures for the 2050s?' I resist pointing out that climate scientists usually talk about the climate, not the weather. While weather can change from hour to hour and reflects short-term changes in the atmosphere, climate describes weather patterns over a longer period of time (>30 years) in a certain region.[166] Of course weather changes are highly unpredictable, but climate patterns can be modelled based on past and current trends.

We move on to CO2, the second favourite topic of the climate change sceptics scene. Academic research shows CO2 is not the only cause of global warming, but it is considered the most important one by the vast majority of climate scientists.[167] Moreover, the high connectivity of different variables means that CO2 release is causing a chain reaction of factors that cumulatively reinforce global warming[168] and lead to related effects such as ocean acidification, in turn leading to losses in biodiversity.

Climate science sceptics like to cast doubt on the so-called Keeling curve, which shows the accumulation of carbon dioxide in the earth's atmosphere. 'CO2 is not the villain it has been portrayed as,' they say at the conference, to applause from lobbyists in the oil industry. Some EIKE participants believe climate change is determined by hundreds of factors such as ocean cycles, volcanic activities and land use, while CO2 effects are only marginal. Others think the rising temperatures are caused by varying solar activities. A third faction doesn't even believe that global temperatures are rising – James Taylor falls into that category. 'You cannot have a global warming crisis if temperatures are abnormally cool,' he tells us at the conference.

Day one of the conference has given me a lot to think about, and there is still another full day to go. But when I arrive at the venue the next morning, I know the game is up. The security guards look at me awkwardly, unsure whether they are angry or amused, before calling the EIKE conference manager. As he walks towards me from the other side of the reception hall I know he has found out who I am. He has a furious expression in his eyes and for a moment I am tempted to run. I take a deep breath and force my feet to stay put. 'Why am I no longer allowed in?' I ask politely, my toes itching to push off for a sprint. 'There was an issue with your name,' he says.

'Can we correct it?' He shakes his head, pointing towards the door. I ask whether I am being kicked out for political reasons, and he says no. But we both know the truth. While EIKE is keen to develop its network, it also tries to defend itself from outside scrutiny and infiltrators.

I am not entirely devastated to be heading home. To compensate for having paid a climate change denier organisation 55 euros to attend its terrible conference, I donate double the amount to Greenpeace. Luckily, environmental activist networks are still more influential than those of the climate change deniers. But research by the Alan Turing Institute shows that climate scepticism has been growing four times as fast as pro-climate content on Twitter in recent years. Tweets by climate change sceptics were shared 16 times more during COP26 in 2021 than during COP21 in 2014.[169] The sceptics' growing power to dominate online discourse, and their ability to block progress, makes it harder for environmental campaigners to be heard. What I took from my conversations with both environmental activists and climate science deniers is that some form of dialogue will become more important in the coming years, especially as the topic is increasingly politicised. Positive change can only happen with environmentally friendly governments in power.

Science is undeniably on the side of climate change activists, whose warnings of an imminent climate emergency are backed by thousands of studies. Nevertheless, deniers and their sympathisers have been able to spread misinformation on a global scale. At first sight, their arguments can sound convincing, especially when you have not looked at the data and scientific studies that underscore environmental concerns for the future. Journalists and political activists need to counter this with better scientific literacy, and be prepared to debunk flawed arguments put forward by climate science deniers. The more I looked into the climate change denial camp, the clearer it became that their strategy was largely based on the systematic spread of half-truths via their global lobbying networks.

BOOSTING ALT-MEDIA

I don't know much about White Lives Matter when I first join them as part of my undercover research. Founded in the US in 2016 in response to the Black Lives Matter protests and declared a hate group by extremism monitoring organisations such as the Southern Poverty Law Center (SPLC) and the Anti-Defamation League (ADL), they grew to become an influential network that counts hundreds of thousands of followers and many affiliated groups worldwide. 'We declare war against the anti-White system and anyone trying to suppress us. We are united by Blood, Culture and Spirit and we will never give up on each other,' an announcement reads as I enter the White Lives Matter Official channel on Telegram.

My avatar 'Claire' is that of a typical pro-White activist: patriotic logo, free speech tagline and comments filled with alt-right insider references: the 'OK' hand sign, YWNRU (You will not replace us) and the Identitarian lambda. I know from experience that Claire will be asked to prove her European heritage and loyalty to whiteness.

Soon after I join White Lives Matter, their administrators urge me and other newcomers to engage in regular 'pro-White activism', both online and offline:

> Join us in our quest for reviving White Consciousness in 2021 by, at minimum, dedicating 2 hours a month to meeting other pro-Whites and standing in brotherly struggle.

If you are physically impaired, you can share this online. If you can't make banners, you can print a sticker. If you can't attend a march, you can get your family and friends to watch Europa – The Last Battle.

Then I receive the official members' manual. Their Open Security guide includes tips for online and offline communications efforts: 'We do everything in our powers to keep you safe, there are a few rules YOU should follow in this increasingly anti-White World.'

ONLINE
- Use a well-reputed VPN with no logs.
- Use an alt/anon phone number not associated with you.
- Turn off app permissions and location settings.
- Never use or reveal your real name, phone number, hometown or where you work online.

OFFLINE
- Attire – balaclava style mask, sunglasses, hat, unidentifiable clothing.
- Body mods – hide tattoos, remove identifiable piercings.
- Careful when and who you share your ideas and political positions with. Don't say anything you don't have to. Do not wear swastikas or anything a glower [a federal agent in disguise] would wear.
- Always be prepared to defend yourself and others. Preferably a sidearm. But sometimes you'll have to settle for a knife, mace, taser, etc. . . . Always have some options.

The introductory materials do not just outline tactics and security precautions. They also give new members specific instructions on how to speak about 'the White Genocide' and 'White Replacement' in media pieces and campaigns. The key talking point is: 'White people are currently only 8 per cent of the world population. A White person in America is 45 to 200 times more likely to be killed or attacked by non-Whites than vice versa.'

'The media doesn't report the truth' I hear again and again from fellow members in the channel. One of Donald Trump's key contributions to the mainstreaming of far-right fringe ideas was his outright hostility towards traditional media outlets, in particular those sitting on the liberal-left or political centre. Across the world, far-right populist leaders and commentators have copied Trump's media denouncement tactic and established a modus operandi of bashing trusted media sources as 'fake news' and 'lying press'. The result? Trust in media is low worldwide.[170] In 2021, Americans' trust in media dipped to the second lowest point in recorded history – just four points above the 32 per cent record low in 2016.[171] Only 7 per cent of US adults said they have 'a great deal' of trust and confidence in newspapers and broadcast reporting. The Reuters Institute Digital News Report 2022 found that almost half of British people now actively avoid the news. This figure has doubled over the past five years in the UK. One reason is fatigue from years of rolling Covid news and political coverage, but rising distrust in British media also plays a role. Only 34 per cent of the UK population trust the country's media, which is a 16 per cent drop since the Brexit referendum.[172] In Australia, the proportion of 'news avoiders' is particularly high among the younger generations.[173]

Off the back of this growing distrust in established media outlets, an entirely new landscape of media websites and social media news channels has emerged: alternative media or 'alt-media'. Today's far-right leverages this arsenal of news sources that frame themselves as pro-free speech and anti-elite. They reach from the English language alternative news sites *Breitbart*, *InfoWars*, *The Gateway Pundit* and *Westmonster* to the German Identitarian outlets *Junge Freiheit*, *Epoch Times* and *Compact* and the Russian-sponsored RT and *Sputnik* offshoots. Connecting the news and grassroots audiences you then have the channels of far-right pundits and influencers on alternative social media sites such as BitChute, Substack, Odysee, Gab, Parler, Truth Social, Gettr, Telegram and Discord.

Once fringe ideas have gained enough traction in 'alt-media', they easily enter the 'mainstream media'. Countless tropes from far-right websites, forums and encrypted chats have already been repeated, endorsed and popularised in mass media outlets such as Fox News and the *Daily Mail*. Tucker Carlson, the host of Fox News's highest rated programme *Tucker Carlson Tonight*, has called white supremacy 'a hoax'. He has also defended 'It's okay to be White' (IOTBW), a slogan born on the alt-right's Politically Incorrect (/pol/) board on 4chan,[174] and described Iraqis as 'semiliterate primitive monkeys'.[175] This is how fringe ideas have reached a broad church of paleo-conservatives whose conservatism expands to both societal and economic issues, right-wing libertarians who embrace capitalism and non-interventionism, and neo reactionaries whose philosophy is anti-democratic and anti-egalitarian.

The spread of alt-media is shifting the parameters of acceptable language and debate. It has effectively moved the Overton Window, allowing for more extreme language and imagery to enter mainstream media commentary.

In the US, right-wing podcaster Joe Rogan let the 'n-word' slip on his 11-million-viewers show. NPR's film critic Eric Deggans blamed Rogan's use of racist language on what he calls the 'Bigotry Denial Syndrome', the misleading idea that oneself is immune to saying or doing something bigoted.[176] After widespread criticism, Rogan said he regretted his repeated use of the anti-Black slur. Similarly, the seven-time NBA All-Star Kyrie Irving apologised after posting wildly anti-Semitic content on

Twitter. He shared the movie *Hebrews to Negroes*, which is based on a book that suggests that 'many high-ranking Jews have reported to worshipping Satan and Lucifer'. Irving later refused to comment on his beliefs on Jews.[177]

An even more prominent example is Kanye West, who now calls himself Ye. The Black US rapper and pro-Trump activist prompted international outcries from anti-racism organisations when he turned up to Paris Fashion Week wearing a 'White Lives Matter' T-shirt. Conservative commentator Candace Owens, who is also Black, posed with Ye for a picture, wearing a matching T-shirt.[178] On another occasion Ye questioned the history of slavery, writing: 'For 400 years? That sounds like a choice.'[179] Ye has long been making headlines for stirring controversy with his hateful statements, including anti-Semitic conspiracy myths about 'the Jewish media' and an alleged 'Jewish agenda'. For example, Ye suggested that the music industry is controlled by the Jews.[180] 'I gotta get the Jewish business people to make the contracts fair. Or die trying', he posted on Instagram. After repeated violations of social media platform regulations, his Twitter and Instagram accounts were blocked and Adidas cancelled his contract.

Ye had twice as many Twitter followers than there are Jews in the world: the global Jewish population is estimated to be 14.8 million, while his Twitter followership was at 30 million. According to CNN, Ye has an obsession with Adolf Hitler and even wanted to name his 2018 album after the Nazi leader.[181] His cryptic tweet saying he would go 'death con 3 on Jewish people' could hardly be read as anything else than a threat to violence against Jews. Ye's statements have already provoked real-world consequences: in L.A., protesters were photographed giving Nazi salutes and showing banners in reference to Ye's anti-Semitic slogans.[182]

Elon Musk is another figure whose comments and tweets have used imagery and ideas from the radical fringes. His takeover of

Twitter has turned the social media platform into an increasingly hostile place for trans people and other minorities. The Tesla founder is not an outspoken anti-trans activist but his words and actions, such as writing that 'pronouns suck' have sent clear signals to the trans community. In the first couple of months after the takeover, the platform saw an 800 per cent increase of anti-LGBTQ slurs. Musk's 'new Twitter' restored hundreds of accounts of far-right and QAnon activists and instead banned a range of left-wing accounts.[183] Unsurprisingly, the far-right have found a new hero in Musk, who himself shared a 'Pepe the frog' meme and tweeted 'the woke mind virus is either defeated or nothing else matters'.[184] He also featured a German World War II soldier in one of his posts, which the alt-right saw as pledge of allegiance.

The mainstreaming of imagery and language from radicalised subcultures shows up in more insidious ways. In December 2022 English broadcaster Jeremy Clarkson made comments about the Duchess of Sussex Meghan Markle, which used deeply violent and misogynist imagery. British press coverage of Markle has also had protracted racist undertones, making his attack even more loaded. In his column in the *Sun* he wrote that he is 'dreaming of the day when she is made to parade naked through the streets of every town in Britain while the crowds chant, "Shame!" and throw lumps of excrement at her', in reference to a *Game of Thrones* scene.[185] 'I hate her on a cellular level,' read another line in his piece. Clarkson apologised later in a tweet and the *Sun* removed his column from the website after the press regulator received 12,000 complaints, but the damage was done.

There are numerous sub-groups of White Lives Matter (WLM) across the world. On Telegram alone, almost every US state and European country has its own chapter, and there are dedicated groups for Australia, New Zealand and Canada. Based on my research, I estimate the numbers of followers to be in the hundreds of thousands. They have dedicated sub-channels on subjects such as 'Christian Aryanism' and 'Adamic Enlightenment'. Other topical channels range from religion, health and home-schooling to anthropology, arts, news and memes. White Lives Matter Official is one of many white identity grassroots channels. Its 6,500 subscribers on Telegram believe that they 'must fight the actionable anti-White force with an even more actionable pro-White spirit'. One group administrator promises: 'In the end, Victory will be Ours. Freedom or Death!' He continues:

> WE ARE THE NORMAL WHITE PEOPLE
> WHO KEEP THIS COUNTRY ALIVE.
> WE ARE THE TAXPAYERS.
> WE ARE THE CHURCHGOERS.
> WE ARE THE 'NORMIES'.
> WE ARE THE 'MANIPULABLE'.
> WE ARE THE ORGANIC BODY
> THE PARASITES FEED OFF OF.
> WE ARE THEIR WORST NIGHTMARE.
> WHITE LIVES MATTER

Once you are in one Telegram channel, Pandora's box is open: you get invitations and recommendations for others. The WLM group focused on the EU and UK shares a propaganda video from the US, where activists wearing masks, sunglasses and caps – in line with the movement's Open Security guide – attach provocative flyers and QR codes across the country. 'The choice is yours. The future is in your hands.' The host of the WLM EU and United Kingdom group writes. 'Are you going to live a passive life where your happiness will be driven by another "happening" on some obscure forum? Or are you going to act mature and responsible and contribute to the salvation of our people?'

In their briefings, White Lives Matter leaders have called on their followers to avoid using slurs, neo-Nazi symbols and violent means to spread the movement's message. 'Delivery and "optics" matter,' one group host writes to us. Their public communications reflect a wider strategy adopted by far-right activists in recent years: to allow their extreme ideas to leak into mainstream discourse, they have rebranded their campaigns and hidden their hateful messages behind a satirical cloak. As US counter-extremism expert Cynthia Miller-Idriss showed in her research, the far-right has 'gravitated away from the singular, hard-edged skinhead style in favor of sophisticated and fashionable commercial brands that deploy coded extremist symbols'.[186] Their extremist campaigns are tailored to resonate with more wide-spread grievances in the population such as freedom of speech or cultural heritage.[187] When undercover with white supremacists in the run-up to the lethal white supremacist protests in Charlottesville in 2017, I witnessed lengthy conversations about how to appeal to mass audiences.

Ideas from white identitarianism have increasingly infiltrated mainstream political discourse. The so-called Great Replacement – the notion that whites are gradually being erased by non-whites to allow a global cabal of elites to take control – first appeared as a radical conspiracy myth in 2010. The term was coined as 'grand replacement' by the French novelist-turned-campaigner Renaud Camus. Today, the myth of an orchestrated white genocide has become so mainstream that even political frontrunners are using it in their campaigns. The French presidential candidate Éric Zemmour propagated the racist conspiracy myth on TV and social media ahead of the 2022 election. A survey the same year found that nearly half of the Republican electorate agrees at least to some extent with the idea that native-born Americans are being deliberately replaced with immigrants.[188]

Where does this revival of white activism come from? In part, the world has seen a massive backlash against Black people following the surge in BLM activism after the 2020 killing of George Floyd. By early 2021 BLM had inspired protests in more than 70 countries across the world.[189] An analysis of over 7,700 protests in the summer of 2020 revealed that 93 per cent of all BLM demonstrations were peaceful.[190] But for white supremacists, they became an opportunity to fearmonger. 'Do not allow our lands to turn into Haiti . . . time to shut the savage beasts down. Shut down Black Lives Matter,' Rebecca Barnette, Women's Division leader of the National Socialist Movement and co-founder of White Lives Matter in the US said.

The BLM protests in the summer of 2020 sparked a return of biologically racist themes in many countries, including the US, UK and Germany.[191] Biological racism is the pseudo-scientific belief that there is a genetic justification of racism. An example is the idea that Black people are genetically inferior to whites in the evolutionary chain or that they are less intelligent and more aggressive, all of which are irreconcilable with modern genetic research. Right-wing news websites and TV shows systematically demonised and dehumanised BLM activists, turning their viewers' hatred and resentment towards the Black community.

Leading politicians have followed suit in portraying BLM as violent, dangerous and threatening to white communities. British Conservative MP Sajid Javid said BLM is not a 'force for good'.[192] Trump called the movement 'a symbol of hate' and described its activists as 'thugs'. Political condemnation of BLM has exacerbated societal tensions on the topic of anti-racist activism. A YouGov survey for the organisation More in Common found that 35 per cent of Britons see BLM as a negative force, while 46 per cent perceive the movement as distinctively positive.[193]

Has BLM increased racial tensions? Fifty-five per cent of Brits believe it has. But organisers of BLM argue that it has just exposed pre-existing fault lines.[194] White supremacists have exploited the moment to orchestrate a backlash and in so doing recruit a new generation of sympathisers to their dedicated alternative media channels; all under the banner of 'White Lives Matter' (WLM) or 'All Lives Matter'.

* * *

The White Lives Matter channel brings me directly to one of their most prominent propagandists in Britain: Mark Collett. He is the founder of the Patriotic Alternative, Britain's biggest white nationalist movement. Founded in 2019, it has local offshoots across the country, hundreds of activists and tens of thousands of followers. It has the declared goal of removing all non-white people from the UK.

The 41-year-old father and self-declared patriot grew up in Leicestershire. Mark was once the director of publicity at the far-right political party British National Party (BNP) and the chairman of its youth wing. As early as 2002 he gained notoriety for calling AIDS a 'friendly disease because Blacks, drug users and gays have it'. In 2020 he organised a worldwide White Lives Matter campaign on International Indigenous People's Day.[195]

'Obviously people have misconceptions about me,' Mark says at the start of our conversation. His voice sounds calm, almost too calm for what he is about to tell me. To Mark I am Claire Lafeuille, a French-British free speech warrior sympathetic to white nationalist movements and a citizen journalist who is about to launch her own podcast series on controversial topics. Does Claire agree with everything Mark says? No. But she also seems naïve enough to be trusted in a one-on-one conversation.

'Let's start with an association game,' I say to him, silently cringing at how shaky my voice sounds. I continue:

'Black Lives Matter.'

Mark takes a split second to respond: 'A communist insurgence intent on wrecking the West and reducing white people to hated second class citizens.'

'Feminists,' I continue. People like Mark often blame feminism for declining birth rates among whites.

'An attack on the traditional family,' he bursts out, taking only a brief break, 'aimed at turning women into something they were never meant to be or will be happy being.'

I swallow hard and struggle to think of the next word.

'Joe Biden,' I say after a few seconds.

Mark's response comes instantly in an amused voice: 'A puppet president who doesn't know what he's doing, probably suffering from dementia that will usher in some of the most anti-white and anti-traditional policies America has ever known.'

I wonder what he thinks about . . . 'Covid'.

In a self-confident voice Mark announces: 'A fake pandemic used to spread fear and to institute draconian new legislation which takes away the rights of people all over world.'

'One more,' I say. 'Climate change'.

Again, no hesitation in Mark's reply: 'A manufactured problem used to raise taxes and to guilt-trip white people into not having children. The real threat to the environment is population growth not climate change.'

It is incredible how Mark somehow manages to make everything about the so-called 'white genocide', whether it is feminism, Covid or climate change. His example powerfully demonstrates how radical ideas connect with and feed each other. As people adopt one set of extremist views like white nationalism, they may weave in additional layers to their conspiracy myths and embrace anti-feminist, climate change denial, anti-vax ideologies.

As Mark gives me a tutorial based on his radical convictions, I wonder what exactly it is that he is afraid of. He says: 'We're seeing this massive demographic change where most European nations become places where the indigenous people are a minority.' He believes that in Britain this will be the case from around 2066. The Patriotic Alternative website even has a countdown until the UK will supposedly be majority non-white. Mark goes on in a sombre voice: 'We're also seeing a sustained attack on white people, upon traditionalism, upon healthy moral values and upon the fundamental building blocks of Western civilisation.'

It is hard to argue with people like Mark. He is convinced that demographic change and racial or cultural differences are responsible for almost every problem in Europe: knife crimes, child abuse, rising house prices and the destruction of green spaces all feature on his list. It does not seem to cross his mind that these problems might stem from other causes. An extensive 2020 review found no association between ethnicity and youth violence in the UK. Instead, it concluded that negative childhood experiences, poor mental health, discrimination and socio-economic problems were the strongest predictors for street violence such as gang crimes and knife offences.[196] A 2020 Home Office report also debunked the claims that child grooming gangs are predominantly black and Asian: 'Offenders come from diverse backgrounds,' it found, but groups tended to be made up of men of the same ethnicities.

I am shocked at the speed and eloquence of Mark's responses in my association game, as if he often practises. Perhaps he does — since his twenties, he has been actively campaigning for far-right and white nationalist causes. Mark has been aware of ethnic differences from school age, he tells me. He grew up in an all-white village, but the nearest major city was the first in the UK where whites became a minority: Leicester. And that made him afraid. 'I realised that I wanted to do something about it because of the profound effect on everyone living in the UK and on my future children.' One of his underlying grievances is that people of European descent have lost their community whereas 'Jews, Muslims and Afro-Caribbeans have their community and sense of identity fostered by our government.' According to people like Mark, 'anti-white racism' is propagated by media, taught to us by the education system and pushed by 'the establishment'.

Mark has a child himself now, and is very focused on recruiting young people into Patriotic Alternative. He tells me: 'We do a lot of community building and leafletting. But activism can be as small as speaking to family and friends.' The website features a call-out: 'Time to Play Your Part',[197] announcing 'We are recruiting in South England'. Every weekend Patriotic Alternative's local offshoots organise outreach activities: they offer camping trips, trail hikes, fitness clubs, bird-watching excursions and paintball sessions for white British teenagers to 'build communities'. Social media posts advertise their activities 'After a hard morning of sand sprints and weight training, the team headed into town for a well-deserved breakfast,' one of their posts reads, showing pictures of a workout session on the beach in northern Scotland and a fry-up.

Mark regularly hosts Call of Duty videogame tournaments, offering a mix of fun and political indoctrination. Sometimes there are minors among the players: some users write they have their 'bedtime' soon or mention they have to go to school the next morning. To most of them, being radicalised simply seems like a game.

'Hello friends,' a user who calls himself Adolf Hitler greets the other players.

'Heil Mark,' another one comments. 'It's sad England isn't white anymore.'

Barkley Walsh is one of Patriotic Alternative's youngest recruits. He followed Mark from the age of thirteen and now runs his own online show called 'Zoomer Talk', which is livestreamed via Patriotic Alternative's YouTube channel. 'I watched a f***ing meme compilation,' he says, half-jokingly, talking about what led him to the movement. 'That is what's f***ing led me to being in a campsite with some of the most notorious neo-Nazis in the country.'[198] The Gen Z recruit is convinced that young people need to stand up for their race: 'You don't see us in advertisements anymore,' he warns. 'All these mixed-race couples. It's all white erasure at the end of the day.' An undercover investigation by Channel 4 *Dispatches* recorded him using anti-Muslim slurs and making an anti-Semitic comment about a Jewish teacher.[199] He has a clear mission: turn young people into fellow 'Zoomer nationalists'. 'Eventually Patriotic Alternative will be the future for us,' Barkley says in one of his talks.

Like many other far-right extremist movements, Patriotic Alternative gained ground massively during the pandemic. Its main Facebook and Instagram accounts were deplatformed in early 2021, soon after reaching over 16,000 followers. But the group has continued to be active on Twitter, Telegram and Gab.[200] The movement has managed to re-unite the splintered British far-right, and absorbed members that range from the more moderate followers of English Defence League founder Tommy Robinson to former members of the terrorist organisation National Action.

On 30 October 2022, a white nationalist-inspired terrorist attack made headlines in the UK. The 66-year-old Andrew Leak firebombed a migrant processing centre in Dover before taking his own life. An hour before Leak carried out his attack, he tweeted: 'We will obliterate them Muslim children are now our target. And there [sic] disgusting women will be targeted mothers and sisters Is burn alive'. His online history shows that he did not just have one enemy but, much like Mark, he connected the dots between different hate ideologies: Leak's posts were agitating against Jews, Muslims, migrants, homosexual and trans people. He also posted about New World Order and Covid-related conspiracy myths.[201]

The pandemic has fuelled radicalisation towards violence. But it has also mainstreamed extreme views and allowed white nationalist online groups to reach new target audiences. Lockdown was 'a blessing for nationalists', the Patriotic Alternative's website declared. Widespread frustration with the status quo was projected onto the establishment and demonised out-groups. Movements like Patriotic Alternative had only to connect personal grievances to white nationalist narratives in order to earn a raft of new recruits. To rack up mobilisation during the pandemic, White Lives Matter activists even started creating alternative homeschooling curricula for white children.

* * *

'Welcome to the Ministry of Homeschooled Education,' is how I am greeted when entering the next Telegram group, which describes itself as 'a Christian Aryan channel to help build and facilitate independent homeschooling'. The hosts invite me to join the project to help 'future generations of White children'.

Originally this group was the 'National Socialist Book Club' but during the pandemic it was repurposed, becoming a homeschooling group chat for white parents, with the aim of creating 'a concise and complete home-schooling guide, textbook and manual', covering topics as diverse as cartography, biology, economics. And proficiency with firearms.

As I skim through their recommended homeschooling materials, I am rapidly filled with horror. The reading list starts fairly moderately with *An Aryan Classical Education: Understanding the Greek Foundations of Western Philosophy*. The Ministry of Homeschooled Education apparently perceives literature by the Ancient Greeks as the necessary starting point for 'Aryan children'. Their reading list then moves on to Latin orators: from Ovid and Caesar to Augustus. But after this gentle introduction to the Classics they get right to the point with books such as *The Negro: A Menace to American Civilization* and *Anti-Semitic Legends*. These profoundly racist books are both classified as 'essential readings' for high-school-level students.

The channel hosts have compiled texts about biological racism and anti-Semitic myths to form a 'complete workbook' for parents' homeschooling efforts. 'This book on its own should be able to teach your child everything they could ever need to know, if you had no access to other educational resources.' It can be used as a substitute for or supplement to standard education, the Ministry for Homeschooled Education assures members, 'to cover a range of educational fields that are neglected or completely skipped' or 'to straighten out and cut through the propaganda of the corrupt education system'.

Patriotic Alternative even provides a letter template that parents can use to remove their children from school. Their home-schooling materials are aimed at kids from five to sixteen years, and topics include maths, Anglo-Saxon history, Charles Dickens and nature. The curriculum also includes racist songs for children.

A class called 'The People of England' teaches that all English people have white skin.[202] 'So, who are the English?' asks a page which features pictures of white girls. 'We have national traditions and regional ones too; we all have white skin but some of us have red hair, or brown hair, black hair or blond hair; some of us have blue eyes, some of us have green or brown eyes – there is a lot of true diversity amongst the English people!'

A lesson with the name Be Proud of Your People asks questions such as 'Who was first to reach the highest point on Earth? The North and South Poles? The bottom of the ocean?' The given answer to each is 'white people'.[203]

* * *

James sounds his horn at a Black woman who is crossing the street in front of us. She is wearing sunglasses and holding a Black Lives Matter sign in her hands. As we pass, he mumbles something inaudible to himself. Even though I don't hear his words, his anger is palpable through the transparent plastic wall that separates us.

I clear my throat. 'Traffic's rather slow today?'

The black-cab driver exhales loudly. He gazes at the crowd of people that is gathering on Piccadilly. 'I don't understand why they still let these people protest.'

'Black Lives Matter?' I ask.

He nods. Then, as if he can read my thoughts, he adds: 'You know, I'm not racist. Really. I've got Black neighbours who are lovely and polite people. They sometimes looked after my kids when they were young. But these Black Lives Matter protestors only cause trouble. Riots, traffic jams, fights with the police. No bloody respect for public order.'

He honks again, this time because of a driver in front of us who is too busy replying to a text message to see the green light.

'But, well, if you criticise them you are immediately called racist.'

James looks at me through his rear-view mirror, as he says this. There is a hint of fear in his eyes, but the rest of his face remains unchanged. I assume he worries that I will judge him or give him a smaller tip.

'It was the same with Brexit,' his raspy voice continues. 'If you voted Leave, you were immediately called a racist. My children stopped speaking to me and my wife for over a month because they were so upset. They didn't call once in the four weeks after the referendum. I knew they were disappointed but what should we have done? Vote Remain just to avoid a dispute? Lie to them and say we didn't vote Leave? I'm too much of an honest person to be doing that.'

His voice trails off and leaves an awkward silence between us. I decide to make a better effort to show my compassion for his undoubtedly difficult family situation. 'I'm sorry to hear that,' I say. The artificial distance between us created by the plastic Covid protector seems less substantial now. 'I'm sure time will heal even the deepest Brexit wounds. I also had a fight with a friend because he voted for Brexit. I was furious with him at first. But now my anger has transitioned into some form of acceptance.'

James nods and lets out an affirming sound. Then we both look out of the window for some time, waiting for the red lights to turn green.

'Your accent tells me you are not from here. Where are you from?' he asks.

'I'm Austrian,' I say. 'But I feel at home in London and I'm a permanent resident now, so I'm here to stay. Sorry.' I wink at him and he smiles what seems like a genuine smile.

'I honestly don't care where you are from, as long as you pay your taxes and make an effort to be a good citizen. It's the people who bring their cultures and crimes to this country that I'm worried about. Last year my daughter was followed home by a Sudanese man who started talking to her on the street in south London. She's only sixteen, you know. We got so scared we had to call the police but they didn't do anything about it. Their investigations led nowhere really.'

He changes gear. 'You know, I sometimes don't recognise my own country anymore. I grew up in the Peak District and my first encounter with a foreigner was when I moved to London. I think it's great to find so many different communities here. But I don't want us to be losing parts of our identity. Look at what's happening with football.'

The debate on footballers taking the knee, a gesture of protest popularised by BLM, has become a centrepiece in the culture wars between liberal progressives and right-wing conservatives.

Tory MP Lee Anderson boycotted all England games in the lead-up to the Euro 2020 final, arguing that taking the knee equalled endorsing an organisation with 'quite sinister motives'.

But racism in football is very real. During the Euro 2020 tournament I tracked hate posts against the Black players Bukayo Saka, Marcus Rashford and Jadon Sancho. When they missed their chances in the penalties, racist harassment surged. They were attacked by their own team's fans. Bukayo Saka's Instagram feed was littered with comments like 'Go back to Nigeria' or 'Get out of my country'. Some users even called him by the N-word and shared memes that depicted him as a monkey.

Targeted hate campaigns against players in the England football team were serious enough for the Metropolitan Police to launch an investigation. The Football Association harshly condemned the racist abuse of Black players: 'We could not be clearer that anyone behind such disgusting behaviour is not welcome in following the team. We will do all we can to support the players affected while urging the toughest punishments possible for anyone responsible'.[204]

England has never won the UEFA European Football Championship and the last time that England won the FIFA World Cup was in 1966. David Beckham's personal appeal aside, the last few decades of English football have been characterised by rather modest success stories. So I was all the more surprised to see the extent to which national euphoria about England's excellent performance in the 2020 Euros was overshadowed by racism and xenophobia.

Self-proclaimed patriotic movements used the English defeat in the finals to spread hate against ethnic minorities. Some spread hateful social media content that blamed any subpar performance on the non-white players, others created memes that depicted them as monkeys or other animals and linked them to conspiracy myths. 'Africa was in the Finals,' commented the racist Telegram group White Well-Being. A post in the European Identitarian group 'Defend Europa' read: 'Diversity is England's biggest weakness'. Even before the finals, white nationalists were busy spreading racist and dehumanising memes.

Football racism is not just a toxic influence on public discourse. It also has a negative impact on players' performance. An *Economist* analysis found that non-white players played better when stadiums were empty during Covid lockdowns. Experts linked this to the absence of racist abuse during games.[205]

James continues: 'What are all these bloody lies about the Royal family being racist?' Without pausing, he goes on, 'It's a debate about nothing, don't we have more serious problems in this country? What happened to freedom of speech if we are not allowed to make a little joke anymore?' He tells me he doesn't like 'mainstream media's glorification of Black Lives Matter', and it is one reason he has resorted to alternative information sources.

James pulls over at Trafalgar Square. There they are again, the Black Lives Matter logos. If only he knew that I am about to join the protestors. He stares at one of the signs that reads: 'Kill the Bill. NO to more police powers'. In the distance we can hear a voice shouting 'Black Lives Matter' into a megaphone.

James is shaking his head in disbelief. '*All* Lives Matter, don't you think?'

I don't reply. His nervous smile as I get ready to pay signals that he reads my silence as disagreement. Despite our profound political disagreements, I force myself to give him a fair tip. Apart from his frequent use of the horn, he has been a good driver and got me to my destination quickly and safely.

* * *

James was not an anti-democratic, dangerous extremist. He seemed like a kind father and law-abiding citizen. But the phrase he used set off alarm bells. A movement called All Lives Matter is a mainstreamed version of White Lives Matter, and political support for ALM has given white identity struggles a public platform. Donald Trump even used the slogan at one of his rallies in 2016, denouncing Black Lives Matter as 'racist'. He would later call BLM activists 'thugs' and tweet: 'when the looting starts, the shooting starts' in reference to the comment by a Southern police officer during the 1960s civil rights movement.[206]

To many people, All Lives Matter might sound like an innocuous, even positive phrase when taken out of context. I ask Black Lives Matter activist Dr J to explain why it is harmful.

'All Lives Matter are refusing to hear what we say,' she replies. 'We are exposing the fact that for too long there has been disparity on the fundamental value of human life.' BLM's vision *is* to make sure that all lives matter, she goes on to explain. If white people had been saying 'All Lives Matter' for the past hundred years it would be different. But in reaction to BLM, the statement 'All Lives Matter' lacks authenticity. 'As opposed to the actual message that all lives matter, what they are really saying is that it doesn't matter to us how you feel about the positionality of blackness across the world. They are reasserting the value of their lives and refuse to hear what we are saying because it offends them.'

Dr J, aka Jamila Lyiscott, is a spoken word artist, a Harry Potter enthusiast and an educator on racism. She is an assistant professor of social justice education at the University of Massachusetts Amherst, and a leading voice of the Black Lives Matter movement. 'Sometimes in class I might pause the intellectual sounding flow to ask: "Yo! Why dese books neva be about my peoples?", she rapped in a viral TED performance that has been viewed over 5 million times.

You don't have to go as far as white supremacist homeschooling materials to find problems with what students are taught. The standard education system and pedagogy are more aligned with colonialism than most of us realise, Dr J explained to me. In her book *Black Appetite, White Food* she wrote: 'We are force-fed whiteness in our everyday lives at the expense of the rich capacity for our differences to powerfully shape our world.'[207] Today she tries to make the classroom a place where everyone can explore their own biases and prejudice. 'You have to get people out of their comfort zone.'

Dr J grew up in Brooklyn, New York in a family of proud Caribbeans. The extent of white privilege in day-to-day life was a gradual realisation for Dr J. 'The energy in the household I grew up in – the music, the décor and the food – was so deeply Black and Afro-Centric that the cognitive dissonance that I felt when encountering the curriculum in school was even greater,' she tells me. She loved her culture and wanted it to be represented, but felt that there was no space for it. 'You see yourself missing and you feel the incomplete narrative. Then you start to learn that what's required is essentially a compartmentalisation of who you are.' As she felt that she could not be her true self in school, she joined poetry slams and spoken word competitions during her spare time. She witnessed how the winners would use the power of their words to beat thousands of participants and make it all the way to Broadway, and yet they were failing English classes in high school. Again, she felt cognitive dissonance and asked herself how that was possible.

A recent study at the University of California, Berkeley found that as of 2019, America was more racially segregated than it had been in the 1990s.[208] In 2014, 75 per cent of white Americans did not have any non-white friends and 65 per cent of Black people in the US did not have any white friends.[209] Dr J says that 'the black-white binary' is still deeply engraved in politics, pop culture and education, and that frequently the latter is portrayed more positively than the former, with the 'purity' of whiteness contrasted with the 'putridness' of Blackness.

Many people are not racist on purpose. Our idea of racism is focused on intention rather than impact, Dr J argues. But stepping on someone's shoe unwittingly doesn't change the fact that it hurts. Indeed, 85 per cent of Britons of colour think the UK is still very or somewhat racist and that the situation for ethnic minorities has barely improved in the last three decades.[210] The numbers speak for themselves. Black infant mortality in Britain is twice as high as for white infants.[211] Black mothers are five times more likely to die during childbirth than white mothers.[212] Black people are twice as likely to be unemployed,[213] ten times more likely to be stopped and searched and four times more likely to be arrested.[214] Black people account for 3 per cent of the population, but 8 per cent of deaths in custody.[215]

Statistically speaking, Black lives don't matter as much as white lives in many countries. This is why the line 'All Lives Matter' reads like an insult to many Black people. It fails to acknowledge the systemic injustices towards Black people and other ethnic minorities. It does not take their plea for a fairer society seriously. The way the term All Lives Matter is used denies or downplays the scale of anti-Black racism, discrimination and violence. White Lives Matter goes one step further. It suggests that it is white people who are being victimised.

* * *

It is the one-year anniversary of George Floyd's death when I meet Marielle, a 24-year-old Austrian with roots in the Ivory Coast. Her own search for identity is what made her study African History at Vienna University and later join the local Black Lives Matter (BLM) movement in Vienna.

Before the BLM protests swept the world in spring 2020, Marielle was not politically active. 'Growing up in Austria, I didn't think about my own identity too much because I was raised in a whites-only environment.' That changed with BLM. 'I suddenly felt things I had never felt before,' she tells me in a Viennese dialect. She takes a deep breath. 'It was hard work to accept that I am different, and that being different can be a positive thing.' In her teenage years she wanted to fit in. She tried to straighten her hair and adapted her clothing to look more like her friends. 'I think my fear of social rejection started very early. When I was a kid I didn't want to speak French with my dad because I didn't want to be different.' Now she proudly wears her hair in an Afro. To her it is much more than a hair style, it is a political statement.

As she gradually understood what it meant to be Black in a predominantly white society, she went from being politically disengaged to being an activist. 'I came to understand my identity via detours. That's perhaps why my views are radical today. Because I realised what institutional, structural and individual racism can do to people.'

Marielle started her activism out of ancestral pain. She began to do research into anti-Black police crimes and the biased juridical system in the US, but she soon realised the problem of police violence against Black people and other minorities was not confined to the US.

In 1999 and 2000, the police carried out their biggest operation in Austria since World War II. Operation Spring was a systematic crack-down against the Black community; 127 people of African descent were taken into custody for drug dealing, illegal immigration and other crimes – many of them without any evidence. Around a third of the arrested were released shortly afterwards.[216] A large proportion of the targeted people in Operation Spring were part of the Viennese Black activist community, who had protested against police crimes after the Nigerian immigrant Marcus Omofuma was killed by three policemen.

Marielle began to post on social media about her own experiences with racism to reach friends who were not interested in politics. 'I tried to explain to them that some people can't afford to be politically uninvolved because we are experiencing the consequences of politics every single day.'

The response was powerful.

Some of her friends apologised to her for the racist language they had used or for jokes they had made in the past. But she also received a lot of hate as a result of her newfound activism. She was insulted, accused of reversed racism, and lost some of her friends.

Ever since Marielle was little, experiences of racism have made her self-conscious about her identity. 'I sometimes notice that no one wants to sit next to me on public transport. At the same time, I constantly have my hair touched by strangers. I'm often too taken aback in the moment to complain.'

In the countryside it is particularly bad, she reports. When she spends her holidays at her grandmother's in Carinthia, southern Austria, she doesn't want to go shopping or take a walk by herself. She has learnt to read people's gazes and sometimes hears them mumble 'What are these Black people doing here?'

Black women usually experience even more marginalisation than Black men. 'This is because in African cultures and therefore in diaspora communities you often find patriarchal structures,' Marielle explains. The Black Panther movement, for example, was deeply sexist and misogynist.[217] The Black communist radical feminist Claudia Jones called this phenomenon 'super exploitation': Black women experience a triple discrimination on the basis of their skin colour, gender and social class.[218]

Marielle suspects that Austria is among the most racist places in Europe. But the problem of discrimination knows no borders.

* * *

In the US, the quest for racial justice is deeply intertwined with the fight against gun violence. Aalayah Eastmond came to understand its impact on Black communities early in her life.

The Black Lives Matter activist is originally from Brooklyn, New York. When Aalayah was eight years old she and her mother moved to Parkland, Florida, where she was one of only a few Black students at the affluent, predominantly white Stoneman Douglas High School. As a high school junior she was shy and spent most of her spare time playing the violin. 'I was reserved and only spoke out when I was asked to,' Aalayah tells me. 'Which was rare,' she adds, 'because many teachers tended to not pick Black students.' She ignored their occasional racist comments.

But everything changed on 14 February 2018. Aalayah was sixteen years old when a gunman opened fire at her high school. Seventeen people were killed in the shooting. Aalayah survived by hiding behind her dead classmate's body.

Her mother told her that her story could change the lives of millions of people. She decided to turn this traumatic experience into a springboard for activism, and has since become one of America's most important voices on gun violence prevention and racial justice. Shortly after the shooting Aalayah spearheaded the 2018 United States gun violence protests. Following the murder of George Floyd she co-founded Concerned Citizens of DC and led several BLM protests against police brutality. She has testified before US Congress several times.

Today Aalayah studies criminal justice at Trinity Washington University. 'Mass shootings only make up 2 per cent of all gun violence,' she says. 'But gun violence is a much wider problem that disproportionally affects Black communities.' Aalayah has experience of this too: her 18-year-old uncle was shot dead in Brooklyn when she was only two years old.

Black Americans, in particular young Black men, are disproportionately impacted by firearm homicides. Black people only account for 12 per cent of the country's population,[219] yet they make up 58.5 per cent of the Americans who lose their lives to gun violence. Firearm homicide was the leading cause of death for Black men and boys aged 15–34, making them ten times more likely to die from gun violence than white men and boys of the same age group. Most children who are killed in firearm homicides in the US are from ethnic minority communities.[220]

'I can't even describe how frustrating it can be when legislators are not listening or pro-Second Amendment campaigners are shutting their eyes and ears.' Making the connections with other gun violence survivors or mothers who lost their sons to shootings is what keeps Aalayah going. But the sacrifices she makes and the risks she accepts are significant. 'My entire family got doxxed on Twitter last year when I was leading protests in DC,' she tells me. Like so many anti-racism activists, she has become the target of White Lives Matter hatred. 'My address was leaked online to all the white supremacists. One day when I was visiting my mum in Florida, I wasn't really thinking and posted on my Instagram that I was home. And that night someone tried to break in.' Her mother had to move house as a result.

Rising polarisation on the topic of race has inspired a new wave of anti-minority violence and harassment both in the form of online hate crimes and real-world terrorism. In the UK, over 100,000 racially motivated hate crimes were reported in 2021/22, an increase by 19 per cent compared to the previous year.[221]

* * *

'I would love to murder the mayor,' writes Jake in the white supremacist group World Elite, which has almost 9,000 followers. He is referring to the Mayor of London, Sadiq Khan, who has become a top target for white supremacists in the UK due to his skin colour and religion. 'I've already done time for murder. So it won't be a far stretch for me!'

Online backlash to BLM results in real world violence. White Lives Matter has resonated with an increasing number of far-right extremist groups who have long wished for a race war. They have openly planned violent retaliation against Black Lives Matter activists over the messaging app Telegram.[222] In June 2020, self-declared Ku Klux Klan leader Harry Rogers drove a car into a group of Black Lives Matter protesters in Virginia.[223] This was just one in a series of vehicle attacks launched by violent counter-protesters.[224]

The Great Replacement conspiracy theory has inspired multiple deadly terror attacks in recent years. It's been cited as an inspiration by innumerable perpetrators, from the mosque shootings in Christchurch (New Zealand) and the synagogue attacks in Halle (Germany) and Poway (US) to the anti-Latinx and anti-Black attacks in supermarkets in El Paso (US) and Buffalo (US).

One of the dangers of this ideology is its apocalyptic outlook. Let's return to Mark Collett of Patriotic Alternative for a moment. Based on our conversation, he appears convinced there are only two possible futures. One is that indigenous people in the UK and Europe will defend themselves and their children, embrace traditional values, and go back to morality. In the other 'they become a degenerate minority that will be hated by the people that come here'. Mark's conclusion is: 'The white people that are left will be victimised for who they are.' There is no third option.

Today's anti-Black racism often goes hand in hand with anti-Semitic conspiracy theories.

'The people trying to replace us are the global elites,' Mark adds in a casual tone, as if he is talking about what he had for breakfast.

'Who are the global elites?' I ask Mark, trying to sound as naïve as I can.

'They own the vast majority of wealth, they own the media, they are in powerful positions. They know that the people who are most likely a threat to their power are people of European descent. So they have to get rid of us to avoid that we come together. They are afraid of our revolutionary spirit.' He believes that the people who are behind demographic change want to stay in a position where they will never be challenged, where they can hold the keys to power forever. 'All of this is coordinated on international level,' he concludes.

* * *

It is a Sunday evening on a mild autumn day in 2021 when I join the extremist roundtable 'Our Subverted History'. I would have rather gone out for a Sunday roast, but this international gathering of ultra-nationalists feels urgent. I am one of 60 participants from across the world who log on via the closed Telegram group The Great British Debate, a white supremacist channel which claims to focus on 'current events, the Covid plandemic, history, animal rights, the environment and faith.'

An attempt to bring together international members of White Lives Matter, the roundtable includes speakers from the UK, USA, and South Africa. This is the first time I've heard a British white nationalist in conversation with a US-based 'naturopath' and certified nutritionist, and a South African author.

It has been promoted in closed chats on social media and the teaser for the event promises that the speakers will present 'critical misconceptions about their nation's historical narrative, and the "True History" that the world needs to know.' Traditional media is denounced as being a propaganda machine for 'the Jews'. So the question is: how can white identity narratives be brought to a wider audience?

'What's happening in Europe at the moment is probably the biggest social experiment ever carried out on any people in history,' Charlie, a local leader of Patriotic Alternative, announces with a thick Irish accent at the start of the conference. 'Our people have had their collectivism, their ethnocentrism and in-group preference torn out of them. They've been propagandised to believe that anyone can be British, German, French.'

The white nationalists speak about the promotion of globalism by 'them', 'the elites'. Charlie makes clear that he has given up his belief not just in the media but in the democratic system: 'They are not going to let us vote our way out.' Instead, he says, 'we need to rise and collectivise together as the English, Scottish, Irish, Welsh. The same is true for the Germans, the French, the Spanish.' He advises whites to promote their own interests and look out for each other. 'Only then will we regain what our enemies have taken,' he continues. 'If not, then unfortunately we will go down the route that South Africa is currently taking. We will become a despised minority within the nations where our forefathers died.'[225]

Dresden Berns, the American 'naturopath' and certified nutritionist, adds: 'The elites highlight crimes by Europeans and omit crimes of non-Europeans. They do that to guilt-trip us and instil a victim complex in non-white people. This creates a Marxist oppressor and oppressed narrative.'[226] 'Cultural Marxism' has become a buzzword for many far-right extremists to describe the application of Marxist theory to culture. It is directly linked to the anti-Semitic conspiracy belief that the political left – allegedly controlled by the Jews – engages in academic and intellectual efforts to undermine Western culture.

A participant named Handsome Truth with the tagline 'Name the Jew or Die' speaks up: 'I'm in the US, the laws are a little bit different here,' he introduces himself. I know he is about to say something repulsive. 'If we have one group of people who have been expelled from 190 countries over 1,030 times,' he breathes heavily, 'then we know what the problem is. It's this parasite that follows us around nation by nation and uses and abuses us.' He goes on: 'They dominate all of our media, they push paedophilia and homosexuality onto our children.'

These anti-Semitic canards are centuries old. Jews make up roughly 0.2 per cent of the world population. Yet, the idea that 'the Jews' control the media, the financial world and political institutions, while also running dark underground trafficking networks has been around for a long time. From the fourteenth-century Bubonic Plague, to the 1929 Great Depression, 9/11 and the 2008 Financial Crisis – Jews have been blamed for many major crises in the history of humankind.[227]

The early twentieth-century publication *Protocols of the Elders of Zion*, which conveys the fabricated idea of Jews seeking global domination, was a major inspiration for Hitler and the Nazi party and is still influential.[228] But today's anti-Semitic allegations often come in the form of memes or manipulated infographics, for example visuals showing CNN, *The New York Times* and BBC team organisational charts that mark journalists with a Star of David to signal that they are all Jewish.[229] The Buffalo attacker's manifesto contained exactly such graphics. 'They spread their lies through all forms of media,' the terrorist wrote.

Handsome Truth claims to have been an activist and journalist 'exposing these Jews' for quite a while now. He admits to having gone to Jewish institutions to harass Jews, calling them paedophiles and telling them they need to leave the US. 'I have lost my ability to rent a car, lost my ability to use Airbnb. I have had my bank account closed, my business account. I can't use

PayPal. I have had these Antifa people come to my house, which is a Jewish militia.' He continues. 'What it comes down to is: we have to start having the balls to call these people out and not get too involved with the low-hanging fruit, who are the pawns of the Jews: could be feminism, the homos, the Mexicans that are flooding our border. But to stay hyper-focused on just getting these Jews out of our country.'[230]

Another discussion centres around the best timing to engage in violence. Charlie cautions against breaking the laws or resorting to violence too early in the fight: 'We only have so many people in our circle who think the way we do and who understand the game that is being played against our people. We don't need any of our people to be putting themselves at unnecessary risk. We need you out of jail, we need you physically fit and we need you networking with in your local area and nationally with likeminded people. That's all we need you to do *for now*.'

The first female voice in the discussion belongs to a woman who goes by the name Apotheke. 'We are fighting an even more sinister, more dangerous and more clandestine psychological and cultural war than World War II. Did we defeat the wrong enemy in World War II?' she asks. Apotheke announces in a passionate voice that 'the war makers and slave owners never changed'. 'We are the generation that is most overeducated and unemployable. The best path to slavery is through institutional education,' she says. Charlie agrees: 'Slavery is still alive and well. We are slaves if you think about some of today's policies: Our money is being recycled and our labour is used for the elites, the same elites that are importing thousands and thousands of migrants.'[231] I listen incredulously: despite everything I've heard, I can hardly believe that an all-white group is talking about being the victims of slavery.

* * *

After this chilling, hate-filled conversation I long to hear something positive. Could there be a more moderate, conciliatory aspect to the white supremacist movement? 'The future you're painting is rather on the gloomy side,' I say to Mark Collett. 'Can we mend those rifts between the liberals and the right?' The white nationalist shows as little hesitation as always: 'No.' His prediction is that groups will only become more polarised due to their irreconcilable differences. 'We are not going to find a middle ground.'

Many anti-racist activists no longer believe in a middle ground either. Too much has happened since 2016 when Donald Trump won the US election, galvanising the international alt-right. Too little has happened since 1619 when the first slaves reached Point Comfort in Virginia. Dr J and Marielle are not against polarisation. 'Just the basic statement Black Lives Matter – the audacity of Black People – has rattled our nation,' Dr J tells me. 'The level of outrage is extraordinary. So yes, if me saying that I matter, leads to polarisation, then we're gonna have to be polarised.' She continues 'It is weird for people to say: "Oh look what you've done, polarised our nation."' She compares the dynamics to an abusive relationship where the victim speaks up and the abuser distracts from their crimes by pointing to the fact that now there is domestic tension.

The Black Lives Matter movement has brought the topics of racial identity, power and privilege to the forefront of today's political debates. It has given hope to communities across the globe who have faced social and institutional discrimination for many decades. Most people who watched George Floyd suffocate under a police officer's knee have recognised the urgency of the movement's cause and many believe there is a real opportunity to tackle the structural racism that still impacts tens of millions of people living in the US and Europe.

But there is also a looming threat that race-based mobilisation will widen the gap between liberal and illiberal elements of society. In recent years, predictions of demographic change have caused many whites to fear for their position of relative power and privilege. Those who have felt that they were already on the losing end of globalisation have been particularly vulnerable to racialised propaganda. The alternative media ecosystems created by white supremacist movements have exploited this, artificially fuelling concerns about the future of white identity.

Alternative communication structures are part of the new-right's 'meta politics' strategy. They want to change politics by first influencing culture and society, following the Breitbart doctrine. Building out alternative media ecosystems has helped extremists to create new realities for their members in closed-off online worlds. Once they have deconstructed society's prevailing mindsets and reshaped world views among a critical mass, they will be able to fulfil their ultimate ambition: bringing about political transformation.

PROVOKING BACKLASHES

Public attitudes are particularly prone to manipulation when large parts of civil society have difficulty keeping up with the pace of cultural and societal change. A wide-reaching societal backlash is the next step in the mainstreaming process. We can observe this in real time with feminism, climate change activism and Black Lives Matter. But the best example is the severe backlash against the LGBTQ community.

Around one in ten people are estimated to be homosexual or bisexual, although the percentage of people who indicate so in surveys tends to be lower.[232] Roughly 0.6 per cent of US adults identify as trans, according to a study by the Williams Institute at the University of California, Los Angeles.[233] These are conservative estimates, which do not take into account individuals who have not yet dared to come out. If we assume the same population ratio across the world, we can estimate that there are over 47 million transgender people worldwide, about the same population as the country of Spain. It is estimated that at least 500 million people worldwide are gay or bisexual.[234]

The queer community is much more visible today than even just a few years ago. The Independent Press Standards Association (IPSO) reported a 400 per cent increase in coverage of trans issues between 2014 and 2019.[235] Trans actress Laverne Cox winning the Primetime Emmy Awards and the public transition of Olympic gold medal winner Caitlyn Jenner made international headlines. Increasingly, TV series and cinema productions feature homosexual and gender diverse protagonists, while trans journalists are finding their voice in a largely cis-gender dominated industry.

But today's stronger visibility and recognition of the LGBTQ community at large has frequently not directly translated into improved lives of people who do not fit societal gender norms. In too many cases, it has provoked a full-blown backlash against the queer community, sometimes in a form that blends old prejudices with new extremist tropes. In 2022, the new 'Don't Say Gay' legislation in Florida caused a major controversy in the US. It started with the conservative American activist Christopher Rufo initiating a large campaign to punish Disney for releasing its new animated series *The Proud Family: Louder and Prouder*. The series introduced a pair of homosexual dads, featuring voice-overs by LGBTQ actors, as well as recurring queer character Michael Collins. After Rufo claimed that *The Proud Family* was grooming children with radical sexual propaganda and helping advance a 'gay agenda', waves of anti-LGBTQ campaigns kicked off. Old anti-LGBTQ tropes had been combined with new QAnon ideas.[236]

While homophobia remains a significant problem, today the most polarised cultural battleground has to some extent moved from homosexuality to gender expression. The state of transphobia in most liberal Western countries is deeply shocking. 2021 was the deadliest year on record for transgender and non-binary people in the US.[237] Transphobic crimes in the UK have quadrupled since 2015.[238] One in four trans individuals in Britain have experienced transphobic physical assault.[239]

Some people reading this book might not agree with trans-inclusive reforms. So I want to make clear that not everyone who expresses concern about the impact of new policies is an extremist. Similar to debates about migration, it can be difficult to draw the line between legitimate concerns regarding border controls, and hateful prejudice against minority groups. One can question whether it is a good idea that children can change their gender. And one can debate under which circumstances trans women should be allowed to participate in sports competitions. But when this discourse uses narratives that systematically demonise and dehumanise minority groups, legitimate debate stops and hateful 'othering' starts. There is little difference between describing women as 'femoids', 'toilets' or 'bitches', calling Blacks 'monkeys', 'rapists' or the n-word, and labelling queer or gender diverse people as 'groomers', 'faggots' or 'trannies'. Verbalising disgust or disrespect, propagating conspiracy myths or denouncing the existence of a group are all expressions of hate.

Trans people are now one of the primary targets of far-right extremists,[240] whose forums are saturated with transphobic language and imagery. 'More pandering to far-left, cancel-culture, "trans" activists,' writes Jim of the Pie and Mash Squad, a British far-right group with links to the football hooligan community. He shares a *Daily Mail* article about ongoing disputes on gender-related language on university campuses.[241] Jim is outraged by the attention trans people were getting at universities and calls them a 'tiny insignificant minority of degenerate, weirdo, attention-seeking, mentally ill, gay men & occasionally women'. Britain First writes on Telegram: 'Don't mess with the all-powerful trans movement. They are very, very powerful and exercise a disproportionate influence on society!'

Online transphobic hatred is not confined to the darker corners of 4Chan or Reddit. It can be found in the comments section of the *Daily Mail*, in popular YouTube channels or even the discussion forums of Mumsnet. Many parents who come to Mumsnet for knowledge, advice and support find themselves in a breeding ground for transphobia. One day, the Mumsnet user Mike voices his concern over the rise of transphobia on the platform. He writes: 'A very good friend of mine and a long-time poster here has spent most of her day crying because this fresh wave of transphobia in a community she thought she was welcome in has finally broken her spirits.' Within a few hours, he receives a cascade of hostile replies such as 'Mike is an all inclusive, self identifying, lady penis' and 'Women do not have penises. Our feminist ancestors would spit on you, you nasty, misogynistic little man.' Another post by a user called CisMyArse reads: 'If your mate is shedding tears cos us women won't accept her be-penised existence, tell her to man-up and stop being a fucking victim'.[242]

Transphobia is not limited to online commentators, and it traverses the political spectrum. High-profile politicians have lent legitimacy to anti-trans attitudes: British Labour MP Rosie Duffield[243] has called trans women 'male bodied biological men' and liked a tweet that labelled trans people as 'mostly heterosexuals cosplaying as the opposite sex'. When Russian president Vladimir Putin was asked to share his thoughts on gender identity, he responded by stressing the importance of traditional family values, 'mother is mother, father is father'. Former Alaska governor Sarah Palin called University of Pennsylvania trans swimmer Lia Thomas 'a dude' who is beating women's swimming records.[244]

Ultra conservatives, Christian fundamentalists and radical feminist activists are unlikely allies at first sight. But they have teamed up in their overt opposition to trans rights. Paleo conservatives and gender-critical feminists, so-called Trans Exclusionary Radical Feminism (TERFS), have formed a new coalition based on their shared feeling that transgender identities are invalid and that women are defined by biology only. There are areas for serious disagreement between the two camps – from abortion rights to 'reproductive sovereignty' of women. But organisations like the radical feminist Women's Liberation Front (WoLF) have become strategic allies to the conservative right: they are frequent guests on *Tucker Carlson Tonight* and celebrated speakers at right-wing events. In 2019, the conservative think tank Heritage Foundation hosted a panel entitled 'The Inequality of the Equality Act: Concerns from the Left', inviting several feminist activists from WoLF to talk about the dangers of trans activism.[245]

The main concern of TERFs is that they believe progress in trans rights comes at the expense of women's rights and threatens female-only safe spaces. Sheila Jeffreys, an Australian radical feminist and former Melbourne University professor framed transgenderism as 'an assault on feminism'. In front of an audience at the UK House of Commons she compared trans people to parasites for 'occupying the bodies of the oppressed'.[246]

The confrontation between trans rights activists and radical feminists dates back to the 1970s. During the Second Wave of Feminism in the 1960s and 70s topics such as rape, domestic violence and workplace safety had become key mobilisation areas in feminist activism. The focus was on biological differences and resulting injustices. Radical feminists were splintering off into two separate groups: those who supported trans women and embraced them as part of the wider fight for equality, and those who denounced their struggles and accused them of hijacking women's rights debates.

In recent years, even sub-groups within the LGBTQ community have attacked the queer community. In 2018, the London Pride Parade organisers apologised after anti-trans protesters forced their way to the front of the parade.[247] Get the L Out is a grassroots lesbian feminist activist group that advocates for lesbians to form their own independent community separate from GBTQ movements. It is their belief that queer politics and transgenderism promotes misogynistic policies and systems that prioritise men's interests. 'We are witnessing how transactivism erases lesbians, and silences and demonises lesbians who dare to speak out,' the group announces on its website. 'We will not be silenced!'[248]

Looking through 'mainstream' news reports on trans people, the amount of offensive and demonising language I find is shocking. Many pieces in large national newspapers depict trans people as sexual predators or mentally disturbed and promote disinformation about the trans community. Headlines describe them as 'extremists',[249] 'demented'[250] and 'dangerous'.[251] The *Daily Mail* has been at the forefront of inciting hatred against the trans community. Almost every article I come across in transphobic groups cites the newspaper. Transphobic comments accumulate underneath headlines such as 'Trans rapist, 25, who groomed a 13-year-old girl asking her on text "do you mind if my hands wander?" days after being released from prison is jailed for 100 months'[252] or 'EXCLUSIVE: "We're uncomfortable in our own locker room." Lia Thomas' UPenn teammate tells how the trans swimmer doesn't always cover up her male genitals when changing and their concerns go ignored by their coach.'[253]

The highly controversial nature of trans-related news helps drive the disproportionately large volume of media coverage that the community receives. Demonising media pieces often get picked up in far-right channels, whose members are quick to quote and share them transnationally. This often means more clicks for the original media piece. Anti-trans activists might even add their own hateful memes and create viral campaigns that take the fearmongering to the next level. 'This *definitely a female person* is revealing *her* very female penis to actual human females, and the school administration is fine with it because trans 👏 women 👏 are 👏 women or some such Emperor's New Dick bulls**' Simon comments in the alt-right Telegram group We the Pepe, sharing a media piece on gender-neutral locker rooms.

Many of today's anti-LGBTQ campaigns show a typical victim-perpetrator reversal. Studies found that transgender people have a significantly higher chance of being sexually assaulted than cis-gender people. Black transgender people were in the most vulnerable group and experienced the highest proportion of sexual abuse.[254] Most acts of sexual harassment, misogynist abuse and domestic violence are not committed by minority communities, they are committed by white cis-gender heterosexual men.[255] But it can be hard to acknowledge that violence and indecency is coming from one's own in-group, so blaming a minority out-group – be that transgender people, Muslims or people of colour – is an easy escape.

* * *

A message pops up on my iPhone. 'Hating fats doesn't make you fat phobic just the same as hating trannies doesn't make you trans phobic,' Simon posts into the Great British Debate. He goes on 'Phobic would indicate fear. I'm not scared of either loathsome group, I just can't stand them.' I close my Telegram and look up.

I am standing in the middle of the Bois de Boulogne, a large park on the edge of Paris. I took an early morning train from London to witness the protest that is about to happen here. It is a cold October day but the sun is piercing through a few clouds in the otherwise blue sky. The few Parisians who got off the metro with me immediately put on their sunglasses and confidently dispersed in different directions, following what looked like a normal daily routine. It is hard to imagine that this place has become the number one crime scene for lethal transphobic hate attacks in Europe. Since 2018, France has seen a dramatic spike in violent transphobia, and several trans women have been attacked and assassinated in these woods.

By French standards I am early. The protest should have started a couple of minutes ago, according to social media of the trans rights movement Acceptess-T. I approach a little crowd of people who look like they all know each other. Some have clearly put a lot of time into their shiny costumes, complex make-up and drag queen styles. Others have come as they are, in jeans and T-shirts. One protester is wearing a provocative T-shirt saying 'gender terrorist'.

Three women with matching glittery eye shadow, pale make-up, black lipstick, rainbow-coloured hair and veils attached to extravagant hats wave to me. They probably see that I am on my own, standing a little awkwardly among animated groups. 'We are the Sisters of Perpetual Indulgence,' one of the women tells me in French, flashing her fake lashes at me. The Sisters of Perpetual Indulgence are a charity and street performance movement that was born in 1979 in Iowa City in the US. Its members – in the beginning just a small group of gay men – dressed up as nuns to raise awareness about the social problems in San Francisco's famous Castro district. Over the years, the Sisters of Perpetual Indulgence expanded across North and South America, Europe and Australia. Today their international orders run campaigns to warn of sexually transmitted diseases, drug abuse and hate crime.

Once I find myself involved in an intimate conversation with the Sisters, the crowd starts growing quickly. Within five minutes, ten people have become 100, within the next five minutes I am surrounded by around 500 people. The queer community in Paris wants to take a stand.

From afar, I spot a little crowd of middle-aged parents holding up a large banner saying, 'Our children are transgender – respect them'. I walk towards them and smile at one of the women. 'We are here to demand justice and fight discrimination,' she tells me. Apart from family members of trans victims, it seems as though there are few cis-gender protestors at the protest.

Carole was the mother of Mathilde, a 19-year-old woman who took her life during Covid because of the lack of perspective and support for trans people in France. Carole tells me about the discrimination and stigmatisation her daughter faced in daily life: at school, in hospital, in sports. 'Transphobia is embedded in the health, education and even in the justice system.' She holds up her 'Trans rights are human rights' sign, as Mathilde's father pats her shoulder.

Mathilde always fought against injustices and discrimination, Carole later explains. 'But in the end, she didn't see a future. There were no solutions to her endless struggles. She thought that she would still have to fight in twenty or thirty years.' As Carole says it, her own emotions overwhelm her. But she ignores the tears that are forming in the corner of her eyes and continues: 'That was too much for her. She felt exhausted. She felt exhausted at the age of nineteen.' Carole and her husband had decided to take her out of school, but it was too late.

I learn that Mathilde took her life before being able to change her identity. As she hadn't yet officially adopted her new gender identity before her death, the mayor refused to put her preferred pronoun on the memorial tablet. 'It's tough for young people, the transition can take a long time and there is no respect for their basic human rights,' Carole concludes. 'We demand respect for our children. We demand that society stops questioning their existence. Everyone should have the right to be who they want to be.' I think of my own little son and hope that the situation will get better by the time he discovers his own gender identity. A 2015 survey by the National Center for Transgender Equality found that 40 per cent of transgender people had attempted suicide, which was nine times the rate of the general population.[256]

A tall woman walks towards me. 'Vous êtes qui?' she asks, and I can sense her suspicion. I explain that I have travelled to

Paris from London to attend the protest, as I am investigating the rising levels of hostility towards the trans community.

'Ah I see. I usually know the faces that turn up to our protests. The media doesn't cover our protests, so we are not used to people from outside the community.' Then she gives me a smile. 'I'm Giovanna, the director of the organisation Acceptess-T.' Her long blonde curls, strong deep voice and slight Spanish accent make Giovanna Rincon quite a presence.

Giovanna clears her throat and walks over to the front of the crowd to give her speech. 'We have reached a dramatic point in France,' she says into the microphone. 'Since 2018 we have lost too many innocent lives to violent transphobia.' The crowd falls silent. 'Vanesa Campos was assassinated here in the woods in 2018. Then in 2020 we lost Jessyca Sarmiento who was killed here. Last year we counted an unprecedented number of trans individuals who took their lives. Fifteen days ago, Ivanna Macedo Silva was barbarically murdered in her own apartment. She was deeply loved by her community and by her family.' Giovanna takes a few steps towards her audience. 'Our emancipation is not negotiable. It is something that should be self-evident. We have to put pressure on politicians now.'

The trans activist hands the microphone to Marilyn, the sister of Ivanna.

'Good afternoon everyone.' Marilyn delivers her speech in her mother tongue, Spanish. She has travelled to the protest from Peru, their family's country of origin.

'My sister should not have died here. She was murdered by violent transphobia.' Marilyn pauses to regain her breath and curb the sobs that are rising from her.

'Thank you for all of you who are here today, for the support by the community. I don't feel lonely anymore.' She explains that her mother has stayed in Peru. 'She is in a bad state.' The microphone in her hand is shaking. 'She is in a terrible state.' As her voice tails off, tears start running down my face. I can't stop them. 'I cannot believe that my sister is dead,' Marilyn says and returns the microphone.

'Justice for Sasha. Justice for Ivanna.' The crowd is chanting, as they are marching through the neighbourhoods of Bois de Boulogne. 'Trans assassinés, État complice!' The protesters blame the surge in trans deaths on the government's failure to keep the community safe. An EU study found that four in five trans respondents felt measures to protect the human rights of trans people are very or fairly rare in their country of residence.[257] Institutional discrimination and hostile public attitudes towards trans people have contributed to the stark rise in hate crimes that they are subject to across North America and Europe.

* * *

Just a few days after returning from the Acceptess-T protest in Paris, I get on the London Tube at Covent Garden. A middle-aged man in a suit and a woman in a smart-casual outfit sit opposite me, gazing at a young trans person in a tight dress and pink eye make-up who stands a few metres away. When they start whispering and pointing at her she becomes visibly uncomfortable. 'Piccadilly Circus' comes the announcement. She gets off.

'Have you seen that story about the transgender prisoner who raped two women?' the man says, loudly enough for fellow passengers to hear him. The story of Karen White, who sexually assaulted fellow inmates in a female prison, made global headlines in 2018 and played into the hands of anti-trans campaigners. The sex offender Stephen Wood had entered the prison system as a trans woman named Karen White but was legally still a man and not actually transgender.[258]

The man on the Tube continues in a confident voice: 'I can't believe we allow men posing as women to enter female-only prisons and bathrooms. They're a threat to women's safety. It's outrageous.' His female friend nods. The man goes on: 'At work they are discussing using pronouns. You know, including them in our email signatures and asking our clients how they want to be addressed. It's so ridiculous. As if an old man like me could be a woman. Do I look like a woman to you?' She laughs. From the corner of my eye, I see the couple sitting next to me exchange looks.

Few topics are currently as politically and emotionally charged as trans activism. Even the *Harry Potter* fan community has been deeply divided ever since J.K. Rowling publicly ridiculed trans-inclusive labelling of women. Rowling's first controversial tweet in 2020 mocked an opinion piece that spoke of women as 'persons who menstruate'.[259] 'I'm sure there used to be a word for those people. Someone help me out. Wumben? Wimpund? Woomod?' she wrote. It didn't take long until the message 'J.K. Rowling is a TERF' was trending across Twitter. Many readers reacted with outrage, some were even seen burning *Harry Potter* books on TikTok.

J.K. Rowling had previously positioned herself as an ally to the LGBTQ community. She had revealed that the School of Magic in her books, Hogwarts, includes students of different sexual orientations and its headmaster Albus Dumbledore was homosexual. But she has also repeatedly liked and shared tweets that are considered deeply offensive by the trans community. For example, she liked a tweet that called trans women 'men in dresses' in 2018. British writer and trans woman Shon Faye reacted by tweeting: 'Trans culture is seeing the beloved author of your generation like a transphobic tweet from a troll account which has repeatedly called you a man.'[260] J.K. Rowling's novel *The Silkworm*, which was published under the pen name

Robert Galbraith, gives clues about her attitude towards trans people. In one scene, a trans woman, Pippa, attempts to stab the protagonist, Cormoran Strike. Her trans status is later revealed and her visible Adam's apple noted. The book makes use of common tropes that vilify trans people and paint them as aggressive and unstable.

'My own daughter adores the *Harry Potter* books but understands that J.K Rowling doesn't like her parent,' Katelyn Burns tells me. Through her glasses, her eyes look at me as if to assess whether I am trustworthy. Katelyn was the first openly trans Capitol Hill reporter and has spent years observing how transphobic attitudes went mainstream. She came out as a trans woman in 2016 after decades of repressing her gender identity, when she realised that she could no longer hide who she was. 'One of the key motivating factors for my transition was that I didn't want to be buried in a suit,' she tells me.

Looking back on it now, she says she knew 'something was up' by the age of seven or eight. 'I didn't have the words for it when I was a kid.' All she could find then was an encyclopaedia that described transsexuality in a derogatory way, equating it with a sexual fetish. She thought 'That's not me!' and decided that she would have to hide her identity, including from her closest friends and Catholic family. She was an athletic child and quickly immersed herself in sports to avoid having to confront her identity.

When Katelyn was eighteen, she met her future wife. She had waited for the love of her life to have sex. 'I told her very early on that I have this thing with women's clothing occasionally. But she responded that she never wanted to hear about it again.' Katelyn knew this woman was the one and didn't want to risk losing her. So she locked away her female side. They got married, had kids and bought a house. To the outside world, she led a normal life. But it didn't feel right and even the best moments were 'dulled' and 'as if felt by another person'.

'I managed to bottle it up for fifteen years,' Katelyn says. Then she embarked on a lifechanging journey to discover her identity. Eventually she had an honest conversation with her wife and told her about her gender dysphoria, repressed gender identity, and suicide attempts. They broke up.

Today Katelyn is 40 years old and lives in Maine with her two children and her cat. She runs the popular Twitter account @transscribe and writes for a variety of news outlets, including MSNBC, *The Washington Post*, *Vox*, *VICE*, *Elle*, *Them* and *Playboy*. Reporting on transphobia is not easy, especially when you are trans yourself. 'One of the things that a lot of people don't understand about people like me is that I write about stuff that's so personally affecting. Every devastating story about trans people devastates me emotionally. Every bad word somebody says about a trans person feels like an insult directed at me.' She has stopped writing exclusively about trans issues in order to get some respite. Now every second article she writes is about something entirely different. In her spare time, she plays video games or reads about history.

Katelyn was asked many times to write her story up in a book, but she decided that she would get too much harassment. She has been doxxed before. 'It comes with the territory of being a trans journalist.' She usually laughs it away, but admits to me that she is scared: the extent and nature of the abuse has evolved over the last few years. 'There are a lot more comments about my appearance these days.' She no longer puts up selfies or pictures on social media because she is afraid of the backlash.

The bell rings and Katelyn leaves to get a food delivery for her cat, who has been making hungry sounds in the background of our serious conversation. When she returns, she says: 'Everyday observers don't understand this part: the legal reality of trans people today is not at all different from what it was back in 2015. Public attitudes have changed, although LGBTQ rights have not.' Indeed, the extent to which attitudes have changed is debateable – a YouGov survey found falling numbers of Britons strongly agree that 'a transgender woman is a woman'.[261]

Katelyn believes that her personal story is a mirror of the status of the trans community at large. 'I entered the decade ostensibly as a happily married man, trying to build my life and career while repressing my gender identity,' she wrote in an article for *Vox*. 'Five years in, I found my true self through persistent self-exploration. And I'm now leaving the decade scared shitless.'[262]

2015 was a turning point in the evolution of transphobia. The 'culture wars' between liberals and conservatives gained momentum in the run-up to the 2016 presidential election that led to Donald Trump's victory. Battles were fought everywhere – in local governments, talk shows, on social media and university campuses. In June 2015, the Supreme Court ruled that same-sex marriage should be legal throughout all US states and territories. The conservative and religious right had lost its biggest national fight over LGBTQ rights. They needed something else to pivot to in an effort to maintain their funding and campaigning networks, Katelyn argues. 'So, instead of packing up and going home, right-wing activists simply shifted their focus to a new, even more vulnerable group: trans people.'

A few months later, a local referendum was held in Houston, Texas, over the city's Equal Rights Ordinance. The aim of the Houston Equal Rights Ordinance (HERO) was to ban discrimination against people on the basis of their race, ethnicity, gender, sexual orientation, age and several other factors. The bill was passed at first, but a major backlash followed, Katelyn explains. 'The right-wing jumped on the trans issue, which was only a small proportion of the ordinance.' Their campaigns were successful and the ordinance ended up being repealed. It was the first time the 'No men in women's bathrooms' slogan popped up. The message essentially became a test run for national anti-trans campaigns.

The following year, North Carolina passed their infamous 'bathroom bill', which was designed to limit transgender access to sex-segregated facilities. It also barred cities, municipalities and counties in the whole state from introducing anti-discrimination laws. The bill backfired spectacularly. North Carolina ended up losing at least 3.76 billion dollars and 3,000 jobs, as corporations, artists, TV productions and sports clubs started boycotting the state.[263] Adidas, PayPal and Deutsche Bank cancelled their plans for expansion in North Carolina. Ringo Starr, Nick Jonas, Bruce Springsteen and Demi Lovato cancelled their concerts. The NBA moved the 2017 All-Star Game from Charlotte to New Orleans and the NCAA relocated the March Madness basketball championship. Despite this rather heavy economic toll, North Carolina wasn't the only state that considered bathroom bills. At least sixteen US states were trying to pass similar laws during that year, but all failed.

Meanwhile, the UK government under former Prime Minister Theresa May went the other way. In 2017, proposals were published to reform the Gender Recognition Act and make self-declaration of one's preferred gender possible. This reform would have allowed trans people to self-declare their gender instead of providing numerous medical records, diagnosis of gender dysphoria and other pieces of evidence. 'A friend of mine was even asked to submit a pornography preference list,' Katelyn tells me.

The concept of self-declaration has been vastly misunderstood. To change their gender officially, trans individuals would have to swear under an oath in a declaration that they plan to live out their life in a different sex or gender. But anti-trans activists had already twisted the narrative. 'On Tuesday Joe can say he is a woman if he wants to follow a woman into the bathroom,' they warned. The self-ID controversy kicked off a moral panic and fuelled aggressive anti-trans campaigning on social media. Eventually the UK's plans for a reform of the Gender Recognition Act were dropped.[264]

While France has seen some of the worsts rates in deadly anti-trans hate crimes and the US some of the most discriminatory laws, the UK has been the messaging epicentre of the global anti-trans movement. Large networks of conservatives and liberals have mobilised to promote disinformation and conspiracy myths about the trans community. The lines of messaging developed jointly by trans-exclusionary networks on the left and right side of the political spectrum soon inspired campaigns in the US. 'Arguments that were made in the UK were convincing to suburban mums in the US. So conservatives started copying British campaigns,' Katelyn observes. 'We started seeing the same communications strategies and language that was used in Britain in radically conservative networks in the US.'

Katelyn believes that some of the wildest anti-trans conspiracy myths originated in the UK. One of them claims that trans people are recruiting transgender kids to molest pre-pubescent children. Another conspiracy myth that has gained ground in recent years views trans activism as a gateway to robotic transhumanism and denounces it as a money-making strategy of big pharma and big tech. This idea is especially ludicrous, as many experts have pointed out that modern technologies are largely designed based on binary, heteronormative conceptions of gender and can hence fuel discrimination against transgender people.[265] Some adherents of anti-trans conspiracy myths also add a layer of anti-Semitism, by singling out Jewish philanthropists who donated to trans rights campaigns.

Jennifer Bilek is among the activists who propagate the idea of LGBTQ rights being a 'front for the techno-medical complex'. 'I consider "transgender" to be a corporate fiction, not real,' Jennifer tells me. She lives in New York, counts over 10,000 followers on Twitter and describes herself as investigative journalist, artist and concerned citizen. According to her, the trans rights movement is a secret operation run by the pharma and tech industries. Their goal, she asserts, is to boost sales of hormone supplements and to promote transhumanism. She calls gender ideology an 'ideology of disembodiment',[266] which seeks to deconstruct 'what it means to be human at core: a biologically, sexually dimorphic species'. Jennifer argues that gender is no more than an obfuscation by the state and trans lobby.[267] 'There is an entire body-denying market opening up for pharma & tech in promoting "body diversity" as empowerment.'[268] She believes that trans gender people are leading the path to robotic human supplementation. 'It's only a hop & a skip to chip implants, human interfacing with AI & corporate mind-reading of individuals, etc. "Transgender" softens you for these changes to humanity.' [269]

* * *

Trystan Reese's life consists of two distinctly separate parts: life before and life after he became known globally as 'the pregnant man' in 2017. There was no return to normality after the headlines. Trystan is a trans man who grew up in Canada but lives in Portland today. He and his husband Biff Chaplow describe themselves as 'the accidental gay parents'. When they had been dating for just one year, they became the primary caregivers of Biff's three-year-old nephew and one-year-old niece to save them from being taken by the Child Protective Services. A few years later, Trystan gave birth to Leo.

It was almost two decades ago that Trystan came out aged nineteen. There was little understanding of trans identities then. Many people were confused about him. 'I was a girl who said I was a boy but still looked and sounded like a girl and was also attracted to other boys,' Trystan writes in his memoir *How We Do Family*. Trystan knew for himself that he was a gay man. But he often got the reaction: 'Oh so you're actually a straight woman?' Today there is more societal awareness and recognition of trans rights. But with every step towards progress also came another headwind of hostility.

'It's a double-edged sword,' Trystan explains to me. 'As people learn more about us, necessarily there is a backlash.' By publishing his queer family story he wanted to play his part in educating the public. 'But with that exposure came attack and pushback.' He had already spent a lot of time educating homophobic strangers about LGBTQ rights but what he experienced after pictures of his pregnant belly went viral was on another level. 'The once-in-a-while message of disgust from strangers quickly became a torrent of negativity,' he writes in *How We Do Family*. 'Every buzz of my phone brought a new level of nastiness.' Some users insulted him, calling him 'a f*cking cancer on this planet' and 'a disgusting circus freak'. Others announced that his baby was going to be deformed. A few even threatened him, warning they were going to call Child Protective Services to have his children taken away from him.[270]

Trystan has learnt to understand his audience. He has learnt that his story works best with people who don't comprehend trans identities but want to, who have questions, are maybe a bit curious or confused. He wants the parents of transgender children to read his book, or people who want to be good allies to the LGBTQ community. 'That's who all of my work is for.' He has given up on the idea of changing the minds of those who are openly transphobic or ultra-conservative. 'Someone like me would never be able to impact them anyways, it might even push them further down the radicalisation rabbit hole.'

The Internet is both the best and the worst thing that happened to trans people. Social media has provided a safe place for transgender people to find community and real-time support that can save lives. But it also left the trans community more vulnerable to targeted online harassment, abuse and disinformation campaigns. The GLAAD Social Media Safety Index (SMSI) found in a 2021 study that most social media platforms are 'effectively unsafe' for LGBTQ users.[271] 'Algorithms are explicitly designed to promote and reward outrage,' Trystan says. 'We often end up being the grease in the gears of social media, we're what keeps the machine moving. It's incredibly painful to be used in that way. And that part does not seem to be getting better for a very long time.'

In 2008, Trystan worked on the major political campaign for gay marriage in California. It lost by millions of votes, but the data showed that if everyone over the age of 60 had stayed home the campaign would have won. At the time he said to his boss: 'Why don't we all just go retire to Hawaii and wait for conservatives to die off?' but his boss reminded him that young liberals become old conservatives.

Younger generations are increasingly embracing right-wing and alt-right views. Generation Z (also called Gen Z or Zoomers), which includes people born in the mid-1990s and early 2000s, is often portrayed as 'ultra woke' and pitted against the supposedly more conservative older generations by the media. However, studies show that Gen Z might be more conservative than the Baby Boomers, Generation X or Millennials on some issues. For example, a UK survey found that close to 60 per cent of Gen Z respondents described their views on gay marriage and transgender rights as 'conservative' and 'moderate'.[272] Generation Z is also more distrusting of government institutions and of each other than any generation before it. A 2018 survey by the Pew Research Center showed that around three quarters of Americans under 30 are 'low trusters'.[273]

'A lot of Zoomers and young Millennials have turned to transphobic content, especially on YouTube,' Katelyn confirms. The so-called Prager University (PragerU) is among the growing hubs for teenagers and students who are fed up with 'political correctness' and the 'wokeness' at schools and university campuses.[274] The founders, who are talk show hosts and billionaire investors, have built an online empire with content tailored for precisely that audience. They see YouTube as a way to provide young people with an alternative education and circumvent traditional media. Some of their videos have attracted more than a billion views, using headlines such as: 'Fossil Fuels: The Greenest Energy,' 'Where Are the Moderate Muslims?' and 'Are Some Cultures Better Than Others?' Among the primary donors of PragerU are American Christian-right oil industry billionaires Dan and Farris Wilks.

PragerU has about 6,500 high school and college student ambassadors in the US who call themselves the PragerFORCE. They host on-campus meetings and help produce viral videos. Will Witt is one of their self-made producers based in Los Angeles. He says he dropped out of the University of Colorado Boulder because he didn't want to be indoctrinated anymore. Now PragerU pays him to troll young people who look like they are progressive liberals – he usually identifies them based on their political buttons, oversize clothes or unconventional hair styles. For one video, he approached students at the Florida Gulf Coast University to ask them 'What is a woman?' The answers he got from surprised and confused students helped him to mock liberals and take on their arguments. Many of the PragerU activists and fans come from liberal family backgrounds and see conservatism as an opportunity for rebellion.[275]

Trystan believes that liberals and LGBTQ campaigners have to continue running campaigns that resonate with young people, or the next generations will fall victim to some of the worst messaging on the right. 'Things don't happen magically or by coincidence. They happen because people are pushing for change,' he tells me. 'We have to be that heartbeat for acceptance, for culture change and for progressivism. We cannot become complacent, or we will lose ground.'

The military is a good example. 'Transgender people have been quietly serving in the US military for a very long time,' Trystan says. 'It wasn't until we had a president who said that transgender people were not allowed to serve that this turned into a controversial debate.' In 2017, former US President Donald Trump announced a ban on transgender troops openly serving. 'He had no idea what was going on. The military has been the single largest employer of transgender people in the country.' Courts halted the ban from taking effect and President Joe Biden overturned it as soon as he took office.

Questions around trans participation in sports have opened up even more controversial and emotional debates. In the wake of the 2022 Olympic Games, trans athletes have become the key target of anti-LGBTQ harassment and hatred. Although Twitter, Facebook and Instagram categorise the LGBTQ community as a protected group that needs to be safeguarded from hate speech on their platforms, trans athletes and sports commentators suffered a fierce backlash through social media during the 2022 Olympic Games.[276]

* * *

Today's backlash against the trans community often pits contemporary gender debates against the assumption that in the past, male and female characteristics were fixed, natural and innate.

But gender has always been understood relatively, existing on a spectrum with many cultural differences in how it is expressed. Our sex is assigned to us at birth although there is often a discrepancy between chromosomal, anatomical and hormonal characteristics. It is common to have a biological mix of 'female and 'male' traits: many people have a hormone imbalance (like polycystic ovarian syndrome) or experience gynecomastia (a male body begins producing oestrogen-based hormones). Around 1.7 per cent of the population are born with physical ambiguity or 'intersex' characteristics.[277]

Feminine and masculine traits are also fluid and can change throughout life. The Tanner scale is a system used to medically classify the development of primary and secondary sex characteristics, such as the size of breasts, genitalia, and development of pubic hair. Many cis women's bodies do not even get to the final fifth Tanner stage unless they go through pregnancy and a lactation protocol. Like cis-gender women, transgender women go through Tanner stages when they transition.

Hundreds of societies and cultures throughout history went beyond the gender binary in their language and cultural norms. Many indigenous tribes have a long tradition of using a third, fourth or even fifth gender. For example, Navajo, Zuni and Lakota tribes in North America, the Inca tribes in Peru, the Xanith in Oman and Chukchi in Siberia count more than two distinct gender categories.

But the fact remains that these nuances have largely been unacknowledged in mainstream Western culture, which has historically understood gender as a rigid binary. Against this backdrop, not all day-to-day incidents of abuse against gender minorities are the result of explicit or deliberate anti-trans hatred. As with racism, offensive language is often the result of attitudes that are implicit, entrenched in our upbringing and wider societal attitudes. Many of us were brought up in settings that harboured a certain amount of fear, disrespect or even disgust towards the queer community. A failure to recognise this prejudice has enabled extreme ideas to spread. And it has also been weaponised by those with an interest in inhibiting social progress.

Trans rights have been pitted against feminism by the media as well as radical activists, as if they were mutually exclusive. This 'divide and conquer' approach has been adopted by right-wing campaigners to strategically split their left-wing opponents. There is a parallel here to race-related debates, where driving a wedge between minorities has been a key strategy adopted by right-wing conservatives. For example, labelling East Asians as a 'model minority' while linking Black and Arab populations to crime has led to in-fighting between minority communities and prevented them from teaming up in their campaigns against racism and discrimination.[278]

Trans rights and sex-based rights for 'biological women' are not actually at odds with one another. The focus on biological differences that gender-critical feminists hold on to is outdated and belongs to a feminism of the past. Even in the 1940s, Simone de Beauvoir wrote: 'One is not born a woman but rather becomes a woman.' Our motivations, behaviours, character traits, sexual partners, emotional desires, choices of clothing, and professional dreams should not depend on the sex that was assigned to us at birth. Modern feminism is no longer focused on biological essentialism but on diversity and self-expression. As a feminist I refuse to be subjected to presumptions that are exclusively based on my genitals and reproductive organs. As a cis-gender woman I refuse to yield to those voices who want to sow divisions in the feminist and LGBTQ communities. Feminists should see trans women as allies rather than enemies. After all, one of their shared aims is to put an end to different forms of gender-related oppression.

Policies that undermine trans rights tend to go hand in hand with laws that jeopardise women's rights. Whether you take

Poland, Russia or Hungary, the oppression of women and the LGBTQ community have been closely tied to each other, as they are part of the same effort to uphold old hierarchies, privileges and family values. Texas is a good case in point too. In 2021, the Texas Heartbeat Act made abortion illegal from the moment a foetal heartbeat is detected. In early 2022, Texas governor Greg Abbott called on citizens to refer parents of transgender kids to the authorities for 'child abuse'. He announced that failure to report minors who receive gender-affirming medical care could result in criminal penalties.[279]

The bathroom bill panic even negatively impacted women who do not conform to rigid ideas about what women should traditionally look like. The case of a cis-gender woman who was insulted while using a Walmart bathroom because another woman mistook her for a trans woman went viral on social media. Her short haircut and baseball cap prompted the stranger to shout at her: 'You're disgusting!' and 'You don't belong here!'[280]

It is important to have an open conversation about the future of trans rights. There are legitimate questions to be asked, relating to medical treatments, fairness in sports and women's safe spaces. But to confront the mainstreamed hatred against an increasingly vilified minority community, we will have to introduce better protection systems for those directly affected. As a society, we have to break through the stereotypes in our binary thinking. What do masculinity and femininity mean to us? Why do so many people experience anger, disgust or fear when they are asked to rethink these terms? And who really benefits when hatred and division are sown between groups who have been historically oppressed?

PERSUADING THE MASSES

Once politically significant parts of the population start believing in the ideas that originated in deviant subcultures, the mainstreaming process is complete.

'So you are convinced by the Pfizer vaccine?' the nurse asks me.

I must have looked slightly confused. I didn't expect the question at Vienna's main Covid vaccination centre. I am on an extended family visit and have decided to get the vaccine now rather than wait for my appointment in London. I'm hoping to pass some immunity on to my little baby while still breastfeeding.

'Well, I wouldn't be here otherwise, would I?'

'I guess so,' she says in an unimpressed voice. 'Most people come here voluntarily. Others are dragged here by their partners or friends.'

I can't think of a good enough reply and just nod. Covid vaccine hesitancy is so common across Europe and the US that plateauing vaccination rates prolonged lockdowns in many countries. A *Financial Times* investigation found that German-speaking countries have the highest shares of unvaccinated people in Western Europe. A few percentage points ahead of Switzerland and Germany, Austria leads the anti-vaxxer ranks. By the start of 2022, over a third of the country's population were still unprotected against Covid-19.[281]

The nurse inserts the needle into my arm as soon as I sit down. She is precise and unhesitating, and it doesn't hurt. I am so relieved to finally have my first jab that I wouldn't have cared even if it had. But as I stood in the waiting area a few minutes later, watching the clock let the recommended fifteen-minute wait pass, the nurse's words echo in my head.

A few days earlier, I had been on the phone with a friend who told me she wouldn't get the vaccine. 'I'm not going to risk becoming infertile. Have you heard of the cycle changes the vaccine causes?'

I listened without interrupting as she spoke without pausing to breathe. 'We don't know anything about the long-term side effects on our body. What if the vaccines cause cancer, what if we all die in a few years? Besides, who knows whether they will even work?'

I can't blame her. I used to be a massive hypochondriac myself. Things came to a head when I moved to Beijing for a year. Being exposed to unregulated chemicals, dangerous levels of air pollution and repeated food poisonings initially turned me into a nervous wreck. As time went by, however, the grip of hypochondria softened. As you can imagine, my life improved dramatically.

My hypochondriac self was never rational. It simply didn't care about statistics or probabilities. Instead, it created the scariest possible scenario and mentally replayed it over and over again. In 2018, I travelled to speak at a conference hosted by NATO in Minsk. After reading the UK travel advice for Belarus, which warned of contaminated village well water and the long-term effects of the Chernobyl disaster in some areas of the country, I bought only imported bottles of water and didn't eat anything for the entire two-day conference. We were staying in the fanciest hotel in Minsk with exclusive caviar, eggs in all variations and freshly ground coffee at the breakfast buffet. When it was time for my speech I almost fainted on stage because my sugar levels were so low. In retrospect, I can see that my refusal to eat was absolutely ridiculous. But irrational anxieties are difficult to supress, and sometimes impossible to overcome.

I can understand my friend's fears about the long-term side effects of the vaccines. Yet, according to this argument, we could not use new nose sprays either, or even enjoy new chocolate bars – what if they cause cancer or infertility? We never know with 100 per cent certainty that the products we purchase every day in the supermarket or pharmacy are safe. We just have to trust that existing trials and quality assessments are good enough.

Most diseases are multi-causal and hard to predict in one individual. Not every heavy smoker gets lung cancer in their lifetime, and not every unvaccinated person will have a severe form of Covid. Like most diseases, Covid is an extremely unfair, discriminatory illness that kills some and leaves others completely without symptoms. But just like with lung cancer, it is possible to reduce the odds of getting seriously ill or dying.

'I don't think I would get seriously ill anyway. Covid is just like a new strain of flu,' my friend told me. It was her right to take that bet. But on a societal level, the vaccines are more than an individual choice. Unvaccinated individuals raise the levels of risk not only for themselves but for others. And it's not just illness that spreads this way. Distrust of science can be contagious too. The pandemic led to sharply declining trust levels in scientists and medical scientists, a US survey suggests. In 2021, only 29 per cent of Americans said they had a great deal of confidence in medical scientists to act in the best of interests of the public, compared to 40 per cent a year earlier.[282] Behavioural studies during the 2003 SARS epidemic and the 2020 Covid pandemic found a close relationship between psychological stress and distrust in science.[283] The people who were strongly impacted by stressors – including medical concerns, social and financial worries – tended to be less compliant with medical guidelines and preventive measures.[284] Distrust in science is a dangerous rabbit hole to fall down: if we don't trust our best scientists, who then can we trust?

* * *

'I'm on a hunger strike,' Marius says. 'No food, just water. For twelve days now.'

He looks at me, unblinking; his eyes tired but his gaze intense. Marius looks frail and exhausted behind the black glasses that sit loosely on his slim face. I wonder if he can last another twelve days.

Marius was born in Romania but has lived in London for a long time. He tells me he used to be an Uber driver until the pandemic started. Now he spends his time in a little gated space of maybe eight square metres that he has carved out for himself on Whitehall. Apart from a couple of camping chairs and a small folding table his territory is filled only with banners and flags that feature slogans such as 'Covid is a scam', '5G is a WMD', 'Defund NASA' and 'Expose Bill Gates'. He calls his set-up 'The Wall of Truth'.

When I join Marius at 'The Wall of Truth', his only audience consists of a young man in shorts and hoodie.

'Nobody is dying at home. Everybody is dying in hospital.' His voice is agitated, as he starts explaining the different signs and banners. 'They are killing us!'

The young man next to me listens to him intently.

Out of the blue, Marius says 'I can prove the queen is a reptile.'

Some passers-by on the other side of the pavement look up.

'The queen?' I repeat, slightly unsure if I have heard him correctly. 'How?

'It's a long story.' He exhales loudly. 'All of the police are hybrids. In the UK more than 85 per cent are hybrids.'

'What do you mean, hybrids?'

As if I've asked something obvious, he casually answers: 'They can read our minds. They use 15 per cent of their brains, while we only use the brain 10 per cent.'

'How do they do that?'

Marius looks into an empty bottle of water. 'Multiplying with reptilians. You know the Nephilim?'

'The giants from the Hebrew Bible?' I ask.

'Yes, the Sons of God. They multiplied with pure humans. It's as simple as that.'

I carefully look away to a family crossing the street, trying to suppress a laugh.

'They run all the governments in the world and now they kill pure humans. They give vaccines to the pure humans and placebos to the hybrids. They give positive PCR tests to pure humans and negative ones to hybrids.'

I turn to the young man next to me. His baseball cap, wide hoodie and red shorts make him look like an American college student.

'Do you believe that?'

The man nods. He introduces himself as Pedro from Mexico. He tells me he met Marius just three days ago but has heard similar stories in the groups he has been following on Telegram.

'But how do they know who is human and who is hybrid?' I ask Marius.

'They use infrared, electromagnetic radiation, so they can see your aura.'

'I see.'

'Look.' Pedro points to the sky. 'You've seen the airplanes that leave these white lines in the sky. These are chemtrails. They manipulate the weather this way. It's poison that comes down on us.'

Marius nods. 'Once a week you see the sky is completely full of white trails.'

He picks up a speck of dust from a tree next to us. 'You can even see it on the street, it looks like white sand.'

A passer-by with a walking stick is observing us. The old man is dressed elegantly as if he has just come out of a meeting. He stops in front of the anti-vax signs and doesn't hide the disgust on his face.

Marius returns his scornful look. 'Are you a reptilian, yes or no?' he prompts.

The old man looks both angry and confused. 'A what?' he shouts back.

Marius repeats his insult: 'A reptilian.'

'I don't even know what you're talking about.'

Marius's eyes are fixed on the old man. 'You are a liar,' he shouts. The old man is a few metres away from Marius's reach and there is a gate in between them, but I get ready to act if the situation escalates.

Luckily the man takes a few steps back himself before saying: 'I've had Covid and still can't walk up the stairs without taking several breaks. You are a disgrace to the people who have died, or who are suffering from Long Covid'.

As we watch the old man walk away, Pedro turns to me: 'Are you vaccinated?'

His face is serious now. I know what the only acceptable reply is.

'I'm not,' I lie. 'Not yet.'

'In my opinion you should not do it. Covid 19 is a flu, nothing else. The vaccines are deadly.' Pedro hesitates. 'That thing they insert with the vaccines slowly travels up to your brain. It makes you magnetic too. I'm not sure how it actually works. He is the master.' He looks at Marius, who by now has collected himself. 'How do the vaccines work? What's the medical explanation?'

I am surprised that Pedro defers to Marius. If I was searching for medical insight, a former Uber driver on hunger strike to raise awareness about reptilians in Buckingham Palace would probably not be my first choice.

Marius looks at Pedro, surprised, for a different reason. 'Graphene oxide is modifying your DNA and in addition to 5G antenna you will become a hybrid. What do you not understand?' he says, sounding almost offended. Of course, what's there not to understand? I think to myself.

More people believe that the Pfizer/BioNTech Covid-19 vaccine is made up of 99 per cent graphene oxide than I would have thought possible. Graphene oxide is a nanomaterial derived from graphite that can be toxic to the human body in large quantities. The graphene oxide vaccine myth started with a paper published by Pablo Campra, a professor at the Spanish University of Almería. The publication went viral online in several languages in July 2021 and even prompted Forbes and Reuters to release fact-checking articles.[285] The claim that the Pfizer BioNTech Covid-19 vaccine includes graphene oxide has been disproven multiple times.[286] The Spanish study has been rejected as scientifically flawed by experts and had non-conclusive results even according to the professor himself.[287]

Furthermore, vaccines are highly regulated, go through multiple independent reviews and full lists of ingredients have to be made public. The most frequently cited alleged 'evidence' of magnetism caused by the vaccines is completely wrong as well. Even if the vaccines included graphene oxide, which they don't, there would be no way they would make metallic objects stick to your arm.[288] Despite all the fact checks, the idea that the vaccines might be poisonous or tools for a mass genocide is here to stay.

Graphene oxide is just one example of dangerous vaccine myth. Another wave of vaccine disinformation was kicked off by the US-based self-proclaimed journalist Ramola D. who published a review of studies that claimed to have found parasites in vaccines. None of the named study authors has serious academic credentials in vaccine research however: one is a geologist, another one is a former osteopath turned anti-vaxxer, the third is the author of *The pH Miracle*, who received a prison sentence for three years and eight months for practising medicine without a license.[289]

Marius lifts his megaphone: 'The queen is a reptile!'

His voice echoes across Whitehall. I resist the temptation to hide my face.

Even Pedro next to me giggles. 'I'm still not sure about the reptiles,' he says, shrugging his shoulders.

I am vaguely amused. By this point, as well as chemtrails and killer vaccines, Pedro has explained to me that the weather is manipulated, paedophile elites run underground tunnels for child-trafficking and the Earth is in fact a flat disc. Believing the Queen was a reptile doesn't seem so far-fetched.

Marius's amplified voice bounces off the government buildings around us: 'Lady Diana wanted to expose her but was killed! Eighty per cent are hybrid humans! They want to erase pure humans. You must understand your family is likely controlled by the reptilians in Buckingham Palace.'

He drops his megaphone and sinks to his knees.

'Within 24 hours I can save this planet from reptilian supremacy, and nobody cares. All I need is one solicitor. Last time when I went to the Crown Court and spoke to the judge, I told him "you are a hybrid" and since then he put my trial to next March. They cancelled all my other hearings.'

Looking at him I feel very sad.

He tells me he has lost contact with his entire family. 'They are against me. My whole family is controlled.' He has tears in his eyes. 'They think I am crazy, my ex-partner too. I loved her and she loved me but she could read my mind.' On a banner he has spelled out his logic:

1. Elite (reptilians from Illuminati clan) who shape the world and put
2. Controllable people (their telepathic slaves) to marry with
3. Normal people for our extinction

As I try to imagine what it is like believing in the apocalyptic world described on the banner, a man in a yellow hi-vis tabard greets Marius and asks if he is all right. He returns a grim look and says 'I have a problem with the government. I can prove the Queen is a reptilian.' The uniformed man looks confused and explains that he works for Westminster Council. Marius turns his back and blocks his ears, singing: 'Blah blah blah. I don't talk to you.' The man assures Marius that he is not part of the government. 'I work collecting rubbish, man.' Marius eyes him with suspicion: 'Prove it. Show me identification.' But when the man reaches for his ID, Marius takes out his camera and starts filming. 'I know you are lying!' By now the refuse collector's initial confusion has turned into annoyance. 'Listen, I just clean the streets. I wanted to know if you've got any rubbish that I can throw away.' He shrugs and walks off.

Beneath the faintly comical scene lurks something very dark. 'I want to kill everyone, all the reptiles,' Marius tells me in a serious voice. His agony is visible and his face turns into a grimace as he says: 'I don't want to live. I either need to destroy them or I die. It's me or them'.

It's easy to dismiss Marius as a mentally ill individual, someone whose problems are psychological not societal. But those things are linked. Levels of frustration, fear and fantasy in large parts of the population have reached dangerous dimensions. During the pandemic more and more people started to believe that Bill Gates and international health organisations were waging a chemical war against all of us. Targeted and spontaneous attacks on scientists, health workers and even hospitality employees spiked and the deeply polarised debate over Covid vaccines and masks has sparked violent, sometimes deadly, confrontations. In Eastern Germany a man attacked a nurse and an assistant at a vaccination clinic for refusing to issue him a certificate without getting the jab,[290] while in New York a hostess at an Italian restaurant had to be taken to hospital after three tourists attacked her because she asked for their proof of vaccination status.[291] On 21 September 2021 a man shot dead a 20-year-old cashier at a gas station counter in the German town Idar-Oberstein for telling him to wear a mask. One month later, an Apple store security guard in New York City was stabbed multiple times by a customer who refused to abide by mask regulations in the shop.[292] And in Georgia, a grocery store employee was killed, and two other people injured in a deadly fight over face masks.[293]

Marius looks at me, as if he is still making up his mind about whether I am his friend or his enemy. For all he knows, I could be a hybrid myself, or worse, a reptile.

'Are you coming to the march tomorrow?' he asks me.

I hesitate. Then he hands me a little piece of paper with the official announcement:

SATURDAY 25TH SEPT – 1PM – HYDE PARK CORNER

Do you want the Government to bring in Plan B? Vaccine passports, mandatory masks, working from home etc.? Or even worse the secret option Plan C – lockdown? If not join us with your feet on the street and vote for PLAN FREE. We are free.

'Sure,' I say. 'I'll see you there.'

* * *

I decide it is time I spoke to a reptiloid myself. Karolin Schwarz has received personal threats from people who believe she is one of them. One email even included a picture of her head with an analysis of her facial traits that proved she was a reptile. She is a well-known journalist and expert on disinformation who regularly comments in Germany's biggest public news network ARD. Spending her days countering disinformation and debunking conspiracy myths has made her a popular target for hate campaigns

The WHO warned as early as in spring 2020 that the Covid pandemic had unleashed a worldwide 'infodemic'. Disinformation about the virus appeared to spread even faster than the virus itself. In Germany, prominent figures like German pop singer Michael Wendler, former radio host Ken Jebsen and vegan cookbook author Attila Hildmann have pushed wrongful and misleading claims about the pandemic and vaccines out to mass audiences. In the UK, famous faces of the Covid denier and anti-vax movement include Piers Corbyn (the brother of the former Labour leader Jeremy Corbyn), former nurse Kate Shemirani and ex-footballer and sports broadcaster David Icke. In Australia, the faces of the anti-Covid vaccine movement include the famous chef and former television presenter Pete Evans, the skydiving instructor Zev Freeman and the Melbourne-based lawyer Serene Teffaha, who launched a class action lawsuit during lockdown.[294] A 2021 report found that twelve US celebrities were behind 65 per cent of the shares of anti-vaccine misinformation. The 'Disinformation Dozen' includes environmental lawyer Robert F. Kennedy Jr. (yes, he is a nephew of John F. Kennedy) and alternative medicine entrepreneurs Ty and Charlene Bollinger. Together they have a combined social media following of around 60 million.[295]

For Karolin the infodemic started long before Covid. 2015 was a global turning point in the virulence of disinformation and conspiracy myths, she tells me. 'Back then the type of disinformation changed, it got more political and more contagious because of social media.' These changes could be seen in events worldwide: in the US in Trump's victory, in the UK in the Brexit referendum and in Germany in the so-called refugee and migration crisis. At the time, Karolin worked for the local newspaper *Leipziger Volkszeitung* and saw the damage wrong information and half-truths could produce on a local level. Misinformation and unscientific conversations had always bothered her. But it was only then that she understood how detrimental systematic disinformation can be for our democracies. 'I longed for us all to be able to agree on a basic reality that is not constantly under attack.' So she decided to create Hoaxmap, a fact-checking site for articles on the topic of migration and migrant crimes.

Fact-checking organisations identify false or distorted content that is shared online, and provide an evidence-based assessment of the claims made. But misinformation has something fundamental in common with medicine in that prevention is preferable to cure. Research has shown that ex-post fact checks do little to reverse the effects of untrue stories.[296] Once a piece of disinformation is out in the world, the damage is done: debunks reach fewer people than misinformation[297] and spread not nearly as quickly as the lies they seek to address.[298] Additionally, irrational beliefs frequently cannot be countered with rational refutation. As my past hypochondriac self knew, irrational fears are not simply cured by facts. In addition, hard-line conspiracy myth communities are frequently not merely grooming new members with alternative facts, but with their alternative offers of identity and belonging.

'Why do people believe in conspiracy theories?' I ask Karolin.

'Many people who believe in conspiracy theories feel special because they are 'the awakened ones'. They think they are among the few citizens who understand what is actually going on. Your identity can become dependent on that idea.'

Beliefs do not exist in isolation, they are embedded in complex webs of emotions and ideas. The single biggest predictor of whether one believes in one conspiracy theory is whether that person believes in other conspiracy theories.[299] Psychologists speak of a 'conspiracy mentality' that makes some people more likely to believe in conspiratorial accounts, even when they are unfounded, illogical or contradictory.[300]

There are many psychological reasons why people believe in conspiracy myths: to fill an information vacuum, to overcome their fears, uncertainties and feelings of powerlessness, to find an antidote to a general lack of perspective, to offer a sense of belonging to a victimised in-group and to blame a scapegoat for everything that has been going wrong. All of these reasons have become more relevant in the course of a global pandemic that has brought us all an extra portion of uncertainty, loneliness and other personal challenges.

Karolin blames the media for having given a platform to those who have been presenting unscientific viewpoints for too long without debunking their claims. For example, Covid sceptics have been invited to TV talk shows to comment on vaccine safety even though they were neither experts in virology nor immunology.[301] 'Their factually ungrounded views were presented as valid standpoints in a debate, which is very dangerous. When we report on NASA, we don't first ask the flat earthers for their opinion either.' She stops to let this idea sink in before continuing: 'There is enough diversity of opinion on how to deal with climate change or the Covid pandemic. Questioning their existence altogether is something very different.'

The systematic spread of disinformation has reinforced vaccine scepticism across the world, frequently interacting with pre-existing networks of 'alternative' beliefs. Social media analysis has shown that anti-vax disinformation has been propagated primarily by the overlapping networks of prominent conspiracy theorists, white nationalists and far-right populist parties.[302] The media outlet London Real was founded in 2011 by the American-British ex-banker Brian Rose, and now has over 1 billion views and 5 million subscribers. Since 2020, this self-proclaimed 'digital freedom platform' with the slogan 'Transform Yourself' has given much airtime to Covid-related conspiracy myths propagated not only by the controversial American biochemist Judy Mikovits but also by the famous British Holocaust denier David Icke.[303]

How do we get believers to question these dubious ideologies? Making fun of them might not be the right way. Karolin believes that hashtag campaigns such as #Covidiots (#Covididioten) have been counter-productive. 'It's a big mistake to ridicule or discredit people who consume disinformation and are vulnerable to conspiracy myths. If they feel unheard or even humiliated, it might push them even more towards conspiratorial content.'

* * *

I hear drums and whistles in the distance. The air smells of smoke and the thousands-strong crowd of protestors is surrounded by men and women in uniform. I expected a high police presence because the previous 'Unite for Freedom' rally had escalated into violence: eight police officers had been injured by protestors throwing bottles at them.[304]

Across Europe and the US, police and media representatives faced threats, harassment and physical assaults at anti-vaccine and anti-lockdown protests. Violence against journalists reached a level that was described as 'unbearable' by many reporters.[305] In Berlin in 2021, a cameraman from the public service broadcaster ARD was hit on the head and a sound assistant was deliberately attacked in an anti-lockdown protest.[306] That September in

Slovenia, anti-lockdown demonstrators even broke into the headquarters of the public broadcaster RTV Slovenija.[307] In the same month, a BBC news crew was cornered and threatened by a group of at least eight protestors in the northern English coastal town Scarborough. The protestors were caught on camera shouting: 'You will hang for what you've done to this country' and 'the nooses are ready'.[308]

The psychological toll on victims of this kind of animosity cannot be overemphasised. In Austria, months of harassment and death wishes directed at Lisa-Maria Kellermayr, a prominent doctor who campaigned for vaccines during the pandemic, led to the woman's suicide in the summer of 2022. She had previously alerted the police about the threats but received only limited help. 'Patients' had tried to enter her clinic with butterfly knives, and one of the threats she had received straight to her email inbox read:[309]

> Subject: I will kill you.
> Hello you stupid piece of shit. You can try to threaten me with lawyers but you won't get me anyways. Instead I have decided to get you. And since I'm already doing this, I will also slaughter all employees in your clinic. I am armed and have a double-barrelled shotgun.

* * *

As I enter the gates of Hyde Park, a woman hands me a flyer which says 'Well done . . . You are in the minority of those awake and who haven't been totally deceived by this global tyranny of evil.' Another protester gives me a book entitled *Covid19 and the Rest of the Story* by Pastor Bill Hughes and a CD of the *Free Forever* album by the folk and gospel group Deep Persuasion.

I think that as long as the protesters don't identify me as a 'mainstream' journalist I will be fine. Unlike in previous undercover trips, I do not have to worry about my appearance this time. The crowd is as eclectic as it gets: I stand between a woman in dreadlocks and baggy jeans, an ordinary-looking old man in a wheelchair, a man with fascist tattoos and a shaved head, and a woman in an elegant retro dress and a Kentucky Derby hat. The protest has attracted people ranging from hard-line conspiracy theorists and neo-Nazi skinheads to alternative medicine proponents, Christian fundamentalists and worried parents. I meet participants aged from their late 80s to as young as six months, pushed in a buggy by their parents.

I read banners proclaiming 'Smash the New World Order', 'Children are dying from the jab', 'Defund the BBC' and 'What was washed most? Hands or brains?' I wonder if I should start making conversation with one of the protestors. Many people seem to be there with family or friends and I feel conspicuous by myself.

Three men in Trump T-shirts are walking right in front of me. They shoot me a suspicious glance and I decide to deflect with a question.

'Are you American?' I ask.

Johnny turns out to be English. He lives in Essex but has travelled to London for the protest.

'You can be a Trump fan without being American. I think we need a Trump in this country,' he explains and tells me that he would consider moving to the US if Trump got voted back in again. His three sons would want to live in the US as well.

I force out the most affirmative sound my tight throat will allow.

He inspects me. 'Where in the US are you from?'

'I'm Canadian,' I lie, unsure how long my accent would allow me to pretend I'm not an EU migrant. I would try for French-Canadian.

'Oh sorry,' he comments and moves on to rant about Canada's PM Justin Trudeau and his liberal policies.

A man in front of us shouts 'Shut down the BBC,' prompting my conversation partner to switch to a different scapegoat: 'the mainstream media'.

'You can't listen to anything the media says,' he rages. 'I'm on Telegram. You should join too. It's easy, you join one channel and then you immediately get links to others. So over time you build up a whole new information system.'

He pulls out his phone. 'Look at these channels.' I see names such as Q News, Flat Earth, QAnon Global, The Great Awakening, as he scrolls down. 'This is where I get my information from. No lying media for me anymore.'

I decide to say good-bye, and for a few minutes I just watch the crowd around me. Dozens of protestors with custom-printed T-shirts pass me: common slogans are 'Save the children' and 'PLANDEMIC', a reference to the conspiracy idea of a 'planned pandemic'.

When I have gathered my thoughts, I walk over to a casually dressed Black man who holds up a banner that says: 'Stop the paedos. Leave our babies alone.' It is interesting to see a Black man walking side by side with a xenophobic Trump supporter.

'What is it with the babies?' I ask him.

'They kill babies to extract adrenochrome.'

'What's adrenochrome?'

'You know adrenaline? Adrenochrome is a concentrated version of adrenaline. It's much richer than adrenaline and becomes a drug. They extract it from babies and children.'

'How?'

'When they torture the babies, they release adrenochrome.'

I struggle to find words. 'But who does that?'

'All celebrities and the Royal Family. They want to stay young and healthy.' He looks ahead into the distance. 'It's terrible.

Have you watched this documentary series on what's been happening behind the scenes in the Royal Family and how they have been living off babies' blood?'

Oh, the Royal Family again. As well as being reptiloids they are now Satanists who drink the blood of babies to stay young. Sounds familiar? That's because the conspiracy myth is centuries old. In the Middle Ages the idea that Jews were harvesting the blood of Christian children for use in religious rituals was widespread.[310] Today, a modern mutation of the myth has re-emerged and found more adherents than one would think possible. At least 24 US political candidates have supported the idea that the global elites are blood-sucking Satanists.[311]

As I stare at Buckingham Palace ahead of us, I wonder if we have entered the 'Digital Dark Ages'. My mind fills with images of terrorist Tobias Rathjen, who opened fire in the German town of Hanau, killing three people, in early 2020. He had also believed in secretive forces that were supposedly using underground military bases to torture young children. I find myself shaking my head. 'Terrifying,' I note. My companion has a very different image in mind, but he agrees. I continue to question the protestor, grateful for his openness: 'So how do they get the children?'

'It's all institutionalised,' he tells me.

'Do you know anyone who's had their child taken?'

'Yes, an English guy living in Portugal. Institutions have taken his only child away.'

I wonder if the real story was that child protection services intervened to safeguard the child from a family member with clinical paranoia.

'What brought you here?' the man asks me. He has been to many protests.

'Freedom!!!' shouts a protester next to us into a megaphone. 'No to the vaccines!'

I hesitate for a second. 'The vaccine passports. What's your name?' I ask to avoid further questions.

'Earth G, and yours?'

'That's a cool name,' I say. 'Claire.'

He stretches out his hand. I take it, trying not to show that I'd much rather bump elbows.

Earth G has a friendly smile. 'Nice to meet you. Meet my wife Kate, she's Swedish.' The blonde woman next to him also shakes my hand.

'I gotta go and find my friend,' I tell the couple and vanish round the corner.

* * *

'Spike can kill you. The Vaxx is a bioweapon. Be aware.'

A few days later my patriotic avatar Claire is browsing through images of alleged vaccine side effects and diagrams of the 'global elites'. I have decided to check out the Telegram channels that Pedro and Johnny recommended. The channels have names such as 'London Protests Official', 'Covid Truth Network', 'Anti-Vaxx Worldwide' or 'Great Awakening Community'. Some are hubs for crowdsourcing (dis)information while others are coordination centres for protests. They seem to be the source of radicalisation and disinformation for many anti-science activists. Wherever I look, the conspiracy myth at the centre of most channels is QAnon.

I originally went undercover with QAnon before it became the world's largest conspiracy myth network. When I joined in 2017, it was a fringe movement in the US claiming that the Clinton family ran a child exploitation network in the underground of Washington DC. But within just a couple of years the network expanded globally, founding offshoots from the Netherlands to Australia. Viral campaigns and game-like crowd investigations to get to 'the truth' were used to recruit new members. A *Guardian* investigation found that by 2020 QAnon had more than 4.5 million aggregated followers on social media, spanning at least 15 countries.[312] There are hundreds, if not thousands, of QAnon-related channels on social media. One of the main Telegram channels is Qnews with 120,000 subscribers who believe that 'communism is the final Covid variant'. By comparison, the Flat Earth channel only counts 44,000 followers. The Covid-19 pandemic accelerated the global rise of QAnon: Covid deniers, anti-vaxxers, lockdown opponents and traditional conspiracy theorists united in frustration, fear and anger. Soon it became all about the 'plandemic' and 'dangerous vaccines'.

Here I am once again, looking at how the self-styled investigators of QAnon go ever deeper down the rabbit hole. Members collect so-called 'breadcrumbs' of information to bake 'the dough' – basically their own version of reality. It feels like being part of a Dan Brown book, where you have to solve different enigmas and mysteries. But the pieces of information are crowd-sourced, often from unreliable places, and the connections between them are frequently arbitrary. To a believer, nothing is allowed to be coincidence anymore, even the initials or birth dates of politicians suddenly have a deeper meaning.

Traditional conspiracy theory communities have modernised and responded to emerging trends. During the pandemic most redirected their attention to it – Even Flat Earthers shifted conversation topic to predominantly talk about Covid conspiracies. They've taken these new myths and merged them with very old ones. 'Every single aspect of Covid is Jewish,' one of their members writes to me, and shares a diagram that showed Jewish CEOs, politicians and scientists who are supposedly all tied to vaccine development and Covid policies.

Anti-Vaxx Worldwide is a more intimate group, with just a few hundred followers. Its members believe 'the COVID VACCINE is the DISEASE'. One tells me to 'be aware of the vaccinated, they have now become the super-spreaders'. I manage to resist pointing out to them that by far the biggest risk for unvaccinated people comes from other unvaccinated people.[313]

* * *

For a month my new daily routine has been to check all the anti-vaxxer and conspiracy myth channels I could gain access to. Scrolling through my daily Telegram feed while enjoying my early morning coffee, I find it hard to believe that many groups are still denying the existence of the virus. 'Covid 19 does not exist and the jib ab is not a vaccine,' I hear from dozens of users. By this point there have been over 250 million Covid cases worldwide and over 5 million have died. Even prominent Covid deniers have caught the virus: the US musician Landon Spradlin who called Covid-19 a 'mass hysteria' died of the virus, as did the British denier Gary Matthews.[314] American Covid sceptic Tony Green who thought the pandemic was a hoax became famous after a family gathering he hosted in Texas turned into a super-spreader event and he lost several relatives to the disease.[315] In Norway, the host of an illegal Covid sceptics event died after contracting the virus most likely at his own event.[316] Staring at my phone, I ask myself: how much proof do Covid deniers still need?

But then I remember that polarisation is never about facts, it's about identity. And the drama of Covid denial played into pre-existing identitarian strife. My research found the anti-vaxxer and conspiracy myth communities strongly overlap with the white nationalist and anti-climate science scenes. Even anti-feminism and anti-transgender activism seem to play a role in many of the channels. The white supremacist World Elite group runs a poll: 'Can you be vaxxed and still be a nationalist?'

Most people think you can't be both. The narratives of Covid deniers and anti-vaxxers have merged into one almost-coherent conspiracy theory: 'What we're dealing with is just another flu strain like every year, COVID 19 does not exist and is fictitious,' one white nationalist writes. He adds: 'I believe China and the globalists orchestrated this COVID hoax (the flu disguised as a novel virus) to bring in global tyranny and a worldwide police totalitarian surveillance state, and this plot included massive election fraud.'

The follow-up question by another user is precisely what has worried the security and intelligence community in many countries: 'What do we do next??'

In December 2021, Piers Corbyn told a crowd of a few hundred people gathered in front of Downing Street that they needed to 'get a bit more physical' with 'lying MPs'. He called on his followers to:

> . . . hammer to death those scum who have decided to go ahead with introducing new fascism [. . .] We've got to get a list of them [. . .] and if your MP is one of them, go to their offices and, well, I would recommend burning them down, OK. But I can't say that on air.[317]

The following month, an undercover investigation by the *Daily Mail* found a group of 200 members of a hard-line anti-vax group had met up in a Staffordshire park to practise smashing police lines and prepare for 'war' on the government. The group called Alpha Men Assemble (AMA) was led by ex-Royal Fusilier Danny Glass who taught the others the basics of military-style combat training. 'We need to hit the vaccine centres, schools, headteachers, colleges, councillors, police, directors of public health in every area,' one of the attending women shouted. 'None of us are going to take the f***ing jab and none of our families are.'[318]

Many conspiracy theorists were fed up with living in a pandemic. Their version of the truth helped them to find concrete villains who could be punished. As I study their online discussions, I observe in real time how the language in many of the channels gets more and more aggressive daily. Adherents want to replace words with actions. By 2021, 79 QAnon followers had committed ideologically motivated crimes in the US alone.[319]

One of the key challenges for security forces is the diversification of potential targets of violence: in the world of QAnon, scientists, pharmaceutical companies, politicians, journalists, minority communities and even Hollywood actors and celebrities all became part of a hugely complex conspiracy. There is not one clear enemy group, so the protection of potential targets for attacks has become an impossible mission.

*　*　*

While some anti-science activists campaign for violence, others are more motivated by the feeling of belonging to an insider network of likeminded people. Pop culture can play a key role in creating intimate bonds between conspiracy theory adherents.

Listening to J.T. Wilde's music, I catch myself bouncing my head and tapping my feet to the beats. The song is actually pretty good, even if the lyrics are ludicrous.

They call us deplorable
And we love the name
They got the bodies in the dirt
And need someone to blame

They got a penchant for greed
And the money to spare

They put the dollars in the coffers
And the lies in the air

Where we go one We go all
I won't push you down
You won't let me fall
One day for sure we will stand tall
Where We Go One We Go All!

We are the patriots,
Trust the plan
Because we have it all
And their fate is in our hands

They had a reason to fool us
But we didn't take the bait
They want to take us to hell
But we got guns at the gate

J.T. Wilde not only sounds like a real rocker, he also looks like one. Long hair falls onto his black T-shirt and he wears a professional headset to speak to me. His room is full of music equipment: guitars, drums, microphones. There is some contemporary art on the walls next to an American flag.

'The movement was a blast,' J.T. Wilde tells me in his raspy voice. He refers to QAnon as the movement. 'I had so much fun. It was like this beautiful, fun game.' His eyes are full of excitement. 'I look at things from a spiritual aspect, it was like being in a dichotomy ... look at this and that and that.' The singer-songwriter looks up to the ceiling, lost in thought for a few seconds before returning his attention to me. Then he says: 'QAnon scared the shit out of me. And it made me write some really cool songs.'

J.T. Wilde grew up in Florida and used to listen to the Sex Pistols and Ozzy Osborne. His example shows that QAnon cannot be classified as having just one political direction. He is against abortion but for LGBTQ rights. He wanted to become a vegetarian. He would call himself fiscally conservative but socially liberal. Although the movement has clearly taken a pro-Trump, patriotic and anti-liberal stance, it has attracted people from the traditional left, right and centre. Has J.T. Wilde always been interested in politics? 'No. I used to be a very spiritual person,' he says and tells me that he had his own personal YouTube channel where he spoke about spirituality and meditation. But today he is convinced 'the political system needs a revolution'.

J.T. Wilde joined QAnon in 2019. 'Without a breakdown there is no break-through. We need to rebuild the system,' he tells me. QAnon gave him belief in radical change and he found a new family in the fellow anons. But he also lost many of his old friends, who were shocked by his extreme views and conspiratorial thoughts. He looks at me intensely before insisting: 'I'm still the same person.' I can sense the frustration in his voice. He is clearly against violence and disavows the more extreme parts of QAnon, saying 'There were things that turned me off about the movement, which is why I am no longer actively involved.' But, he jokingly adds, 'I'm the most extreme rocker in America. The conspiracy theorist rocker.'

J.T. Wilde's songs became so popular with QAnon followers that you could hear them at anti-lockdown and anti-government protests. 'My *Enjoy the Show* Album is a concept album for the Q movement,' he claims. 'The themes are about patriotism, unity and rooting out corruption in our government and media establishment.' His music has been removed from Spotify and Soundcloud[220] – platforms he believes are also part of the conspiracy.

He says that there is a real thirst for knowledge about the inner workings of government. 'Q has filled that void in a lot of ways.' J.T. Wilde is convinced that President Joe Biden is a menace to the democratic foundations of America. 'Our constitution had never been as threatened as it is now under the current administration,' he tells me.

Ironically, QAnon is a movement that has exhibited deeply anti-democratic behaviour and has been supported by sovereign citizens and militia movements who don't accept the rule of law. Were the mob of Donald Trump supporters playing his song when they stormed the Capitol in January 2021? 'Possibly,' he admits. But he thinks the Capitol protest was all a trap planted by the security services or the Clintons to paint the movement as dangerous.

As with Marius, Pedro, Johnny and Earth G, the list of government bodies, media outlets, scientific institutions and private companies Wilde doesn't trust is long. At the top of it are the pharma industry and academics involved in developing the Covid vaccines. He believes the vaccines are an attempt to genetically manipulate and control the population. 'Nanobot technology,' he says without being able to explain to me how this would work. 'You could see it as another domination experiment, like the CIA Project MKUltra during the Cold War.' When I try to press him for details however, he acknowledges that all this is pure speculation.

Despite an obvious lack of evidence, he is clearly afraid of getting his Covid jab: 'I don't plan on getting the vaccine until *they* hold me down and put it in my arm.' I nod and ask: 'So who is *they*?' He laughs. 'Ha, that's always the first question. *They* are running the show.' He tells me that our world has a mega structure. 'The people that were behind the money 100 years ago, are still behind the money. They are running the entire world.'

He hasn't mentioned any specific group, but in my work with security and intelligence forces I have witnessed how this kind of rhetoric can inspire hatred and violence against those who have historically been the most common scapegoats for conspiracy theories: Jews. Like White Lives Matter, QAnon has made use of old anti-Semitic tropes, including the idea of a child-molesting, blood-sucking cabal of global elites – often implicitly assumed to be Jewish.

Over the past year, QAnon followers have surged in tandem with anti-Semitic hate crimes. Globally, anti-Semitism has seen a strong uptick both online and offline since the outbreak of the pandemic. In the first half of 2020 alone 789 anti-Semitic incidents were reported in the UK.[321] This is more than the full-year record for 2010, which saw 639 anti-Semitic incidents and back then was the second-highest annual total since the Community Security Trust (CST) began recording hate crimes against Jewish communities in 1984.[322] The strong upward trend in anti-Semitic hate crimes is expected to continue with the spread of conspiracy myths that place Jews at their centre. In 2021, CST recorded a total of over 2,000 hate crimes for the first time.[323]

* * *

Will Moy has been at the forefront of the battle against disinformation in the UK. He runs the fact-checking website Full Fact – a key abuse target for Covid conspiracy theorists.

'The level of anger has gone up remarkably,' Will tells me. 'The sheer amount of attention that has gone into claim and counter-claim about the pandemic has been huge, and the anger and abuse have come along with it.' Attacks on Full Fact's own staff, in particular women, have been significant enough that they have been actively working on reducing abuse of staff members.

'We also get reasonable feedback,' Will explains. 'It's important not to lump everybody who provides feedback under harassment, but a lot of the cases really are. There are many people who would be happier if we were not here.'

In the decade that Full Fact has been running, there have been four general elections, three referendums, a migration crisis, waves of terrorist attacks, Brexit, the pandemic, war in Ukraine, and historic levels of inflation with catastrophic economic results. 'Essentially the country has been in crisis mode for a large part of Full Fact's existence,' Moy says. 'It's an interesting question as to what normal looks like and I look forward to finding out.' The upheaval and resulting uncertainty we have faced as a society has made us collectively more prone to conspiracy myths.

A look at history shows that disinformation has always thrived in times of crisis. The plague in the fourteenth century was blamed on the Jews who were accused of having poisoned wells. In the times of cholera in the 19th century the myth spread that doctors had created the disease so they could harvest the bodies of the dead. And it's not only health crises that have given rise to similarly themed infodemics. Past economic crises and security crises have provoked the same collective coping mechanisms: the Great Depression of 1929 and the Financial Crisis of 2008 both fuelled anti-Semitic conspiracy myths.[324] The trauma of 9/11 was a foundation stone for the complex master conspiracy myth of QAnon.

But Covid took disinformation to a new level. The combined health and economic crisis had more impact on our day-to-day existence than any public event most of us have witnessed in our lifetimes. It required us to change our lifestyles, and was therefore perceived as a threat to private life. For many people, denial was simpler than facing the truth that had prompted this intrusion. Collectivising that denial is a lot easier in the digital age than it was in times of the plague, or even than it was during the Financial Crisis little over a decade ago.

Full Fact was launched in an era of political spin. There was a lot of concern at the time about politicians misleading the public and bad journalism, especially surrounding discussions about the Iraq War and the Financial Crisis. 'But the Internet was not a significant player in information consumption in the way it is now,' Will Moy notes. 'Today the top three news sources include Facebook.' BBC Radio 4 is only number 16 of the list – far behind Facebook, Twitter, Instagram and Whatsapp.'[325]

Will has an unconventional background. Most fact-checkers come from journalism, but he originally worked for a blind member of the House of Lords, the non-party affiliated Lord Colin Low of Dalston. 'As he was blind, I would read all the briefings for him and some of them were just rubbish,' Will says. He adds: 'On the basis of that rubbish, really important decisions about how the country is run were made.' Watching lobbyists mislead politicians and wanting to challenge them is what made him found Full Fact.

At the beginning of the pandemic, it became clear that the things that went viral fastest were the most absurd – whether it was advice to swallow bleach to heal from Covid, or the idea that Bill Gates was launching an international population surveillance experiment using vaccines.

In times of crisis the so-called Dunning-Kruger effect usually fuels the spread of disinformation. The Dunning-Kruger curve shows that we are most likely to be overly confident in our own knowledge and judgement when we know very little about a topic. At the beginning of Covid all of us knew very little about the pandemic and were therefore more prone to conspiracy myths and unscientific explanations. As we became better informed most people could manage the situation's complexity and ambiguity better. But many were prevented from making that shift by a rising tide of disinformation: they didn't know what they didn't know.

Will is convinced that fact-checking can help to tackle the ongoing infodemic. 'There are specific groups of people with specific hesitations who need to be listened to,' he argues. Middle groups who sit on the fence are, for example, minority communities who feel that scientific trials were not demographically diverse enough. If you don't have Black people represented in a vaccine study, why should Black people feel safe with the vaccine?

'That's a reasonable concern and needs to be addressed,' Will notes.

He also mentioned pregnant women. 'They have a set of concerns because they have been given one piece of advice followed by another piece over the last twelve months.' New drugs also tend to not be tested on pregnant women for ethical reasons, making it hard to know how safe they are for developing foetuses.

Science is never unambiguous, according to Will. 'Almost all useful information is more complex than that. A fact-checker's job is not to make the world black and white. It's to reinsert shades of grey where campaigners paint the world black and white. Very often part of our job is to express the ambiguity.'

The good news is that according to recent research, fact-checking can work. A National Academy of Sciences study which tested the effects of fact-checking on audiences in Argentina, Nigeria, South Africa and the UK found that the positive effects of fact-checking were still detectable two weeks later.[326] But correcting facts won't necessarily change beliefs that are rooted in someone's identity and worldview. That takes a different approach.

'Worldviews are not accumulations of atomised facts,' Will says. 'If you are convinced that Buckingham Palace is run by reptilians, then someone has to engage you on the level of that narrative rather than fact-checking whether the Pfizer vaccine contains graphene oxide or not.'

Will agrees that there are extremely persistent subcultures 'who are deeply convinced that medical evidence is wrong or falsified and that we are being lied to'. Those who hold firm opinions are usually the hardest group to reach for fact-checkers. If you fundamentally distrust official information, it is close to impossible to change your mind with official-sounding information.

But a fact-checker's job is not to convince people that the vaccines are safe, Will explains. It's to give people a good basis on which to make up their own minds. 'We are not a public health campaign. We're not trying to persuade anyone to do anything.'

Will is a free-speech advocate. He is convinced that it is the best guarantor of good information in public discourse. 'Open societies depend on open debate . . . It's just in the short-term it's messier,' he tells me. He is a realist about present challenges, however: 'I don't think we've yet worked out how we maintain that open debate with increasingly fragmented audiences online.'

The threshold for stopping people from saying things has to be set higher than simple misstatements of fact, he argues. The intentions and consequences of spreading disinformation matter. 'If you go to the fire brigade and you say there is a fire while there isn't, that's a criminal offense – not because it's [factually] wrong, but because you prevent the fire brigade from going to an actual fire.'

He believes removal policies should be driven by behaviour rather than content. Individual pieces of wrong content, he argues, should not be removed. Instead, toxic behaviour should be regulated – for example users engaging in coordinated, systematic disinformation campaigns. 'This is a form of power abuse,' he says.

The real gamechanger in today's online information is how easy it has become to reach large audiences at low cost without anyone noticing you are doing it. You can also mislead people about who you are and what your goals are by hiding your intentions and identity. 'If you wanted to talk to a million people a decade ago you had to get a newspaper out or a billboard,' Will says. 'So everyone would notice you are doing it. Now you can talk to a million people and fly under a radar screen.'

Internet scale is a massive challenge. Will observed the same claims spreading from country to country. 'The sheer volume of what gets created online in any one day is beyond what humans can tackle,' he says. 'The fragmentation of audiences means that it's impossible to even be aware which key claims are shaping public opinion.'

Full Fact has invested in artificial intelligence teams who are automating monitoring, identifying when people repeat untrue claims and even automating fact-checking in some cases. But while solutions are getting better, the problem might be getting worse. Future technologies are bound to add new challenges for fact-checking and myth-busting. For example, deepfakes and natural language generation will make it harder to identify the author behind a piece of content.

'Ultimately we will need to build chains of trust from when something is originally produced all the way through to when it's finally seen,' Will believes.

Earlier chapters explored well-established fault lines between liberals and conservatives – feminism, LGBTQ rights and racial justice – and looked at how the environmental debate has become a new outlet for old conservative impulses. But during the research for this chapter, I saw that today's anti-science movements such as QAnon have moved beyond any conventional left vs right, or liberal vs conservative divide. In an era in which fact-checking and evidence-based approaches are up against unparalleled levels of fantasy, paranoia and outright lies, the key conflict of our time increasingly seems to be between crazy versus not so crazy.

WAGING PROXY WARS

Time passes very differently. A day feels like two, a month like four.

The thought that a month has passed doesn't make you tremble anymore. No one here knows when the war will end. But there is already an established routine and a new way of being.

The pain, the fear and above all the love that you feel with every bell, siren and message grows stronger. In this very long and ruthless month we have lost many, many, but unfortunately it is not yet the time to mourn them.

Those I encourage you to think about now are those we thought we lost before the war, not in death, but in disputes. Those with whom our relationships have grown stronger, more caring and more loving than ever during the war. Those who have forgiven you and whom you have forgiven. The ones you think about during the day and ask ten times a day if they've eaten.

This month has taken away too much, but it has given back something we didn't have before, and it would not have happened without war.

What's important now is to keep each other from forgetting that war isn't a routine or a way of life. Dream together about what you will do after the war, plan your life after the war together, do not hesitate and do not be stingy with the words 'I love you and miss you so much.'

Den Kubriak, Ukrainian fighter, April 2022

Six weeks into the Russian invasion of Ukraine, Den joins me from Kyiv via the encrypted messaging app Signal.

I am looking at a tall 33-year-old man with a full beard. As we introduce ourselves, he takes off his military jacket. When I ask him how he is doing, he smiles and points at his bald head. 'The worst thing that happened to me is this.' Clearly, he has not lost his sense of humour.

As a young father of three children, Den could have opted out of fighting when the war broke out. But he rushed to join the military. 'It all came very fast. No one really had the time to prepare,' he tells me in excellent English. His wife and kids are in elsewhere in Europe now. As soon as US intelligence had warned of an imminent Russian invasion in February, he decided to get his family out of the country. He knew it would be too late once the first shot had been fired.

Before the war things were good. 'Life was amazing,' he tells me, a big smile on his face. 'I really got into running and regularly travelled to a different country to go for a 10km run in nature and then return home to my family the next day.' On a typical day, he would get his kids ready for school, drop them off, go to work and pick them up again. Den's parents ran a radio station network in Ukraine, he told me. He had been a journalist and worked in communications before the war. 'I owned a digital marketing company,' he says. 'I guess I still do, technically,' he adds. 'But it's kind of out of business these days.'

As a journalist, Den had received hostile environment and combat training to prepare him for potentially reporting from war zones. But he had no experience in real battles and had never planned to use his training in a live conflict. 'Almost no one here did. A few people in the military had fought in Donbas but that's about it. We all had little or no experience.' But the stakes were too high for Den to justify inaction. He didn't join the Ukrainian forces out of bravery but out of love, he tells me.

'There are so many things I'm afraid of: I'm afraid of water, I'm afraid of heights. But when Russia invaded, I didn't even stop to think whether I should fight.'

As we speak, US intelligence are warning that Russian forces are planning to use chemical weapons in Kyiv. They have already used them in Mariupol. He is not afraid of dying. 'No one here is,' he tells me and shows me his gas mask. 'You can't be prepared for something like chemical weapons though,' he says. 'They enter through the skin.' He takes a long draw from his e-cigarette. 'Putin can do whatever. He is isolated, doesn't have full understanding of the war dynamics and has no moral boundaries.' Den exhales a mouth ful of vapour. 'We have to accept that they will again use chemical weapons, that they might even use nuclear weapons. At least we won't be surprised then.'

For Den, winning the current conflict with Russia does not mean you won a war. 'They will come back two, three years later,' he says. Putin will continue his aggression against Ukraine, Georgia and the Baltic countries. Den is convinced that the war he is fighting is not just about Ukraine. 'Our victory will not just be a victory for Ukraine but for all of Europe.' It's about a fundamental clash of values. The Kremlin at war with minorities, free speech and liberal-progressive values. 'In Ukraine we sometimes make politically incorrect jokes, but Russia actually means it.'

In the lead-up to the invasion, US intelligence services had warned that Russian troops might target Ukrainian LGBTQ activists in assassinations, kidnappings and arrests. The Biden administration was surprised at how formalised the target and kill lists of the Russian intelligence agencies GRU and FSB were.[327] Den confirms: 'In Bucha and other cities we went to, we would find printed out lists of people to be shot.' He tells me that these included anyone who challenged the Russian agenda and values: journalists and teachers, but also those involved in any progressive activist movements or minority communities. Russian and Belarussian dissidents exiled in Ukraine were also prime targets. Homosexuality is a criminal offence in the eastern Ukrainian city of Luhansk, which has been occupied by Russian forces since 2014.[328] Even before the invasion in 2022, Pride group members living in eastern Ukraine had been interrogated and pressured into reporting other LGBTQ activists.[329]

When Putin warned of alleged Western efforts to 'cancel' Russian culture, he linked them back to a wider war against traditional values. In his rant against Western 'cancel culture' he even namedropped J.K. Rowling, claiming she was punished because she 'did not please fans of the so-called gender freedoms'. But the *Harry Potter* author was quick to respond: 'Critiques of Western cancel culture are possibly not best made by those currently slaughtering civilians for the crime of resistance, or who jail and poison their critics,' she wrote in a tweet.

There is a long tradition of Russian connections to anti-LGBTQ activism in Europe and the US. For example, the US Christian-fundamentalist institution World Congress of Families is closely linked to the Russian orthodox church. In particular, the oligarchs Vladimir Yakunin and Konstantin Malofeev have in the past acted as important bridges between Russian funding and anti-liberal campaigns against same-sex marriage, abortion and trans rights in Europe and North America.[330]

Putin has repeatedly attacked progressive policies and 'sociocultural disturbances' in the West. In 2019 the Russian leader claimed liberalism had become 'obsolete', and in 2021 he called teaching gender fluidity to children a 'crime against humanity'.[331] Putin has been trying to rally 'those yearning for the certainties of the past and offended by the constant instability of the liberal present', *New York Times* columnist Ezra Klein wrote. The logic that Ukraine belongs to Russia today, he argued, is similar to the logic that defends the social hierarchies of the past.³³²

* * *

April weather does not entirely justify sunglasses or winter hats. The sun isn't strong enough yet, while the cold isn't piercing enough anymore. But as cameras are zooming in on me standing in between hundreds of protestors waving Russian and German flags in central Frankfurt on 10 April 2022, I am happy to be wearing both items. A face mask would have been handy too, but my intuition told me that too many in the crowd would not appreciate it.

It is 1 p.m. in Frankfurt, and the pro-Russia protest is slowly taking shape on Opernplatz. I have never seen more police cars at a protest. No one wants a repetition of last weekend's vehicle convoy in Berlin, where around 700 cars showed support for the Russian invasion of Ukraine. Cars decorated with Russian war symbols met slogans against mask mandates and mandatory vaccines.³³³ Today's protest faces tight restrictions, including a ban on Russian propaganda symbols such as the Z, the V, the Soviet Union flag, the Cross of St George and St George's ribbon.

In the beginning, the protest is as I expected: speeches about alleged harassment of Russian kids in German schools are followed by the Russian and German national anthem. Angry verbal exchanges are fired across the lines of policemen that keep pro-Russia protestors from the pro-Ukrainian counter-protestors. Protestors with Russian flags wrapped around their bodies and patriots' white-blue-red lines drawn onto their cheeks start moving towards the historical landmark Hauptfriedhof, the 'Main Cemetery' of Frankfurt.

One of my first encounters at the protest is with Gabriel. I know almost instantly where Gabriel stands politically. It might be his wild undercut in combination with a neatly shaved beard. Or maybe it is the Guy Fawkes mask dangling from his back. In recent years, far-right and conspiracy myth communities have hijacked this symbol of the 1605 Gunpowder Plot, an attempt by a group of provincial English Catholics to blow up Parliament in London.

My first guess is that Gabriel is a Querdenker ('lateral thinker'). The German Querdenker movement was founded in the wake of the pandemic, and today counts hundreds of thousands of sympathisers who participate in online group chats and show up at anti-Covid protests in German cities, often with T-shirts, banners and flags that show QAnon narratives, slogans and symbols. They are made up of a wild mix of far-right extremists, traditionally left-wing anti-vaxxers, old-school conspiracy theorists, new-born Covid deniers and hard-line sovereign citizens who reject the democratic order.

I decide to give it a shot. 'When did you wake up?' I ask him, adopting the language of the QAnon and anti-vaxxer community. It works. 'I already woke up before Covid.' He tells me that his distrust in the way the country was run started before the first pandemic lockdowns. 'With all the bullshit and lies we were being told I already suspected that something was going to happen.' He says catching Covid almost changed his mind. 'I had Delta and almost bit the dust. I swore I would get the vaccine as soon as it would be available.' He pauses to look at me intensely before saying: 'Luckily I had enough time to understand what these jabs really are.'[334]

'Did you go to the Covid protests yesterday?' he asks me. I shake my head and explain that I am only here for the weekend. I thought about my story before joining the protest. My name is Mary and I am from Bavaria, with Russian heritage. As I speak about my trip to Frankfurt, he only half listens anyway. 'Russia! Best country. Russia! Best country,' he sings. He occasionally exchanges 'Russia!' for 'Serbia!'

Every now and then he stops to wave to residents standing on their balconies or leaning out of their windows to watch the spectacle. Some of them are waving back, others are swearing back. One man cheering at us is only wearing a bathrobe. 'Come down and join us!' Gabriel shouts over the Russian music playing in the background. It isn't hard to tell that he is a hyper-social human being, chatting and smiling at everyone. I can imagine the adverse effects that lockdown must have had on him.

While half-running to keep pace with Gabriel's steps I learn that he is running several Telegram groups. He shows them to me on his phone. 'It's amazing. We are growing rapidly. I only set this one up a few months ago and have already reached over 350 members. I also run a few other groups.'[335] He tells me they are all connected, posting mainly about pro-Russia and anti-vaccine activities. 'Do you want to join?' he asks and gives me his phone number. 'We're private. But I can let you in, if you text me.' We agree to get in touch after the protest.

Crude conspiratorial Telegram groups appear to be the bridge connecting many of the Germans who have shown up in support of the Russian war today. I meet several other protesters who mention Telegram as their go-to source of information and mobilisation. A German man with a Russian wife, a Kurdish social worker with a radical pro-Russian friend and a middle-aged woman who is outraged by media portrayals of the war, which she thinks are a hyper-biased and distorted version of what is '*really*' going on.

'The number of police cars here is insane,' a man walking in front of me is passionately speaking into a professional headset and microphone that is attached to his head of grey hair. 'You would never see that at a fag protest.'[336] The homophobic slur catches my attention. When the man stops talking for a few moments, I take the opportunity: 'Are you doing a livestream?' He laughs out loud and shakes his head. 'I was just on the phone.'

We walk and talk about the protest, ignoring the loud chanting next to us. 'I hope Russia will be able to realise their ambitions. I'm hoping for a Russian victory,' the man told me.[337] It doesn't take long to find out that he is not just for Russia, but also against Covid measures, alternative energy and the closure of coal-fired power stations. Another Querdenker, I conclude. Just when he starts complaining to me about the alleged fairy tales told by the United Nations and the 'global executive elites',[338] a dynamic-looking man with designer-looking glasses introduces himself as Martin, an independent journalist.

Without warning, Martin starts filming us with his iPhone. I am surprised by his bold approach, but he appears to be half-accepted, half-hated by the community of pro-Russian protesters.[339] The grey-haired man is on the friendly side, seemingly enjoying having a camera pointed at his face. 'May I ask you what you are protesting for?' Martin asks him, the camera only a few centimetres away from his subject's nostrils. That can't be a flattering angle, I think. The reply comes, 'For free speech in the broadest sense. The news reporting on all kinds of topics has become increasingly one-sided, especially in the homogenous leading media outlets. I don't just mean the public broadcasting but also the private media firms. There are only a few exceptions.'[340]

The Querdenker appears prepared for the question of which media outlets he uses to stay informed. Without hesitation he replies: 'Deutsche Welle, hr-iNFO' – two reliable German news sources that conspiracy theorists would often denounce as 'mainstream media'. I am surprised, but then he adds: '*Junge Freiheit*, *Cato* and the Internet.' This sounds more like it, I think, as he mentions the new right media outlets.

If homophobia has been a notable trait among the most ardent Putin supporters, the same goes for misogyny. 'What do you think about Putin beating his wife?' Martin asks the man, referring to sources of the German spy agency BND that accused Putin of domestic violence.[341] There is a short pause, as the man is thinking about his reply. 'Who does not beat his wife? Or how often does this happen? Is that really a relevant criterion now?'[342]

Martin turns to me. 'Can I interview you as well?' he asks.

'Rather not,' I say and put on a shy face.

'Yes, many don't want to show their faces in front of a camera. What does that say about us?' the grey-haired protester jumps in.

'Why don't you want to speak in front of the camera?' Martin insists.[343]

Once I can be sure that the Russian supporters are out of our reach, I explain to him that I am also covering the protest as a researcher. When I tell him my real name, he exclaims: 'Oh I know you, you wrote *The Rage*!' I put my index finger to my lips to shush him and nervously look behind me.

A short man with a shaved head is walking towards us, shouting: 'NATO wants this war! It's the same as with the war against terror. You only have to look at where terror incidents happen. They've all been staged.' The man's eyes are furious, as he gestures towards the police line-up next to us. 'And then they invented the pandemic and the war against their own people. Now their own people woke up, so they needed another crisis.'[344]

* * *

Later that evening, I log into Telegram and add Gabriel's phone number.

His bio says only one word: 'unvaxxed'.[345]

As I scroll through his profile pictures, I come across a rich mix including a Putin quote denouncing Western Satanism, a meme depicting vaccinated people as zombies and an expression of interest for 'unvaxxed singles'.[346]

I hesitate over one of Gabriel's quotes: 'To all teachers, politicians, journalists, vaccination doctors, police officers and other supporters who still play along. Go to hell.'[347]

I persevere. My message is short and simple. 'Hi, this is Mary from the protest. I would like to be part of your group.'[348] Sent.

'Heyyyyy ☺' His reply is quick and friendly, as I remember him from the protest.

'Of course you can,' he writes adding a winking face emoji.[349]

His warmth strikes me. It is in stark contrast with the deep hatred and distrust he voices in his posts: 'I'M DISGUSTED BY THIS WORLD. I CAN'T EVEN TRUST IN WHAT I EAT, SEE, HEAR, OR BREATHE. EVERYTHING IS POISONED BY THE SYSTEM.'[350]

In a different world, an apolitical one, we could have been friends.

I join Gabriel's closed Telegram group 'T3chno4Fr33dom Spirit'.

'Good morning! Putin has been against these NWO Satanists from the very beginning,' says the first message I come across. NWO (short for New World Order) is a reference to a conspiracy myth that first arose in the 1990s and has gained traction rapidly since the outbreak of the pandemic. Its adherents believe that the world is run by a tyrannical cabal of globalist elites that manufacture terrorist attacks and diseases like Covid to allow them to introduce repressive policies, and that they have already created hundreds of concentration camps in the US ready to lock up dissidents.[351]

A day after the protest, Gabriel sends me a screenshot of his Instagram account, where he has uploaded a video from the pro-Russian protest in Frankfurt. 'Published it yesterday, it already has over 10.8K views,' he tells me.³⁵² Whether they centre on Ukraine or Covid, his campaigns are successful on social media. On Telegram he encourages his followers to participate in a mass campaign against a potential vaccine mandate that is being considered by the German government. 'We have to continue in any case, even once we win the battle against mandatory vaccines,' he writes. 'Until these Satanists get their well-deserved punishment and until we have re-elections with the AfD hopefully coming out on top.'³⁵³ Another member agrees: 'No reason to stop now. This terror regime has to go!'³⁵⁴

The overlaps between QAnon, Querdenker and pro-Russia communities are striking. A COSMO survey found that 43 per cent of the unvaccinated in Germany believe that the war in Ukraine is just a distraction from the pandemic.³⁵⁵ According to a different survey carried out by the Center for Monitoring, Analysis and Strategy (CeMAS), the percentage of Germans who believed war-related conspiracy theories was even higher: 56 per cent.³⁵⁶ I regularly observe QAnon posts being shared in pro-Russian groups, and vice versa. 'Covid prompts us to question everything, from the face mask to our history,' one member of Gabriel's group declares. 'Covid is an intelligence test.' Some members believe they have been prepared for it with popular movies like *The Matrix*, *The Truman Show* or *Inception* that deal with questions of whether we live in an illusion, a fake world or even a dream. This is despite the fact that QAnon also designates Hollywood as a key culprit in the global conspiracy. The post continues: 'Q-Plan next level. The great awakening. The liberation of humankind.'³⁵⁷

Gabriel's channel is only one example of a much bigger phenomenon. For years, Russian propaganda and disinformation have played a key role in thriving far-right and conspiracy myth channels in the West. Kremlin-linked efforts have included paying troll armies to amplify extreme messages, or simply to act as chaos agents. Russian information warfare focuses on casting doubt on what's true by flooding the information space with lies and strengthening the narratives of the extreme fringes. In doing so, Kremlin-backed activities have helped to widen existing societal divisions and sow distrust in media outlets and political processes across Europe and North America. We have seen the same patterns of Russian interference in the US presidential election won by Trump, the Brexit vote, and several European elections.[358]

Movements like the east-German 'Freie Sachsen' have staged anti-government protests on the basis of Kremlin-fuelled conspiracy myths. Their out-group thinking combines old enemies with new ones. Soros and Rothschild are accused of benefiting from Covid and the Ukraine war. Ukrainian President Volodymyr Zelensky is portrayed as a marionette of the West who acts in the interests of NATO and the NWO.[359]

Alina Lipp is one of Germany's most prominent pro-Kremlin influencers. The 28-year-old former member of the Hannover Green Party has a German mother and a Russian father. She has been invited to talk shows on Russian state media and anti-vax protests organised by the Querdenkers in Berlin.[360] Her Telegram channel 'Neues aus Russland' ('News from Russia') with over 180,000 followers casts doubt on atrocities against Ukrainian civilians, framing them as false flag operations by the West. 'The West simply wants this war at any cost and is looking for some sad horrible story with which they can justify an attack,' she claimed in one of her videos.[361]

Alina Lipp is by no means the only self-styled journalist who spreads Russian war propaganda and anti-democratic views in her own country. Patrick Lancaster is to the US what Alina Lipp is to Germany. The 39-year-old man from Missouri is a US

Navy Intelligence veteran who has found a second career in crowd-funded journalism. He has spread Russian war propaganda and flirted with the audiences of prominent conspiracy theorists such as Alex Jones.[362]

When I return to Gabriel's group, the atmosphere is cheerful – the German government has dropped plans for mandatory vaccines. But the demonisation of everyone loosely affiliated with the government, the pharma industry or 'mainstream' journalism continues. 'Vaccine mandate failed,' Gabriel writes. 'But who are they really, these people who rule over people's dignity . . . these Satanists. They will NEVER manage to get to the non-vaccinated, healthy rational thinking people. Whatever it takes.'[363]

German health minister Karl Lauterbach has been a prime target for hatred and conspiracy myths. A search for the words 'criminal' and 'Lauterbach' on Telegram shows just how commonly these two words appear in German far-right and conspiratorial groups. Lutz Bachmann, the founder of the anti-immigration street protest movement Patriotic Europeans Against the Islamisation of the Orient (PEGIDA) even called Lauterbach a 'mass murderer' in one of his posts.[364] In Gabriel's group Vanessa rants about him, warning that face masks are slave masks, vaccines are deadly injections, Covid is no more than a strong flu and we are in the midst of the third World War. 'We are constantly being scorned. When will you finally understand?'[365]

As always, lies spread online are not without real-world consequences. As I scroll though the Lauterbach accusations, groups of self-described patriots with a mix of far-right, apocalyptic prepper and Covid denial ideas are communicating via Telegram and meeting in real life to discuss an attack, exchanging ideas on how to produce poisons, organise weapons and stage attacks on politicians.[366] Soon after, news breaks that German police are arresting a terror network of twelve people who have planned to cause a nation-wide power outage, kidnap Lauterbach, kill his security staff if needed, and stage a coup to topple the government.

In December 2022, the German intelligence service's largest anti-terror operation in modern history uncovered an even bigger violent anti-government plot. A network of roughly 50 far-right extremists, Reichsbürger (sovereign citizens) and QAnon sympathisers was accused of preparing for Day X on which they intended to stage a violent coup against the German parliament with the aim of re-establishing the 'German Reich' and reintroducing the pre-World War II borders. The network consisted of a bizarre mix of people from different backgrounds, but their institutional embeddedness shows that this was by no means an isolated fringe group. They included a 72-year-old former aristocrat, a former MP of the far-right populist AfD party and several ex-elite soldiers. Their ideology reconciled old Reichsbürger ideas with newer QAnon conspiracy myths. The head of the movement, Heinrich XIII, of the former royal House of Reuß, had allegedly contacted Russian representatives to ask for their support in the planned plot.[367]

* * *

'Pro-Putin sympathisers in Germany are made up of Querdenker anti-vaxxers and conspiracy theorists, AfD voters and Russian Germans,' Bogdan Rackow tells me. The 28-year-old Ukrainian has been shocked by the extent to which large parts of Europe's population buy into Russian propaganda. Today he lives in Berlin, but he spent the first seventeen years of his life in Kyiv. Some of his friends and family members are currently fighting on the frontlines or hiding in bunkers in Ukraine. When the invasion started Bogdan founded a fashion brand that works with Ukrainian designers to create anti-war themed merchandise. The profit is spent on protective gear for civilians in Ukraine to help them survive.

'For many Ukrainians the current war is the continuation of a much longer fight against Russian domination,' he tells me. His parents were election observers in the early 2000s. During the Ukrainian presidential election of 2004, Russian interference and election fraud allegations sparked the Orange Revolution. Less than a decade later, Ukrainians took to the streets once again in the Maidan protests in 2013, which transitioned into the so-called Revolution of Dignity. It was a popular outcry against then President Yanukovych's sudden decision to walk away from a free trade agreement Ukraine was supposed to enter into with the EU. The subsequent Russian invasion of eastern Ukraine and annexation of the Crimean Peninsula in 2014 were marked by today's clash of values. 'Russians fighting in Donbas were not just opposed to the Maidan movement,' Bogdan says. 'They were fundamentally against what the entire West represents. They preferred what Putin stands for.'

The bell rings and Bogdan jumps up. He lets in his new couch surfers, a Russian-Ukrainian couple who were on holiday when the war broke out and decided not to return to their homes in Moscow and Kyiv. Bogdan never felt resentment towards the Russian population. His grandmother was Russian and he still has many Russian friends. 'At the moment I don't have enough emotional capacity to feel hatred,' he says.[368] 'But I do wonder what it will feel like after this war is over.' Bogdan has been confronted by many Russians loyal to Putin's regime on social media. Reactions to his bold 'FCK Putin' brand on TikTok are deeply divided. 'Social media has characterised this war like no other,' Bogdan notes. 'It is exacerbating existing polarisation globally.'[369]

Bogdan made an effort to understand both sides in the war. He even watched the documentaries and propaganda materials that were circulated online in pro-Putin circles. 'Putin's comments on de-Nazification shocked me most.' Growing up in Kyiv, he said that he never met a single neo-Nazi. 'There is a small percentage of far-right extremists and neo-Nazis in Ukraine, like in any other European country. But I always associated the far-right much more with Russia.' Extremism researcher Alexander Ritzmann at the European Foundation for Democracy confirmed this assessment: 'The statement that Ukraine has proportionally more neo-Nazis is definitely propaganda. In Russia you find much higher numbers of neo-Nazis than in Ukraine.'[370]

But it's undeniable that far-right extremists have played a role in the frontlines on both sides of this war. A report by the Soufan Group already warned in 2019 that conflict over Ukraine was attracting white supremacists from across the world to join both pro-Russian separatist and Ukrainian nationalist fighting units. In a sense, the Ukraine war has become to white supremacists what the Afghanistan war in the 1980s was to jihadists. The violent conflict has been exploited by extremist groups as an opportunity to expand the global white supremacist movement and gain battleground experience.[371]

Much of Russia's war propaganda against Ukraine has focused on the Azov Battalion, a militia group that is fighting alongside the Ukrainian army and has been associated with white supremacist ideas. But while the largely autonomous battalion has been the protagonist in much of Russia's propaganda, its political impact in the Ukraine has been extremely limited. Azov's political wing National Corps only won 2.15 per cent of the vote in the last elections of 2019.[372]

Meanwhile, the Kremlin has directly supported a number of violent far-right groups. Around 1,000 members of the Kremlin-backed Wagner Group have become pro-Russian fighters in the war.[373] Tech Against Terrorism, a UN counter-terrorism initiative, found evidence of their close ties with the extreme right.

For example, Rusich is a militant white supremacist group within the Wagner Group founded by the neo-Nazi paratrooper Aleksei Milchakov. The Rusich logo features a Slavic Swastika known as Kolovrat.[374] Milchakov himself has become known for sadistically collecting the ears of his enemies. The militia group has published a cartoon of a Russian soldier returning home to his family with blood-drenched gifts stolen from Ukrainians. The caption reads: 'If you are a real man and a Russian, join our ranks. You will spill litres of blood from vile Russophobes, and become rich and cool.'[375]

I want to find out more about the ominous Wagner Group and its ideological leanings, so I join them on Telegram. The first post I spot in their channel WAGNER Z GROUP/ PMC WAGNER Z gives me goosebumps. It shows a badge with the devil and the Wagner Group's signature, saying 'Our business is death and business is good'. The comment below has a skull and reads: 'Where we are there is peace, W.'

Most of the messages in the Wagner Group chat are about the war in Ukraine, giving real-time updates in Russian to its over 19,000 followers. Many posts are encouraging Russian soldiers to keep fighting and stay loyal to each other. A typical message would read:

> Brothers 👋 Good Morning 👍 To all those of our soldiers who are now in the line of fire 💪 To all who are in the war, strength to you, endurance, 👍 Brothers! Warriors! Come back alive, healthy 👍👋 Let's all support our guys together 👋 Good and cheerful morning, Brothers 👋 I wish you all a great fighting spirit like mine 👍

But the Wagner Group members are also interested in Western politics, supporting far-right populist candidates in Europe and glorifying Trump in the US. One meme reads:

Trump:	'We have a president who has no idea what's going on, has no idea what he's doing, and has no idea what he's saying or where he is.'
Biden:	'What are we doing now?'
Wagner Group:	'It looks like the Republican won't have much trouble in the next US presidential election.'

The Wagner Group is one of several Russian far-right movements who are involved in battles in Ukraine. Russia's fighting units have attracted members of the neo-Nazi party Russian National Unity (RNU), the Eurasian Youth Union, the Russian Imperial Movement, the Slavic Union and Movement Against Illegal Immigration. Other Russian far-right groups that have been involved in the war are Svarozhich and Ratibor battalions, which – like Rusich – wear badges that show Slavic swastikas.

Many of the support networks for American and European neo-Nazis can be traced back to Russia. The traditional neo-Nazi scene in Germany and other European countries is known for its ties to Russian MMA (mixed martial arts) brand White Rex. I first encountered White Rex MMA fighters on an undercover field trip to a neo-Nazi rock festival in the German town Ostritz in 2018. Its business model is geared towards the professionalisation of the white power combat scene, which has given its leader Denis Kapustin influence within Europe's militant far-right.

Russia has also become a safe haven for prominent Western neo-Nazis such as Rinaldo Nazzaro. The 46-year-old American has been directing the violent white supremacist group the Base from Russia, as the BBC exposed in an investigation. Nazzaro, who went by the names Norman Spear and Roman Wolf, moved to St Petersburg with his family in 2018. His adoration for Putin is summed up by a T-shirt he likes to sport featuring the Russian president and the words 'Russia, absolute power'. The group is subject to major FBI investigations and a UK ban after plotting attacks against its political opponents with the end goal of starting a race war.[376] I have personally appeared on one of their death lists.

These are details that the Kremlin's propaganda leaves out. But Bogdan doesn't believe it matters much in the end. 'It's hard to argue with facts,' he concludes. 'This war taught me something about knowledge. Most people already know where they stand before something happens. Facts are useless then.'

* * *

A day later I am sitting in the German Federal Foreign Office as it hosts a G7 conference on disinformation. Rather than the ongoing physical fighting, we talk about the information war. 'The truth is under attack,' Germany's foreign minister Annalena Baerbock announces.

Russia has launched an all-out information war. In April 2022, the Russian intelligence agency the FSB accused the Ukrainian secret service of planning a terrorist attack against the pro-Kremlin Russian journalist Vladimir Solovyev in Moscow. Six Ukrainian neo-Nazis were arrested and the FSB released pictures of the alleged evidence they found in their raid: apart from improvised explosives, Molotov cocktails, firearms, munition, drugs and fake Ukrainian passports, the photos also showed three editions of the game 'Sims 3', an unlikely item for a group of neo-Nazi insurgents. This prompted speculation from some UK journalists that the whole raid was an FSB set-up and that a Russian operative must have been told to organise three SIM cards and mistakenly ordered the game Sims instead.[377]

If these kinds of state activities have been less than convincing, far-right and conspiracy myth channels have had more success with Western audiences and are among the Kremlin's greatest tools in its information war. Over the past few years, it has managed to galvanise anti-democratic and anti-liberal populations in the US and Europe using the Russian state-sponsored media outlets Russia Today (RT) and Sputnik, including playing a significant role in recent election influence campaigns in countries like Germany and Sweden.[378]

QAnon has vastly amplified Russian propaganda in the West. 'Bucha. Where is the evidence? Russia is accused of having murdered roughly 300 civilians in Bucha. But there is no evidence whatsoever,' QAnon Austria shares with its 13,000 plus followers on Telegram.[379] 'The Bucha lie: The West wants a World War. Just when it looked as if a peace treaty between Russia and Ukraine was within reach, the events of Bucha are shaking up world politics again.' Pictures of wounded puppets, supposedly taken in Bucha, circulate in the QAnon channel alongside claims that all war footage shown on 'mainstream media' has been fabricated. Some users are convinced that pictures and videos of Russian atrocities are based on video game visuals or old footage from other conflicts. A 2022 survey by CeMAS found that every fifth German believes the Ukraine war is a conspiracy.[380]

The viral bio lab conspiracy myth is a good example of the mainstreaming of extreme ideas. First, anonymous social media accounts promoted the myth that the US sponsored bio lab programmes in Ukraine to study pathogens and toxins to use as bioweapons. Soon, Russian media outlets and government officials were talking about it, linking the alleged biolabs to Hunter Biden and George Soros. But the idea only got picked up in English language social media once a fringe QAnon figure started tweeting about it. The former restaurant manager and army National Guard veteran who was known on Twitter as @WarClandestine posted from rural Virginia: 'China and Russia indirectly (and correctly) blamed the US for the C19 outbreak.

And [they] are fearful that US/allies have more viruses (bioweapons) to let out.' He went on to claim that Russia had started the invasion to destroy US biolabs in Ukraine and prevent another global pandemic.[381]

Once the idea had been amplified by QAnon online networks, it made its way into minor US alternative media outlets. #USBiolabs was now trending on Twitter and TikTok. Finally, it appeared on Fox News and was given a platform by major news commentators, reaching millions of viewers and influencing public attitudes towards Russia.[382] The idea went global, even reaching Australian politics when Sean Ambrose, a Senate candidate for United Australia Party (UAP) in New Souths Wales tweeted: '[. . .] let us not forget that he [Putin] expelled the Rothschild Banking families from Russia and is now shutting down the child sex and human trafficking and the US biological weapons facilities in the Ukraine.' A stage of mass adoption had been reached.

In many Western countries, belief in a cabal of 'global elites' who are pulling the strings behind closed doors has gone hand in hand with both Covid denial and Ukraine war denial. The British founder of the English Defence League, Tommy Robinson, echoes the idea of an orchestrated Ukraine conflict in his Telegram channel: 'You really do have to ask the question WHY the invasion of Ukraine happened at this point in human history. At the point where – the COVID vaccine efficacy and usefulness of the vaccine is in mainstream doubt. It's now politically damaging those who supported and enforced medical apartheid. War is always a distraction. War is deceit.'

Surveys show that 30 per cent of the German population believe that the world is directed by secretive forces. This idea is especially widespread among AfD voters.[383] A 2020 NPR/Ipsos poll found that 17 per cent of Americans believed in the idea that 'a group of Satan-worshipping elites who run a child sex ring are trying to control our politics and media'.[384] In the UK, over a third of the population believes that elites in Hollywood, governments, the media and other powerful circles are secretly participating in major child trafficking and abuse networks.[385]

Reading this book, you might have picked up on the connection that links anti-vaxxers marching in London to Trump supporters storming the US Capitol and pro-Russia protestors in Frankfurt: QAnon. The elephant in the room is the question about the relationship between the Kremlin and QAnon. This needs further investigation. But it is crystal clear that Russia's state propaganda machinery has fuelled conspiracy myths embedded within the wider QAnon master conspiracy network. Russian disinformation often travels straight from the Kremlin to QAnon to reach its final destination: Western right-wing media.

Like most conspiracy myth communities, QAnon is marked by high levels of opportunism and ideological flexibility. Its stance on China illustrates that. Originally, its networks struck a strong anti-China tone in their content, linking the Chinese government to the WHO and Bill Gates in bizarre conspiracy myths revealing 'the truth about Covid'. This was compatible with their unconditional support for Trump and his China aversion. But it soon became clear that Beijing would be an ally to their other hero, Putin. In the wake of the Ukraine war, they shifted their views on China, finding innovative ways to navigate contradictions and overcome cognitive dissonance. Now Xi was painted as a genius 'white hat' who had been playing a role but was indeed on the same side as Trump and Putin all the time.[386] One QAnon post from 2022 read: 'Vlad & Xi are "onboard", if you haven't noticed yet. Same team, and it ain't against "The Plan" in any way, shape or form, but for it.'[387] Transformed from evil conspiratorial leader who wanted to control the world into a mysterious and ingenious ally, Xi had been rehabilitated. It was a major plot twist.

It is often said that in war, truth is the first casualty. The Kremlin's strategy has been to discourage Ukrainians while keeping Russians in the dark. Traditionally, the Russian information warfare playbook has been based on telling enough random lies that the information space becomes flooded. Facts are distorted and obfuscated out of existence. No one can distinguish between truth and fiction anymore. Even an argument about the colour of the sky could break loose. 'Nothing is true and everything is possible,' as Russian propaganda expert Peter Pomerantsev has said. The idea is to create a foggy information landscape that prevents the public from forming a coherent narrative. If 'the truth is unknowable', their only viable option is 'to follow a strong leader'.[388]

This tactic has been successfully mirrored by the US alt-right and the European New Right. From Trump to Le Pen or from AfD to Freedom Party of Austria frontrunners, it has also become the modus operandi of Western far-right politicians supportive of Putin. Steve Bannon, former head of *Breitbart News* and chief strategist for Donald Trump, pioneered this tactic in Western politics. 'The Democrats don't matter,' he said in 2018. 'The real opposition is the media. And the way to deal with them is to flood the zone with shit.'

* * *

The Russian invasion of Ukraine is where all the nodes of this book came together. Putin successfully projected the global far-right's struggle against the perceived degeneracy of Western society onto the war. In many ways, it became a proxy escalation of the Culture Wars. Russia's autocratic, anti-liberal regime on one side and EU-backed Ukrainian liberal democracy on the other side.

Putin's hatred of the progressive-liberal ideas and policies that have shaped Western democracies has made him popular within American QAnon circles and European far-right networks. His state propaganda and disinformation machinery has long sought to destabilise Europe and North America, and there has been a mutually beneficial relationship between the Kremlin and Western radical fringes.

For years, Putin has been signalling to the global far-right that his fight was theirs. White nationalists, anti-democracy conspiracy theorists and Christian fundamentalists in the West have found a hero in him. His strong-man image and hostility towards progressive modernity have resonated well with those who felt lost in their liberal democratic homes.[389] I witness this myself on Telegram, observing how European and American white supremacist members of the 'It's Okay to Be White' group cheer on Putin for advocating Christianity, Tradition, Family, and Nationalism.

The Russian neo-fascist thinker Alexander Dugin has been dubbed 'Putin's brain'. His philosophy and vision is said to have inspired the leader's politics.[390] In his 2021 book, whose title refers to the 'Great Reset' conspiracy, *The Great Awakening vs The Great Reset,* Dugin issues a war declaration against 'the twin diseases of liberalism and Western political modernity'.[391] Dugin urges US citizens of 'the Heartland' to act against the 'demented usurper Joe Biden', 'the Antichrist and his Soros-backed minions' who allegedly want to destroy humankind and create a 'one-world transhumanist dystopia'. He calls on his readers 'to relentlessly attack, on all theoretical and practical fronts, the global elites of the coastlands, who try to impose their perverse, anti-human ideals by ruthlessly eradicating the long-standing cultures and traditions of all peoples in the world'.[392] Dugin's rhetoric demonstrates how activism against the liberalism of the 'global elites' has served to bring together members of different extreme groups and conspiracy myth communities.

Movements fighting against the same 'progressive enemies' have also joined forces in UK campaigns lately. An anti-LGBTQ campaign targeting drag queen reading events in the summer of 2022 was an example of opportunistic collaboration between different extreme subcultures. The format 'Drag Queen Story Hour' was a reading tour organised for children and young adults in public libraries across the UK. A hateful and disruptive campaign that linked the event series to child grooming was started first by Covid conspiracists but was soon led by the white nationalist movement Patriotic Alternative.[393]

Russian propaganda is carefully targeted depending on its audience. While RT and Sputnik were promoting vaccinations in their Russian language editions, they spread vaccine-related fears and doubts in their English and German language versions. Perhaps Putin's most potent weapon is his deep knowledge of how to sow discord and chaos to empower the radical fringes. Russia's information war has weaponised internal tensions in the West to mainstream radical anti-liberal, anti-democracy, anti-science narratives. The underlying goal is to destabilise the European continent and distract the US by creating chaos. To them, the anti-establishment distrust which built up during the pandemic has been a valuable resource.

The Ukraine war may well be a watershed moment in the wider Culture Wars. Morningside Institute researcher Matthew Rose noted in his 2021 book *A World After Liberalism* that 'after three decades of dominance, liberalism is losing its hold on Western minds'.[394] The illusion many people were raised with, that there is a liberal world order that is irreversible and whose rules cannot be challenged, has fallen apart.[395] But the battle is far from over; we are in an ongoing fight to preserve democratic values in the face of an autocratic aggressor who has amplified radically illiberal voices across the world.[396] This is also how Zelensky has framed the Ukraine war: a fight not just for national independence, but for progressive modernity. At the end of his address to US Congress in March 2022 he switched to English: 'Today, the Ukrainian people are defending not only Ukraine, we are fighting for the values of Europe and the world, sacrificing our lives in the name of the future.'[397]

WHAT CAN WE DO?

If extremism has gone mainstream, then we can no longer rely on traditional approaches to tackle it. As US counter-extremism expert Cynthia Miller-Idriss put it: 'The tools that authorities use to combat extremists become less useful when the line between the fringe and the center starts to blur.'[398] Policymakers, intelligence services, law enforcement and tech firms need a fundamentally new strategy. And we as individuals also need to take part, because we are the political middle, or what is left of it.

There are many potential ways to tackle the rise of radically backward ideas and social polarisation. We can learn lessons from long-standing efforts to prevent terrorism. We can distil insights from strategic communications units and successful deradicalisation programmes. But ultimately, we have to admit that we are facing a challenge that is new in both its scale and nature.

Many of the policymakers and security teams I engaged with over the past few years have been overwhelmed with the speed at which change has occurred. We are in a stage of experimentation, where most decision-makers fighting disinformation and hate are digital migrants. Some of them might have never used TikTok or 4chan, and few will understand the mindsets of young digital natives. Yet it's their responsibility to come up with one-fits-all solutions to regulate cyber space.

As digital citizens, we all have a part to play. Many of you will have seen friends or family embrace anti-vaxxer ideas or voice transphobic views, often with innocent motivations and moderate intentions. But what happens if they continue climbing down the rabbit hole? What if they start demonising scientists and dehumanising a minority group? How can you prevent them from turning legitimate fears and frustrations into irrational, hateful actions?

If we have learnt one key lesson from past efforts to counter radicalisation, it is that we have to stop treating symptoms and deal with underlying structural and psychological sources. Policy-makers need to ask: Who is most vulnerable to being groomed by radical groups, especially in light of the long-lasting socio-economic and mental health effects of the Covid crisis? Tech firms should ask: how do our algorithms amplify the most radical voices and what can we do to support those that stand up for respectful dialogue on the most controversial topics? And all of us could ask ourselves: when was the last time I spoke to my friend who voted differently in the Brexit referendum, had a different opinion on the Covid vaccines, or disagreed with my views on Russia?

For this chapter I had conversations with five experts affiliated with the Institute for Strategic Dialogue whose focuses vary from educational and civic action responses to the future of tech. Together we came up with fifteen recommendations to counter the mainstreaming of extreme ideas.

TACKLING TOUCHPOINTS

The Psychological Touchpoint

Radicalisation usually starts with a set of grievances. Think of the extreme anti-vaxxer Marius or the pro-Russian Querdenker, Gabriel. They turned deeply human fears of death and solitude into fuel for dangerous conspiracy myths.

'Researchers and policy advisors need better tools to analyse widespread anxieties and grievances in real-time,' ISD's founding director Sasha Havlicek says. She has a background in conflict resolution and has pioneered innovative solutions to tackling extremism. When policymakers understand who is most vulnerable during a crisis, they can offer them ways out of their psychological, social or economic struggles before extremists do. As we saw, J.T. Wilde was searching for purpose and community in the lonely lockdowns, which he found in making music for QAnon. Pedro was desperately looking for answers and reassurance in the scary early days of the Covid crisis and turned to online forums and a hallucinating Marius instead of a medical professional. Why did no one divert them on their journey to extremism?

Narrow prevention approaches that focus on a single ideology are no longer fit for purpose. We have seen the emergence of hybrid ideologies such as eco-fascism, Satanic misogyny and QAnon-inspired nationalism. They exploit different psychological touchpoints at once: for example, anxieties about masculinity and fear of demographic change, or socio-economic precarity and mental health struggles. Mark Collett's mosaic of white nationalist, anti-feminist and conspiratorial beliefs is an example of this phenomenon, as is Gabriel's Covid denial and denouncement of NATO and 'global elites'.

These new cocktails of wildly mixed ideologies are a side-effect of changing extremist communication. There has been a shift from traditional centralised propaganda output by movements such as Al Qaeda and ISIS towards user-generated and crowd-sourced content.[399] I saw this decentralised approach in real time as each of my avatar accounts on Telegram would receive new invites to a wide array of bizarre channels daily. As extremists have become their own content curators, there are as many ideological streams as there are extremists. Sasha calls for policymakers to recognise this shift towards forms of extremism which are 'self-organised and post-organisational'.

The Social Touchpoint

Extremists have used gamification and entertainment to attract people who are not politically or ideologically motivated – at least initially. Imagine being among the minors who joined Patriotic Alternative's video game tournaments or the QAnon members who see themselves as part of a large community-based effort to solve a puzzle. Many hobby communities and online cultures have been hijacked by radical worldviews and conspiracy myths – from 4chan's anime boards to Discord's gaming chat rooms. Is it our task to reconquer them?

'It's not that simple,' Jacob Davey tells me. He is an expert in hate movements and extremist online subcultures, and the author of ISD's 'Gamers Who Hate' report.[400] He also used to spend late nights gaming and on forums when he was younger. His experience has taught him that it would be a mistake to treat radicalisation in online hobby communities as a one-directional process where extremists seek to exploit vulnerable people. 'Of course, many extremists are deliberately co-opting youth culture to increase their appeal,' he explains. 'But internet culture *is* mainstream youth culture. By nature of being online, most members of digital extremist subcultures are already involved in other web subcultures.' They may be gamers, but also cosplayers, skaters, or fitness freaks.

Digital culture consists of millions of communities. The gaming community alone counts at least 2.81 billion people worldwide. Not every gamer is an extremist and not every extremist is a gamer. 'We need to find more nuanced ways to understand identity formation within those communities, including the co-radicalisation effects,' Jacob concludes. He suggests starting by mapping cultural overlaps and community-building dynamics online. 'If we drew a Venn diagram of the online extremist ecosystem, we would see significant overlaps with gaming, trolling and other internet subcultures.'

What does that mean for intervention? 'The extremist bleed-overs into other online communities provide us with more opportunities to engage with radicalised individuals,' says Jacob. 'It means that there are multiple entry points for intervention.' What could a prevention approach on Discord, Steam or 4chan look like? First. we need credible influencers who speak the language and know the cultural touch points of an at-risk community. They should then be equipped with the knowledge and tools needed to debunk, disengage and derail conversations that incite hatred or spread disinformation in their online subculture. 'I would love to see more creative solutions in the online space,' Jacob tells me. 'But we need to be careful and make sure interventions can be done safely and ethically.'

The Technological Touchpoint

'The food was great! Unfortunately, Putin spoiled our appetites by invading Ukraine!' Restaurant reviews on Google Maps have become a new way for activists to fight misinformation. Russian dissidents and international campaigners have adopted creative ways to get their messages into Russia and bypass Kremlin-controlled social media outlets. They communicate via emojis, integrate hidden messages in merchandise or leave notes in Google reviews. These are positive examples of how innovation can help to circumvent censorship. But those who spread disinformation have become equally inventive.

Conspiracy theorists have co-opted cooking channels on YouTube and white supremacists have invented their own words to evade detection. For example, 'skypes', 'googles' and 'yahoos' can all be used as code words with hidden hate speech meanings.[401] Some extremists have skilfully adapted their language, testing the borders of legality and acceptability on platforms. Others simply migrated to alt-tech platforms like Parler, Gab, Truth Social Gettr, BitChute, Substack and Odysee, which have framed themselves as safe havens for freedom of speech. Encrypted messaging apps like Telegram, Discord and WhatsApp are also used to bypass security services and coordinate campaigns in private.

Harmful content on social media – overt or incognito – needs to be removed, while those driving violent radicalisation should be deplatformed. But ultimately, removal policies will always be a cat-and-mouse game that does little to resolve the underlying psychological mechanisms at work. Algorithms are designed to hold our attention and exploit human nature. 'They essentially amplify content that evokes strong feelings and targets it at those constituencies that are most emotionally susceptible,' Sasha says. ISD's research found that sensationalist and radical content consistently outperforms truthful and moderate posts. 'If the playing field is not level, the balance is cast in favour of radical activists.'

For nearly a decade, most policies have been about removing, moderating, deprioritising or countering content that is harmful. 'Policymakers have now started to understand that the scale of the online radicalisation problem is not just a function of content but of the business models of these platforms,' Sasha explains. Big tech platforms may be agnostic, but they are not neutral, they are designed to curate the most extreme posts. 'This is at the heart of the mainstreaming of radical ideas,' Sasha says. 'So the algorithmic "outrage machine" needs to be tackled first of all.'

Sasha is confident about the way forward. Algorithms are human-made; they can be changed. 'European governments have introduced more regulatory mechanisms that tackle algorithmic bias and the US is creating more transparency and accountability on social media platforms.' While the response of authoritarian regimes is censorship and removal, liberal democratic approaches should focus on transparency and accountability around decision-making, product design and algorithmic processes. 'We should never lose the human rights perspective that is at the heart of the values we are fighting for,' Sasha says.

RALLYING STAKEHOLDERS

Connecting Global and Local Practitioners

Remember the striking parallels between the storming of the German Reichstag, the US Capitol and the New Zealand parliament? Extremists have developed a strategy that combines global networking with hyper-local mobilisation. In marketing, this would be called a 'glocal' strategy. International meme databases are adapted to local contexts, regional campaigns are amplified to go viral by radical sympathisers from across the world. The only way to respond to this competitive advantage is to get better at building 'glocal' counter-radicalisation cooperation on a policy and interventions level.

The Strong Cities Network (SCN) is an initiative that does precisely that. The network has brought together mayors and policymakers from 140 local governments of megacities, states, counties and small municipalities to share insights about globally and locally observable patterns and lessons learnt in the field of extremism prevention.[402] 'Our research shows that the social bonds and grievances that drive radicalisation are often hyper local,' Jakob Guhl says. He is a disinformation and extremism expert who has observed the mainstreaming of many fringe ideas 'But lessons learnt from specific local instances can be highly relevant for communities in different geographic settings, even internationally.' For example, the SCN developed a terror response toolkit that used as best practice New Zealand's political communications strategy from the aftermath of the Christchurch attack.

The places where people spend most of their time are local: their workplaces, religious communities, sports associations, and leisure centres. As high-trust environments, these places are in a good position to engage with individuals who might be on the path to radicalisation. 'Employers tend to enjoy high levels of trust among people who work for them,' Jakob says. The Business Council for Democracy (BC4D) is an innovative new approach started by the Hertie Institute, the Robert Bosch Institute and ISD Germany to bring digital citizenship education to employees. In cooperation with the Confederation of German Employers' Associations, the BC4D's courses have been trialled in six German companies, including Volkswagen and the leading recycling service company ALBA Group. This leads us to the role of the private sector more generally.

Engaging the Private Sector
Extremists have a history of hijacking brands for their radical campaigns.[403] New Balance tennis shoes and Fred Perry polo shirts are examples of fashion brands that were co-opted by white supremacists and neo-Nazis. These brands usually face PR crises as a consequence and have to take measures to distance themselves from racist provocateurs. But private sector companies have been linked to extremist campaigns in less visible ways. For example, when they provide the payment services for extremist funding, host the online infrastructure for their communications or sponsor their activities via online ads.

'Firms should be held accountable for supporting extremist propaganda or disinformation campaigns,' Sasha tells me. Environmental Social Governance (ESG) has become a buzzword in the private sector. Companies increasingly focus on performing in these categories to satisfy socially conscious investors. Environmental activism has increased awareness among consumers, which in turn has pressured industries to minimise their carbon footprint. 'As a business it is now hard to get away with a sloppy "E" without accepting significant reputational damage,' Sasha comments. 'But the "S" and "G" bits of "ESG" are still relatively unexplored.'

Researchers need better assessment models to understand how, along with the environment, democracy can also be impacted by investment. Just as experts can measure the carbon footprint of a product or service, a formula for assessing democratic accountability could be created. 'None of the private sector companies are going to be happy if our liberal democratic societies drift towards autocratic structures of governance,' Sasha says. They have an interest in investing in a liberal future. Sasha believes that 'we need to start by raising better awareness of democratic accountability through public-facing campaigns, so the consumers are informed about the governance impact of their purchase decisions'. It will only be a matter of time until investors and businesses follow suit.

Forming Activist Coalitions

Extremists have been good at rallying around one shared goal: their fight against 'the liberal establishment' and 'woke' elites. Their campaigns driving racism, misogyny, anti-LGBTQ activism, climate change denial and Covid disinformation are successful because they have formed unlikely alliances – recall the white nationalists at the climate change denier conference, and the anti-vaxxers at the pro-Russian protest.

But efforts to fight these intertwined phenomena have been quite isolated Anti-racists, feminists, LGBTQ campaigners, environmentalists and fact-checkers have all fought separate battles. There is little cooperation between Black Lives Matter and Fridays for Future, for example. It's not just policymakers and companies that need to work together. Campaigners for progressive causes should form coalitions too. 'Although extremists have connected their dots, we haven't figured out how to bridge different activist fronts and use synergies across our networks,' Sasha says. How can the political middle ground collaborate for a liberal democratic future?

Most of us have an interest in protecting the environment, fighting racial prejudice, advancing women's rights or countering LGBTQ discrimination. 'If we want to protect the social and scientific progress made on all of these fronts from being reversed, we need to pool our resources,' Sasha argues. 'We should coordinate our responses across the activist fronts that focus on climate action, migration policy, human rights, disinformation analysis and radicalisation prevention.'

ADDRESSING GENERATIONS

Gen Alpha

How can we prevent children from joining Mark Collett's video game tournament, or teenagers from being drawn to an incel site? 'Focusing on the intersection of psychology and digital literacy is key to building resilience among the youngest generations,' Jennie King tells me. She is an education expert and has co-authored the curriculum for the 'Be Internet Citizens' programme, which seeks to raise resilience among teenagers against online harms including hate and disinformation. The educational toolkit has been formally accredited for UK schools and youth centres. 'We wanted to create a framework where young people can question their own biases,' Jennie says. Be Internet Citizens encourages teenagers to explore questions such as: How can the architecture of the Internet push you in a radical direction? What could make someone susceptible to hateful content? How do you interrogate your own gut reaction to what you see online?

In an educational setting it is important not to go into details about specific conspiracy myths. Intrigued young people may look them up online, exposing themselves to harmful content.

'Things that start as fascination can quickly snowball,' Jennie notes. Instead of explaining and debunking specific myths, she says that 'the focus should be on [teaching] eternal competencies and skill sets that can be applied from trend to trend'. There is a confidence crisis in the education sector. 'Many teachers feel ill-equipped to understand today's digital media landscape,' Jennie says. Yet, most digital literacy skills are not entirely new, but rather are traditional competencies applied in a new setting: critical thinking, lateral reading, self-awareness and emotional intelligence. 'We try to highlight these to lower the barrier of entry for educators.' The most important contribution that teachers and parents can make is to help children and teenagers recognise the recurring patterns and manipulation tactics used by radicalising narratives.

Another way to build resilience among Gen Alpha is to focus on the human dynamics behind online interactions. This means encouraging exposure to different socio-economic, cultural and ethnic backgrounds from a young age. Jennie says this can be done by connecting schools from demographically different areas, and by forming diverse teams of students who collaborate on projects they care about. 'Encouraging young people to work together on a social action project of their choice is a way to broker diversity, not as the stated objective of a project but as a by-product of an activity.' Co-design and co-development are more effective in creating emotional connection and intercultural awareness than theoretical lectures about diversity.

Gen Z

Gen Z is sometimes called the 'meme generation'. Long text is given little attention, visual aesthetics are key for most digital natives. Seventy-seven per cent of people aged 16 to 24 automatically reach for their phone when nothing else is occupying their attention, according to a Microsoft Corp study. Compare this to only 10 per cent of the generation over 65. Gen Z are accustomed to a multitude of visual, auditory and kinaesthetic stimuli competing for their attention. Studies have found that our average attention span has gone down in the social media era, although there is an ongoing debate about whether it is now shorter than that of a goldfish or not.[404,405]

Extremists have been quick to understand and exploit this trend. While ISIS generated visually striking propaganda materials to appeal to Gen Z, it was the alt-right that pioneered the use of memes for radicalisation purposes. Extremist movements across the world – from Salafi jihadists and Brazilian far-right campaigners to Indian ultra-nationalists, Egyptian neo-Nazis and Moroccan monarchists – have now started to imitate alt-right aesthetics, having witnessed their success with the younger generations.[406] 'There seems to be a universal desire for and appeal to internet culture,' Jakob explains. 'We need to do better to reach the same young target audiences.'

This prompts the question: How can political moderates compete with trolling Salafis and neo-Nazis for the hearts and minds of young people? Today's extremist communities mock serious attempts at intervention in their cultural dynamics. So one way to get their attention is to use humour. Jakob suggests a comedy writers' room which brings together comedians who create viral content and influencers who enjoy credibility among their followers. Studies show that celebrities from minority groups can be particularly effective in reducing hate and prejudice towards these communities. After Muslim elite football player Mohamed Salah joined Liverpool F.C. anti-Muslim hate crimes in the geographic area of Liverpool dropped visibly and Liverpool F.C. fans posted 50 per cent less anti-Muslim content on Twitter.[407]

The approach of Facts for Friends is similar: the start-up's goal is to make fact-checking sexy. It bridges the gap between fact-checkers and social media platforms by serving visually appealing and fun 'fact snacks' to the 'meme generation'.[408] The initiative uses young influencers, so called 'Factfluencers', to translate information from official fact-checking websites such as Full Fact in the UK or Correctiv in Germany into sharable posts on Instagram.

Digital Migrants

It would be wrong to assume that only the youngest generations are being manipulated. A 2022 survey conducted in Germany showed that Telegram users between 30 and 50 years of age were most susceptible to pro-Russian propaganda and conspiracy myths.[409] Adults over the age of 50 were called disinformation 'supersharers', as they were responsible for 80 per cent of 'fake news shares' during the 2016 US election.[410] Marius and Earth G were both in that age group. Another study found that on average, Facebook users over the age of 65 share seven times more links to fake news sites than younger users.[411]

Cognitive decline and loneliness don't explain why older generations are sharing disproportionate amounts of disinformation. Digital literacy gaps in older generations are also part of the picture, and need to be addressed.[412] Many older people are tech savvy enough to like or share a social media post or article, but may not have the skills to distinguish between credible and distorted media sources. Many of us will have a grandparent or great uncle who has bought into disinformation. As family members or friends, we could ask them to engage with questions such as: Where exactly did that piece of content they shared come from – is it a known news source? What are trustworthiness indicators for the information they read online? How does uncertainty make people look for patterns?

'As with young people, we need to help them to break down the common traits of conspiracy myths that have occurred again and again in human history,' Jennie says. Providing historical examples of hateful narratives rather than fixating on specific contemporary myths can be a powerful approach for older generations. But interventions also need to account for their shifting social goals and psychological drivers, and avoid being stigmatising or patronising. Jennie argues that 'we need to be sympathetic to the fact that being groomed or manipulated can happen to all of us'. Showing emotional empathy towards the underlying psychological purposes that conspiracy myths fulfil is an important starting point for any intervention.

TURNING THE TIDE

Reconquering Language

In recent years, extremists have done something fundamental to our language, or rather our perception of language, co-opting terms associated with liberal values for their own ends. Think of the January 6 rioters who said they stormed the US Capitol in the name of 'democracy', or the anti-vaxxers who persecuted medical professionals while claiming they were fighting for their 'human rights'. At the same time, extremists have created negative associations with other liberal terms such as 'diversity' and 'multiculturalism', in order to discredit their opponents. They are equally adept at weaponising old terms, such as 'elitism', and repurposing newer ones, like 'lockdown'.

'Language has come to mean something else,' Sasha says. She recommends that we all call out language manipulation as and when it happens. 'Ukraine offers an opportunity to turn the tide,' she notes; the first step is showing the inherent contradictions and hypocrisy in Kremlin-sponsored propaganda and its alt-right fan communities. Jacob agrees: 'Let's expose the obvious doublespeak in the hijacking of human rights-centred language.'

Mislabelling and reframing drives a powerful wedge between communities. This is not just happening on the fringe. Jacob explains that the strategic distortion of language is a popular weapon in the way that the Culture Wars are reported on. For example, Critical Race Theory is a term that has been twisted by right-wing campaigners to go far beyond its original meaning. 'It has been framed as a political tool of the left as opposed to what it is: cross-disciplinary education about race history,' Jacob says. Likewise, 'grooming', a term associated with sexual abuse, has been used to describe classroom education about sexual orientation.

Every digital citizen should help to expose language manipulation, regardless of where on the political spectrum it happens. Strong political and civic leadership is needed to encourage a positive framing of democratic, liberal and human rights terminology. Jacob says, 'We need to ask: Who is credible in championing this?' One way to reclaim co-opted and twisted terms would be to work with charismatic figures from both the left and right side of the spectrum and with influencers who have bi-partisan support, such as military, religious and sports figures.

Reporting Opportunism

It is no secret that the radical fringes are opportunistic shapeshifters. Double-think is an integral part of the modus operandi of a lot of conspiracy myths communities. Networks like QAnon shift and twist their narratives as political events unfold – remember how it changed its stance on Xi when it became expedient to do so? High ideological flexibility makes extremism a moving target and can pose a challenge for deradicalisation.

But this opportunism can also be an opportunity. I have watched QAnon members leave the movement when they began to sense that its narratives simply didn't add up, or were in conflict with its actions. Often the journey of leaving behind a conspiracy myth starts with cognitive dissonance, as members can no longer reconcile their beliefs with their experiences. For example, some Covid deniers changed their beliefs after seeing an unvaccinated family member or friend die or get seriously ill.

'Uncovering extremist opportunism and contradictory thinking can work for some people who are at risk of endorsing radical ideas, especially those who haven't been fully sucked into a movement, but are eying it up,' Jacob agrees. He argues that this can be done using partnerships between relatable experts from different constituencies that are particularly prone to disinformation, and whose messages could be supported by platforms such as TikTok, Instagram or Netflix. This might not help to deradicalise the extreme fringes, but it can mitigate the mainstreaming effect.

Prebunking Disinformation

Prebunking disinformation has been shown to be much more effective than debunking. The point of prebunks is to empower people to spot factual distortions before they occur. Imagine how many people might have been kept away from Covid denial and vaccine conspiracy myths if these had been prebunked at the beginning of the pandemic. Perhaps Pedro would have just walked by Marius, paying him little attention, once he noticed familiar patterns of disinformation on the banners. Maybe Marius would not even have set up his protest, because he would not have let conspiracy myths consume his life.

The leading US counter-misinformation project First Draft distinguishes between three types of prebunks: fact-based, logic-based and source-based. Their step-by-step guides can help journalists, fact-checkers, governments and research institutions to use prebunks in areas where they expect waves of misinformation.[413] Experts can often foresee what the next wave of misinformation might be. Prebunking has been effectively used in the Ukraine war to counter pro-Kremlin disinformation.

Based on a combination of NATO intelligence and expertise on Russian propaganda strategies, Western journalists have regularly been one step ahead in publishing facts before Russia could distort them, such as with Putin's attempts to frame Ukraine as rife with Neo-Nazism in order to justify his war of aggression.

Jacob suggests that in the future, radicalisation experts could team up with journalists and geopolitics researchers to predict what will populate the news cycle next, and recognise the potential for misinformation. 'This could help prepare society for the topics extremists will likely jump on next.'

GOING FORWARD

Rebuilding Trust

'Has trust plummeted because we no longer have a public square?' Sasha asks. The information system is fragmented. There is no longer a single space in which debate happens. Previously you had to compete for your right to speak, and the opportunities to broadcast your beliefs to the public were limited. Now we speak (or tweet!) whenever we want, but only to the likeminded. There is no shared experience of information-gathering or exchanging of ideas beyond our own political bubble. Sasha is convinced we need to find new ways to re-establish a 'town square' where dialogue happens.

'The radical fringes have taken a very long-term strategic approach in their campaigns,' Sasha says. Think of the white supremacist alternative homeschooling curricula – these efforts to shape the minds of the youngest generations by providing them with 'alternative facts' may not yield results for a decade, but their effects could be powerful. 'Meanwhile we – the political middle – are not thinking about [long-term] cultural shift. We are thinking in election cycles.'

Moderates have failed to understand that trust – whether in government, in science, or in members of other social groups – is derived from culture. Trust is not primarily about facts; it is deeply emotional and identity-based. 'Extremists have understood that,' Sasha warns. 'So has Russia'. They tap into something deeply visceral instead of purely speaking to people's intellect. Those who want to promote trust in democracy, tolerance or liberal values will have to go far beyond fact-based campaigns, and likewise produce content that appeals to human emotions.

Another key step is to re-establish confidence in trustworthy media outlets. One idea would be to set up an independent, neutral institution to issue licences to trusted news sources. Many professions need licences to operate: from the hospitality sector to hairdressing salons and medical practices. Cutting clients' hair, serving customers food and alcohol or treating patients requires an official permit. So why is something as fundamental as providing information not regulated by independent quality assessments? A similar system could work for journalists and media outlets. Licences might need to distinguish between different types of journalism: from live coverage and analysis to traditional reporting and op-ed style commentary. They would have to be open to newcomers and follow a transparent, consistent protocol aimed at eliminating bias.

Real-Time Research

'Impact-oriented research is crucial in shifting policy and behaviour,' Jakob says. Extremists are early adopters of technologies and youth culture. 'Because both tech trends and web culture move at such a rapid pace, researchers need to be alert at all times to understand how extremist tactics are evolving.' Real-time research is key to avoid falling behind. ISD's 'Hosting the Holohoax' report was a good example of how this can inspire policy changes. This research project which tracked online

Holocaust denial was part of a larger campaign led by a consortium of think tanks and NGOs to pressure Facebook and Twitter into adjusting their inadequate policies tackling anti-Semitism.[414] By providing ample evidence of the ineffectiveness and incoherence of policies across different platforms, the campaign was successful in pushing first Facebook and then Twitter into introducing new sets of policies. An even more tangible example was the 'Bankrolling Bigotry' research, which traced the online financing and fundraising structures of hate groups in the US, identifying over 50 funding mechanisms.[415] According to Jakob, following the report's publication, more than a dozen of these platforms suspended the accounts of extremist groups.

Ultimately, monitoring different types of hate is also important to predict trends. 'A rise in anti-Muslim, anti-LGBTQ or misogynist mobilisation can serve as a proxy for increased community polarisation,' Jakob argues. It can help to determine the likelihood that law enforcement, tech firms and intelligence agencies need to allocate more resources to specific prevention mechanisms or community cohesion programmes. And it can inform soft-target protection when threats against specific minority communities, politicians or activists increase. Online monitoring can be triangulated with other data sources, such as polling statistics or hate crime data.

Reacting to Tech Trends

AI has gone mainstream and the metaverse is round the corner. It is only a matter of time until we will see multiple new challenges emerge in the extremist threat landscape. 'Looking at the past, governments have been terrible at horizon scanning,' Carl Miller tells me. He is the co-founder of CASM Technology at Demos and author of *The Death of the Gods*, which investigates what the rise of new technologies means for the distribution of power in society.

One of the biggest upcoming challenges stems from the rise of digital autonomous organisations (DAOs), Carl warns. DAOs are blockchain-based decentralised platforms that can be used as mobilisation hubs and investment vehicles. They have the potential to disrupt all existing regulatory frameworks, as they have no legal profile, no bank account that regulators can block and no physical office that can be located. At the moment, intense excitement is building up in bitcoin communities. According to the DAO analytics site DeepDAO, there are thousands of DAOs and they collectively hold billions of dollars.[416] Commercial DAOs could quickly inspire political and activist DAOs to follow suit. There is already a 'Free Julian Assange DAO'. Carl predicts that it is only a question of time until extremist groups make use of this new form of Tokenomics-based architecture. 'DAOs give them a new way of collaborating, raising and holding money, and exerting ideological influence outside of any online harms response framework,' he says. 'This new threat appears at a moment in time where – after ten years of tweeting and raising awareness – we got governments to regulate tech platforms.' Carl warns that policymakers need to think about the question: How will policymakers regulate DAOs? 'I don't see enough worry from regulators.'

AI-based technologies such as deep fakes can exacerbate our disinformation crisis and further fuel radicalisation. But Carl believes that deep fakes are overhyped. 'On the surface it is shocking to see a deep-fake video that looks believable, [but] a range of measures exist already to address this.' Identifying deep fakes is technologically feasible. Carl is more worried about AI-based language tools that can be applied to virtual agents and automated chats. 'We are getting very close to passing the Turing Test now,' he says. 'The fact that we can create a machine that convincingly sounds like a human is concerning. Can you imagine what extremists or political campaigners can do with this technology?'

Virtual Reality (VR) and the metaverse provide potential weapons for information warfare as well as terrorist attacks. Think about a terrorist attack that streams to live audiences in a VR setting created for this purpose. Terror is always theatre. It is more effective in instilling fears and inspiring copy-cat attacks when viewers feel like they are part of it. First-person-shooter style livestreams were pioneered by the Christchurch shooter in 2019 and have been imitated by multiple terrorists since then. They made viewers feel like they were in a Live Action Role Play (LARP). The metaverse could be the next step to further blur the lines between reality and fiction. And in the metaverse, tens of thousands of people can be in same virtual environment.

But there is also enormous potential for AI and VR to be used in the fight against radicalisation and disinformation. Early detection mechanisms of violence predictors in language are becoming more sophisticated, and that's just the beginning. There are many creative ways to use new technologies as prevention tools. For example, populations at risk of anti-Semitic radicalisation could be taken on virtual reality tours through concentration camps to prevent Holocaust denial. As the last World War II survivors are about to die out, holographs of eyewitnesses could be recorded to provide future generations with first-hand accounts of historic events.

Ultimately, no one has yet figured out how policy can keep up with tech. Carl believes that this requires foresight as well as legal innovation. 'NGOs that focus on different types of online harms – from monitoring violent extremism, countering disinformation or championing child safety – should be involved in the design of new tech tools,' he says. This could help to integrate mechanisms that protect new technologies from potential misuse for radical political purposes – like the anti-forgery function any commercial photocopier has, which prevents its users from copying money.

'History doesn't repeat itself but it often rhymes,' Mark Twain allegedly said. Ultimately, by studying the ways culture and technology are changing, we can recognise the stressed syllables in the rhyme of radicalisation and predict its future.

ACKNOWLEDGEMENTS

Going Mainstream might have been the most challenging out of the books I've written so far. It spans a range of highly controversial topics that are part of an unfolding story and could be updated with the latest news headlines on a daily basis. I wanted to go beyond what's visible from the outside and get close to the people at the forefront of hyperpolarised debates that are tearing apart the political middle. At the same time, the threats I received after the publication of my previous book *Going Dark* in combination with the Covid lockdowns made new undercover fieldtrips and live investigations extremely difficult.

First of all, I would like to thank my excellent editor Sarah Braybrooke as well as my brilliant agent Luke Ingram of the Wylie Agency for being my co-pilots on this ambitious project. Whether by asking critical questions or by coming up with innovative answers, they kept the plane from crashing. Without their guidance and invaluable feedback, this book would not exist. I would furthermore like to express my gratitude to the entire Bonnier Books UK team for their trust and support. I am also deeply grateful for the helpful comments provided by this book's first readers Alessa Lux and Ulrike Ebner-Stella.

Many thanks to all activists, experts and extremists featured in *Going Mainstream*, both those interviewed on record by my real self and those who opened up to my avatar accounts. I did my best to understand the motivations, grievances and desires that are driving every individual who appears in this book. To protect the privacy of undercover interviewees, I used pseudonyms for all non-public figures.

A massive thank you also goes to the entire Institute for Strategic Dialogue team, in particular the organisation's founding director Sasha Havlicek. I feel incredibly lucky to be part of ISD's world-leading network of experts in the field of radicalisation, extremism and disinformation prevention. I would also like to thank my DPhil supervisors Harvey Whitehouse and Chris Kavanagh for allowing me to write this book whilst completing my doctoral project on a different topic at the Institute for Cognitive and Evolutionary Anthropology at the University of Oxford. They have been incredibly inspiring role models and mentors. Finally, a big thank you to my family and friends who have been by my side even in times of doubt, dismay and drama.

NOTES

1. Hannah Ward-Glenton, "Germany's political landscape is shifting, with the far-right AfD party ahead in the polls", CNBC, 3 October 2023, online https://www.cnbc.com/2023/10/03/germany-shifts-to-the-right-with-anti-immigration-afd-ahead-in-polls.html
Conrad Seidl, "Umfrage sieht FPÖ auf Platz eins und nur noch ein Drittel hinter der Regierung" Der Standard, 25 September 2023, https://www.derstandard.at/consent/tcf/story/3000000188274/umfrage-sieht-fpoe-auf-platz-eins-und-nur-noch-ein-drittel-hinter-der-regierung
2. Jon Henley, 'Voters in west divided more by identity than by issues, survey finds', the *Guardian*, 17 November 2021, Online: https://www.theguardian.com/politics/2021/nov/17/voters-in-west-divided-more-by-identity-than-issues-survey-finds?CMP=Share_iOSApp_Other.
3. Harvey Whitehouse, 'Dying for the group: Towards a general theory of extreme self-sacrifice', *Behavioural and Brain Sciences* Vol. 41 (2018): 1–62; W.B. Swann, J. Jetten, A. Gómez, H. Whitehouse and B. Bastian, 'When group membership gets personal: A theory of identity fusion', *Psychological Review* Vol. 119 (2012): 441–456; and W.B. Swann and M.D. Buhrmester, 'Identity Fusion', *Current Directions in Psychological Science* Vol. 24, No. 1 (2015): 52-57.
4. Harvey Whitehouse, 'Dying for the group'.
5. See for example BBC Reality Check Team, 'Joe Rogan: Four claims from his Spotify podcast fact-checked', BBC, 31 January 2022, Online: https://www.bbc.com/news/60199614.
6. Mike Levine, '"No Blame?" ABC News finds 54 cases invoking "Trump" in connection with violence, threats and alleged assaults', ABC News, 30 May 2020, Online: https://abcnews.go.com/Politics/blame-abc-news-finds-17-cases-invoking-trump/story?id=58912889.
7. Edelman, '2022 Edelman Trust Barometer: The Cycle of Distrust', Global report, online: https://www.edelman.com/trust/2022-trust-barometer.

8. In an interview with *BBC Newsnight*'s US correspondent David Grossman, see: https://www.bbc.com/news/world-us-canada-56004916.
9. See original footage featured in *Insurrection* by Andres Serrano, min. 15.
10. See original footage featured in *Insurrection* by Andres Serrano, min. 22.
11. See original footage featured in *Insurrection* by Andres Serrano, min. 27.
12. Capitol riots timeline: What happened on 6 Jan one year ago', BBC, 6 January 2022, Online: 'https://www.bbc.com/news/world-us-canada-56004916.
13. 'Capitol riots timeline: What happened on 6 Jan one year ago', BBC, 6 January 2022, Online: 'https://www.bbc.com/news/world-us-canada-56004916.
14. See original footage featured in *Insurrection* by Andres Serrano, min. 48
15. See original footage featured in *Insurrection* by Andres Serrano, min. 01:01:00
16. See original footage featured in *Insurrection* by Andres Serrano, min. 01:05:00
17. Robert A. Pape et al., 'American Face of Insurrection', Chicago Project on Security and Threats, 5 January 2022, Online: https://d3qi0qp55mx5f5.cloudfront.net/cpost/i/docs/Pape_-_American_Face_of_Insurrection_(2022-01-05).pdf?mtime=1654548769.
18. Ibid.
19. Hilary Matfess and Devorah Margolin, 'The Women of January 6th', Program on Extremism at George Washington University, April 2022, Online: https://extremism.gwu.edu/sites/g/files/zaxdzs2191/f/Women-of-Jan6_Matfess-and-Margolin.pdf.
20. Robert A. Pape et al., 'American Face of Insurrection', Chicago Project on Security and Threats, 5 January 2022, Online: https://d3qi0qp55mx5f5.cloudfront.net/cpost/i/docs/Pape_-_American_Face_of_Insurrection_(2022-01-05).pdf?mtime=1654548769.
21. 'Guy Reffitt: First trial of US Capitol riot ends with conviction', BBC, 9 March 2022, Online: https://www.bbc.co.uk/news/world-us-canada-60670105.
22. Fortesa Latifi, 'January 6 Insurrection: One Year Later Families Are Still Divided', *Teen Vogue*, 4 January 2022, Online: https://www.teenvogue.com/story/january-6-insurrection-families.
23. 'Teen Says He's in Hiding After Turning in Dad Guy Riffitt for Alleged Role in Capitol Riots', *Inside Edition*, 25 January 2021, Online: https://www.insideedition.com/teen-says-hes-in-hiding-after-turning-in-dad-guy-reffitt-for-alleged-role-in-capitol-riots-64511.

24. Fortesa Latifi, 'January 6 Insurrection: One Year Later Families Are Still Divided', *Teen Vogue*, 4 January 2022, Online: https://www.teenvogue.com/story/january-6-insurrection-families.
25. Barbara F. Walter, *How Civil Wars Start: And How to Stop Them* (N.Y.: Viking, 2022).
26. Robert Pape, 'Deep, Destructive and Disturbing: What We Know About Today's American Insurrectionist Movement', CPOST (NORC) at University of Chicago, 2021, Online: https://d3qi0qp55mx5f5.cloudfront.net/cpost/i/docs/Pape_AmericanInsurrectionistMovement_2021-08-06.pdf?mtime=1628600204.
27. Ibid.
28. David Gilbert, 'QAnon and Trump-Flag Waving Anti-Vaxxers Tried to Storm New Zealand's Parliament', *VICE*, 9 November 2021, online: https://www.vice.com/en/article/m7vabx/new-zealand-anti-vaccine-mandate-protest.
29. M. Götschenberg, H. Schmidt und F. Bräutigam, 'Razzia wegen geplanten Staatsstreichs', *Tagesschau*, 7. December 2022, online: https://www.tagesschau.de/investigativ/razzia-reichsbuerger-staatsstreich-101.html.
30. Adrienne Vogt, Matt Meyer and Meg Wagner, 'Paul Pelosi, Nancy Pelosi's husband, attacked at couple's home, CNN, 28 October 2022, online: https://edition.cnn.com/politics/live-news/nancy-pelosi-husband-paul-attack/index.html; and Jasmine Aguilera and Solcyre Burga, 'What to Know About the Attack on Paul Pelosi' *TIME*, 31 October 2022, online: https://time.com/6226378/paul-pelosi-assault-what-to-know/.
31. Andrew Woodcock, 'One in 20 people has fallen out with family member over Brexit, poll reveals', the *Independent*, 8 October 2019. Online: https://www.independent.co.uk/news/uk/politics/brexit-family-friends-argument-remain-leave-eu-opinion-poll-bmg-survey-a9147456.html.
32. Sona Otajovicova, 'Doppelmord in Bratislava – Angriff auf die LGBTQ-Community in der Slowakei', DW, 25 October 2022, Online: https://www.dw.com/de/doppelmord-in-bratislava-angriff-auf-die-lgbtq-community-in-der-slowakei/a-63552798.
33. Grahame Allen and Yago Zayed, Hate Crime Statistics, House of Commons, online: https://researchbriefings.files.parliament.uk/documents/CBP-8537/CBP-8537.pdf.

34. 'Germans shocked by killing of cashier after COVID mask row', Reuters, 21 September 2021, online: https://www.reuters.com/world/europe/germans-shocked-by-killing-cashier-after-covid-mask-row-2021-09-21/; and Doha Madani, Andrew Blankstein and Ben Collins, 'California dad killed his kids over QAnon and "serpent DNA" conspiracy theories, feds claim', 12 August 2021, online: https://www.nbcnews.com/news/us-news/california-dad-killed-his-kids-over-QAnon-serpent-dna-conspiracy-n1276611.
35. 'What We Know About the Attack on Nancy Pelosi's Husband', *The New York Times*, 31 October 2022, online: https://www.nytimes.com/2022/10/28/us/politics/nancy-pelosi-husband-assaulted.html
36. Julie Posetti, Nabeelah Shabbir et al., 'The Chilling: Global trends in online violence against women journalists' UNESCO, April 2021, Online: https://en.unesco.org/sites/default/files/the-chilling.pdf.
37. Scottish Government, 'Misogyny – A Human Rights Issue. The Working Group on Misogyny and Criminal Justice's independent report on their findings and recommendations', 8 March 2022, Online: https://www.gov.scot/publications/misogyny-human-rights-issue/pages/4/.
38. Stefan Stijelja, 'The Psychosocial Profile of Involuntary Celibates (*Incels*): A Review of Empirical Research ...', Centre for Research and Intervention on Suicide, Ethical Issues and End of Life Practices, Université du Québec à Montréal, September 2020.
39. H. Lee, I. Son, J. Yoon and S-S. Kim. 'Lookism hurts: appearance discrimination and self-rated health in South Korea'. *Int J Equity Health*. 2017;16(1):204. 25 November 2017. doi:10.1186/s12939-017-0678-8.
40. Daniel Hamermesh (2013). *Beauty Pays: Why Attractive People are More Successful*. Princeton University Press; and Shahani-Denning, C. (2003). 'Physical attractiveness bias in hiring: What is beautiful is good', *Hofstra Horizons*, 15–18.
41. Rod Hollier (2021), 'Physical Attractiveness Bias in the Legal System', The Law Project. Online: https://www.thelawproject.com.au/insights/attractiveness-bias-in-the-legal-system.
42. Jacob Ware, 'The incel threat', *IPS Journal*, Democracy and Society, 26 November 2021.
43. Liam Casey, 'Alek Minassian wanted to kill 100 people, but "satisfied" with 10 deaths, court hears', *The Canadian Press*, 9 December 2020. Online: https://www.cp24.com/news/alek-minassian-wanted-to-kill-100-people-

but-satisfied-with-10-deaths-court-hears-1.5223076?cache=xuafaggwnsf%3FclipId%3D89530.

44. 'Retribution: YouTube video', *The New York Times*, 24 May 2014, Online: https://www.nytimes.com/video/us/100000002900707/youtube-video-retribution.html.
45. Greta Jasser, Megan Kelly, Ann-Kathrin Rothermel, 'Male supremacism and the Hanau terrorist attack: between online misogyny and far-right violence', ICCT Publication, Online: https://icct.nl/publication/male-supremacism-and-the-hanau-terrorist-attack-between-online-misogyny-and-far-right-violence/.
46. Based on the author's own analysis of primary source materials.
47. Harry Farley, 'Danyal Hussein: A teenage murderer with far-right links', BBC, 6 July 2021, Online: https://www.bbc.com/news/uk-england-london-57722035.
48. Tom Ball, 'Massive rise in use of Incel sites that call for women to be raped', *The Times*, 3 January 2022, Online: ttps://www.thetimes.co.uk/article/massive-rise-in-use-of-incel-sites-that-call-for-women-to-be-raped-hddbq5mgc.
49. Chris Vallance, 'Rape posts every half-hour found on online incel forum, BBC, 23 September 2022, online: https://www.bbc.co.uk/news/technology-62908601.
50. Sian Norris 'More than Half of Incels Support Paedophilia', *Byline Times*, 29 September 2022, online: https://bylinetimes.com/2022/09/29/more-than-half-of-incels-support-paedophilia-finds-new-report/.
51. Alessia Tranchese and Lisa Sugiura, '"I Don't Hate All Women, Just Those Stuck-Up Bitches": How Incels and Mainstream Pornography Speak the Same *Extreme* Language of Misogyny', *Violence Against Women*, Vol 27, no. 14 (2021): 2709–2734.
52. Jacob Ware, 'The incel threat', *IPS Journal*, Democracy and Society, 26 November 2021.
53. Consuelo Corradi, 'Femicide, its causes and recent trends: What do we know?', European Parliament, Briefing requested by the DROI Subcommittee, November 2021.
54. See Karen Ingala Smith's project Counting Dead Women, online: https://kareningalasmith.com/counting-dead-women/; and Karen Ingala Smith and Clarrie O'Callaghan, 'Femicide Census: there's a disturbing reason for the falling numbers of murders', the *Guardian*, 27 February 2022, Online: https://www.theguardian.com/society/2022/

feb/27/femicide-census-theres-a-disturbing-reason-for-the-falling-number-of-murders.

55. Emily Lefroy, 'Horrifying TikTok trend shows men "fantasising" how they'd kill women', Yahoo! News, 22 March 2022.
56. Interview with UK-based teachers who preferred to remain anonymous as well as Jennie King, ISD's Head of Civic Action and Education.
57. Megan Kelly, Alex DiBranco and Dr Julia R. DeCook, 'Misogynist Incels and Male Supremacy', New America, 18 February 2021, Online: https://www.newamerica.org/political-reform/reports/misogynist-incels-and-male-supremacism/executive-summary/.
58. Eviane Leidig, 'Why Terrorism Studies Miss the Mark When It Comes to Incels', ICCT Publication, 31 August 2021, Online: https://icct.nl/publication/why-terrorism-studies-miss-mark-when-it-comes-incels/.
59. Rosie Carter, 'Young People in the Time of COVID-19: A Fear and Hope Study of 16–24 Year Olds', Hope not Hate, July 2020, Online: https://hopenothate.org.uk/wp-content/uploads/2020/08/youth-fear-and-hope-2020-07-v2final.pdf.
60. See https://www.reddit.com/r/RedPillWomen/.
61. Chelsea Rudman, '"Feminazi": The History of Limbaugh's Trademark Slur Against Women', Media Matters for America, 3 December 2012.
62. Ipsos, 'One in three men believe feminism does more harm than good', 4 March 2022, Online: https://www.ipsos.com/en/one-three-men-believe-feminism-does-more-harm-good.
63. Amanda Barroso and Anna Brown, 'Gender pay gap in US held steady in 2020', Pew Research, May 2021, Online: https://www.pewresearch.org/fact-tank/2021/05/25/gender-pay-gap-facts/.
64. Josie Cox, 'The trust crisis facing women leaders', BBC, 30 November 2022, Online: https://www.bbc.com/worklife/article/20221129-the-trust-crisis-facing-women-leaders
65. See for example Lucina Di Meco and Saskia Brechenmacher, 'Tackling Online Abuse and Disinformation Targeting Women in Politics', Carnegie Endowment for International Peace, 30 December 2020, Online: https://carnegieendowment.org/2020/11/30/tackling-on-line-abuse-and-disinformation-targeting-women-in-politics-pub-83331.
66. Nathan Rott, '#Gamergate Controversy Fuels Debate on Women and Video Games', NPR, 24 September 2014.
67. Britt Paris and Joan Donovan, 'Deepfakes and Cheap Fakes: The Manipulation of Audio and Visual Evidence', Data & Society, 18

September 2019. Online: https://datasociety.net/library/deepfakes-and-cheap-fakes/.

68. See for example, Jane Dudman, 'Far from empowering young women, the internet silences their voices', the *Guardian*, 24 October 2018, Online: https://www.theguardian.com/society/2018/oct/23/empowering-young-women-internet-abuse-harassment; and Mona Lena Krook, 'How sexist abuse of women in Congress amounts to political violence – and undermines American democracy', *The Conversation*, 21 October 2020.

69. See for example Megan Specia, 'Britain's Parliament Is Rocked by Sexist Episodes. Again', *The New York Times*, 3 May 2022, Online: https://www.nytimes.com/2022/05/03/world/europe/britain-parliament-sexual-harassment.html; and Kathrin Wesolowski, 'Frauen als Feindbild: Wie mit Falschmeldungen Hass gegen Politikerinnen geschürt wird', Correctiv, 15 December 2020, Online: https://correctiv.org/faktencheck/hintergrund/2020/12/15/frauen-als-feindbild-wie-mit-falschmeldungen-hass-gegen-politikerinnen-geschuert-wird/.

70. Maya Oppenheim, 'General election: Women MPs standing down over "horrific abuse", campaigners warn', *Independent*, 31 October 2019, Online: https://www.independent.co.uk/news/uk/politics/general-election-woman-mps-step-down-abuse-harassment-a9179906.html.

71. Julia Smirnova, Anneli Ahonen, Nora Mathelemuse, Helena Schwertheim and Hannah Winter, 'Bundestagswahl 2021: Digitale Bedrohungen und ihre Folgen', ISD Global, February 2022, Online: https://www.isdglobal.org/wp-content/uploads/2022/02/ISD_digitale-bedrohung.pdf.

72. 'Grünen-Klubchefin Maurer von Corona-Maßnahmen-Gegner angegriffen', *Der Standard*, 7. April 2022, Online: https://www.derstandard.at/story/2000134774936/gruenen-klubchefinsigrid-maurer-von-corona-massnahmengegner-angegriffen.

73. Emily Crockett, 'After the killing of a British MP, it's time to admit violence has a misogynist problem', *Vox*, 17 June 2016, Online: https://www.vox.com/2016/6/17/11962932/jo-cox-british-mp-assassination-murder-misogyny-violence.

74. Nick Lowles, Nick Ryan and Joe Mulhall, 'State of Hate 2022: On the March Again', Hope not Hate, March 2022, Online: https://hopenothate.org.uk/wp-content/uploads/2022/03/state-of-hate-2022-v1_17-March-update.pdf.

75. Robert Verkaik, 'Sarah Everard's killer is in jail, but the misogyny that enabled him still thrives in the Met, ex-officers say', *i* News, 14 October

2021, online: https://inews.co.uk/news/long-reads/sarah-everard-killer-wayne-couzens-jail-misogyny-met-police-still-thrives-officers-1246906.
76. Joe Ryan, 'Reports of misogyny and sexual harassment in the Metropolitan Police', Debate Pack Number CDP 2022/00456, House of Commons, March 2022, Online: https://researchbriefings.files.parliament.uk/documents/CDP-2022-0046/CDP-2022-0046.pdf.
77. 'Boris Johnson does not support making misogyny a hate crime', BBC, 5 October 2021, Online: https://www.bbc.com/news/uk-politics-58800328.
78. 'Hate Aid as part of the Landecker Digital Justice Movement, Statement on the Proposal for the Regulation of the European Parliament and of the Council on a Single Market for Digital Services (Digital Services Act) and amending Directive 2000/31/EC (COM(2020) 825 final)', April 2022, Online: https://hateaid.org/wp-content/uploads/2022/04/hateaid-dsa-statement.pdf.
79. Judit Bayer and Petra Bárd, 'Hate speech and hate crime in the EU and evaluation of online content regulation approaches', European Parliament, July 2020, Online: https://www.europarl.europa.eu/RegData/etudes/STUD/2020/655135/IPOL_STU(2020)655135_EN.pdf.
80. Gaby Hinsliff, 'Why on earth are the chore wars not done and dusted?', the *Guardian*, 29 November 2019, Online: https://www.theguardian.com/commentisfree/2019/nov/29/chore-wars-couples-women-housework.
81. D. Schneider, 'Market earnings and household work: New tests of gender performance theory', *Journal of Marriage and Family* 2011, 73(4), 845–60.
82. International Labour Organisation, 'ILO: Women do 4 times more unpaid care work than men in Asia and the Pacific', 27 June 2018.
83. Kate Whiting, 'The motherhood penalty: How childcare and paternity leave can reduce the gender pay gap', World Economic Forum, Davos 2022, 19 May 2022 and Joeli Brearley, *The Motherhood Penalty: How to stop motherhood being the kiss of death for your career* (London/N.Y.: Simon & Schuster, 2022).
84. D. Schneider, 'Market earnings and household work: New tests of gender performance theory', *J Marriage Fam* 2011, 73(4), 845–60.
85. Simone de Beauvoir, *The Second Sex*, 2009, p.481.
86. Kate Davidson, 'In 18 Nations, Women Cannot Get a Job Without Their Husband's Permission', *Wall Street Journal*, 9 September 2015, Online: https://www.wsj.com/articles/BL-REB-34010.
87. Angela Henshall, 'Four ways paid paternity leave could boost family income', BBC, 19 June 2016, Online: https://www.bbc.com/worklife/

article/20160617-four-ways-paid-paternity-leave-could-boost-family-income#:~:text=A%20Swedish%20government%20study%20showed,can%20increase%20by%20almost%207%25.

88. Caroline Kitchener, Kevin Schaul, N. Kirkpatrick, Daniela Santamariña and Lauren Tierney, 'Abortion is now banned in these states. Others will follow.', *The Washington Post*, 26 June 2022.
89. Jill Filipovic, 'A new poll shows what really interests "pro-lifers": controlling women', the *Guardian*, 22 August 2019, Online: https://www.theguardian.com/commentisfree/2019/aug/22/a-new-poll-shows-what-really-interests-pro-lifers-controlling-women.
90. Tiffany Fillon, 'Poland: Where "women pay a high price" for populist laws', France24, 19 February 2022, Online: https://www.france24.com/en/europe/20220219-poland-where-women-pay-a-high-price-for-populist-laws.
91. Balázs Pivarnyk, 'Family and Gender in Orbán's Hungary', Heinrich Böll Stiftung, 4 July 2018, Online: https://www.boell.de/en/2018/07/04/family-and-gender-viktor-orbans-hungary.
92. Catharine Lumby and Amira Aftab, 'Australia still has a long way to go when it comes to sexism', the *Guardian*, 4 December 2018, Online: https://www.theguardian.com/commentisfree/2018/dec/04/australia-still-has-a-long-way-to-go-when-it-comes-to-sexism.
93. See https://pregnantthenscrewed.com/.
94. Arj Singh, 'Roe v Wade reversal shows women's rights are "never guaranteed" and must be protected globally, senior MPs say', *i* News, 3 May 2022, Online: https://inews.co.uk/news/politics/reversal-roe-v-wade-shows-rights-never-guaranteed-must-protected-globally-senior-mps-say-1609093.
95. See Programm der Alternative für Deutschland für die Wahl zum 20. Deutschen Bundestag, 2021.
96. Advance Pro Bono, 'Prevalence and reporting of sexual harassment in UK public spaces: A report by the APPG for UN Women', UN Women, March 2021, Online: https://www.unwomenuk.org/site/wp-content/uploads/2021/03/APPG-UN-Women_Sexual-Harassment-Report_2021.pdf.
97. Fiona Smith, '"Privilege is invisible to those who have it": engaging men in workplace equality', the *Guardian*, 8 June 2016, Online: https://www.theguardian.com/sustainable-business/2016/jun/08/workplace-gender-equality-invisible-privilege.

98. See AAUW, 'The STEM gap: Women in Science, Technology, Engineering or Mathematics', AAUW, 2020, Online: https://www.aauw.org/resources/research/the-stem-gap/.
99. Melissa Dancy et al., 'Undergraduates' awareness of White and male privilege in STEM', *International Journal of STEM Education*, Vol 7 (52), October 2020, Online: https://stemeducationjournal.springeropen.com/articles/10.1186/s40594-020-00250-3.
100. See HESA statistics: https://www.hesa.ac.uk/news/01-02-2022/sb261-higher-education-staff-statistics.
101. Laura Bates, 'Female academics face huge sexist bias – no wonder there are so few of them', the *Guardian*, 13 February 2015, online: https://www.theguardian.com/lifeandstyle/womens-blog/2015/feb/13/female-academics-huge-sexist-bias-students.
102. The original French message was: 'Bonjour Pauline, j'espère que tu vas mourir et si je te croise tu verras'.
103. Yanna J. Weisberg, Colin G. DeYoung and Jacob B. Hirsh, 'Gender Differences in Personality across the Ten Aspects of the Big Five', *Frontiers in Psychology* 2 (178), May 2011, Online: https://www.ncbi.nlm.nih.gov/pmc/articles/PMC3149680/; and Leonora Risse, Lisa Farrell and Tim R.L. Fry, 'Personality and pay: do gender gaps in confidence explain gender gaps in wages?', *Oxford Economic Papers*, Vol 70 (4), October 2018, pp. 919–949, Online: https://academic.oup.com/oep/article/70/4/919/5046671; and Christian Jarrett, 'Do men and women really have different personalities?', BBC, 12 October 2016, Online: https://www.bbc.com/future/article/20161011-do-men-and-women-really-have-different-personalities.
104. Marco Del Giudice, Tom Booth and Paul Irwing, 'The Distance Between Mars and Venus: Measuring Global Sex Differences in Personality', *Plos One* 7 (1), January 2012, Online: https://journals.plos.org/plosone/article/comment?id=info%3Adoi/10.1371/annotation/2aa4d091-db7a-4789-95ae-b47be9480338.
105. https://news.un.org/en/story/2019/06/1040291.
106. 'Italy migrant boat: Captain says she disobeyed orders due to suicide fears', BBC, 1 July 2019, Online: https://www.bbc.com/news/world-europe-48818696.
107. 'Italy's Salvini slams Sea-Watch incident "act of war"', Deutsche Welle, 29 June 2019, Online: https://www.dw.com/en/italys-salvini-slams-sea-watch-incident-as-an-act-of-war/a-49415160.

108. 'Italy migrant rescue boat: Captain Carola Rackete freed"', BBC, 2 July 2019. Online: https://www.bbc.com/news/world-europe-48838438
109. Oliver Milman, 'Ex-Nasa scientist: 30 years on, world is failing "miserably" to address climate change', the *Guardian*, 19 June 2018, Online: https://www.theguardian.com/environment/2018/jun/19/james-hansen-nasa-scientist-climate-change-warning.
110. Zach Boren and Damian Kahya, 'German far right targets Greta Thunberg in anti-climate push', *Unearthed*, 14 May 2019, Online: https://unearthed.greenpeace.org/2019/05/14/germany-climate-denial-populist-eike-afd/.
111. Suzanne Goldenberg, 'Secret funding helped build vast network of climate denial thinktanks', the *Guardian*, 14 February 2013, Online: https://www.theguardian.com/environment/2013/feb/14/funding-climate-change-denial-thinktanks-network.
112. Suzanne Goldenberg, 'Conservative groups spend up to $1bn a year to fight action on climate change', the *Guardian*, 20 December 2013, online: https://www.theguardian.com/environment/2013/dec/20/conservative-groups-1bn-against-climate-change.
113. ISD and CASM Technology, 'Deny, Deceive and Delay: Documenting and Responding to Climate Disinformation at COP26 and Beyond', ISD, June 2022, online: https://www.isdglobal.org/wp-content/uploads/2022/06/Summative-Report-COP26.pdf.
114. ISD and CASM Technology, 'Deny, Deceive and Delay: Documenting and Responding to Climate Disinformation at COP26 and Beyond', ISD, June 2022, online: https://www.isdglobal.org/wp-content/uploads/2022/06/Summative-Report-COP26.pdf.
115. Jennie King, 'Climate is the New Front in the Culture Wars', ISD digital dispatches, 11 May 2021, Online: https://www.isdglobal.org/digital_dispatches/climate-is-the-new-front-in-the-culture-wars/.
116. See World Economic Forum, 'The Great Reset', Online: https://www.weforum.org/focus/the-great-reset and https://www.weforum.org/agenda/2020/06/covid19-great-reset-gita-gopinath-jennifer-morgan-sharan-burrow-climate/.
117. Eisha Maharasingam-Shah and Pierre Vaux, '"Climate Lockdown" and the Culture Wars: How Covid-19 sparked a new narrative against climate action', ISD, October 2021. Online: https://www.isdglobal.org/wp-content/uploads/2021/10/20211014-ISDG-25-Climate-Lockdown-Part-1-V92.pdf.

118. Extinction Rebellion, *This is Not a Drill: An Extinction Rebellion Handbook*, Penguin 2019.
119. Kate Connolly and Matthew Taylor, 'Extinction Rebellion founder's Holocaust remarks spark fury', the *Guardian*, 20 November 2019, Online: https://www.theguardian.com/environment/2019/nov/20/extinction-rebellion-founders-holocaust-remarks-spark-fury.
120. Damien Gayle and Ben Quinn, 'Extinction Rebellion rush-hour protest sparks clash on London Underground', the *Guardian*, 17 October 2019, Online: https://www.theguardian.com/environment/2019/oct/17/extinction-rebellion-activists-london-underground.
121. See for example: https://www.rationaloptimist.com/blog/how-global-warming-can-be-good/ and https://www.chartwellspeakers.com/matt-ridley-climate-change-good-harm/.
122. Chris Mooney, 'The Hockey Stick: The Most Controversial Chart in Science, Explained', *The Atlantic*, 10 May 2013, Online: https://www.theatlantic.com/technology/archive/2013/05/the-hockey-stick-the-most-controversial-chart-in-science-explained/275753/.
123. Cf. 'UK "Climategate" inquiry largely clears scientists', 31 March 2010, Online: https://web.archive.org/web/20211104133523/https://www.deccanherald.com/content/61233/uk-climategate-inquiry-largely-clears.html.
124. Adam Forrest, 'One in 15 Conservative MPs believe climate change is a "myth", poll finds', the *Independent*, 6 November 2021, Online: https://www.independent.co.uk/climate-change/news/climate-change-myth-conservative-mps-b1952290.html.
125. Susanne Götze and Annika Joeres, 'Koalition der Klimawandelleugner', *Der Spiegel* 25 January 2020, Online: https://www.spiegel.de/wissenschaft/mensch/koalition-der-klimawandelleugner-a-c1a03be4-8921-4898-a4f3-a11a1c814008; and Quarks Science Cops, 'Der Fall EIKE: So dreist tricksen Klimawandel-Leugner:innen', *Quarks*, 13 November 2021, Online Podcast: https://www.quarks.de/podcast/quarks-science-cops-der-fall-eike-so-dreist-tricksen-klimawandel-verharmloser/.
126. Forschungsgruppe Wahlen, 'Politbarometer September III 2021', Forschungsgruppe Wahlen, 17 September 2021, Online: https://www.forschungsgruppe.de/Umfragen/Politbarometer/Archiv/Politbarometer_2021/September_III_2021.
127. Paula Matlach and Lukasz Janulewicz, 'Kalter Wind von Rechts: Wie rechte Parteien und Akteur:innen die Klimakrise zu ihren Gunsten missbrauchen Eine Analyse über falsche Fakten, Feindbilder und

Desinformationsnarrative im Umfeld der Bundestagswahl 2021', ISD, December 2021, Online: https://www.isdglobal.org/wp-content/uploads/2021/12/ISD_Analyse_Kalter-Wind-Klimadebatte-2021.pdf.

128. Damian Carrington, 'The four types of climate denier, and why you should ignore them all', the *Guardian*, 30 July 2020, Online: https://www.theguardian.com/commentisfree/2020/jul/30/climate-denier-shill-global-debate.

129. Statista, 'Risk index of natural disasters in Indonesia for mid 2022, by type', May 2021, Online: https://www.statista.com/statistics/920857/indonesia-risk-index-for-natural-disasters/.

130. Greg Fealy, 'Apocalyptic Thought, Conspiracism and Jihad in Indonesia' *Contemporary Southeast Asia*', Vol. 41, No. 1, Special Issue, April 2019, pp. 63–85, Online: https://www.jstor.org/stable/26664205.

131. Eisha Maharasingam-Shah and Pierre Vaux, '"Climate Lockdown" and the Culture Wars: How Covid-19 sparked a new narrative against climate action', ISD, October 2021. Online: https://www.isdglobal.org/wp-content/uploads/2021/10/20211014-ISDG-25-Climate-Lockdown-Part-1-V92.pdf.

132. Adam Houser, 'CFACT's Morano: King of the skeptics', CFACT website, 17 December 2009, Online: https://www.cfact.org/2009/12/17/cfacts-morano-king-of-the-skeptics.

133. Adam Sacks, 'We have met the deniers and they are us', *Grist*, 11 November 2009, Online: https://grist.org/article/2009-11-10-we-have-met-the-deniers-and-they-are-us/.

134. Cf. NASA; 'Global Climate Change: Vital Signs of the Planet', Online: https://climate.nasa.gov/vital-signs/sea-level/.

135. N. Mimura, Sea-level rise caused by climate change and its implications for society. Proc Jpn Acad Ser B Phys Biol Sci. 2013;89(7):281–301. doi:10.2183/pjab.89.281.

136. S.A. Kulp, B.H. Strauss, 'New elevation data triple estimates of global vulnerability to sea-level rise and coastal flooding', *Nature Communications* 10, 4844 (2019). https://doi.org/10.1038/s41467-019-12808-z.

137. 'Climate Change Update: Senate Floor Statement by US Sen. James M. Inhofe(R.-Okla)', *inhofe.senate.gov*, January 4, 2005. Archived March, 2011. Archive.is URL: https://archive.is/daqGZ, https://www.cbsnews.com/news/warned-over/.

138. Simon Bowers, 'Climate-sceptic US senator given funds by BP political action committee', the *Guardian*, 22 March 2015, Online: https://www.

theguardian.com/us-news/2015/mar/22/climate-sceptic-us-politician-jim-inhofe-bp-political-action-committee; and Cf. Open Secrets' Oil and Gas Top Recipients, Online: http://www.opensecrets.org/industries/recips.php?ind=E01&cycle=2002&recipdetail=S&mem=Y&sortorder=U.

139. Sebastian Haupt, 'Zitierkartelle und Lobbyisten. Vergleichende Perspektiven auf die Klimawandelleugner', in *Forschungsjournal Soziale Bewegungen*. Band 33, Nr. 1, 2020, S. 170–184
140. Susanne Götze, Annika Joeres, 'Leugnerkabinett. Viele Klimaskeptiker bezweifeln auch die Coronagefahren', in Heike Kleffner, Matthias Meisner (Hrsg.), *Fehlender Mindestabstand. Die Coronakrise und die Netzwerke der Demokratiefeinde*, Herder, Freiburg 2021, S. 135.
141. Kate Connolly, 'Germany's AfD turns on Greta Thunberg as it embraces climate denial', the *Guardian*, 14 May 2019, Online: https://www.theguardian.com/environment/2019/may/14/germanys-afd-attacks-greta-thunberg-as-it-embraces-climate-denial.
142. "Treibhäuser des Klima Alarmismus – Mit welchen Tricks deutsche Universitäten abweichende Meinungen niederhalten", 3 April 2020. Online: https://eike-klima-energie.eu/2016/04/03/treibhaeuser-des-klima-alarmismus-mit-welchen-tricks-deutsche-universitaeten-abweichende-meinungen-niederhalten/.
143. Quarks Science-Cops, 'Der Fall EIKE: So dreist tricksen Klimawandel-Leugner:innen', *Quarks*, 13 November 2021, Online Podcast: https://www.quarks.de/podcast/quarks-science-cops-der-fall-eike-so-dreist-tricksen-klimawandel-verharmloser/.
144. 'Polar Bear Population: How many polar bears are there?', Arctic WWF website, Online: https://arcticwwf.org/species/polar-bear/population/.
145. Damian Carrington, 'Earth has lost half of its wildlife in the past 40 years, says WWF', the *Guardian*, 30 September 2014, Online: https://www.theguardian.com/environment/2014/sep/29/earth-lost-50-wildlife-in-40-years-wwf; and Michael Greshko, 'What are mass extinctions, and what causes them?', *National Geographic*, 26 September 2019, Online: https://www.nationalgeographic.com/science/article/mass-extinction.
146. Gerado Ceballos, Paul R. Ehrlich and Rodolfo Dirzi, 'Biological annihilation via the ongoing sixth mass extinction signaled by vertebrate population losses and declines', *PNAS* 114 (30), July 2017, Online: https://www.pnas.org/content/114/30/E6089.
147. Cf. the WWF's Species directory: https://www.worldwildlife.org/species/directory?direction=desc&sort=extinction_status.

148. 'Die Heartland Lobby', Correctiv, 2 April 2020, Online: https://correctiv.org/top-stories/2020/02/04/die-heartland-lobby-2/.
149. Christian Esser, Manka Heise, Katarina Huth and Jean Peters, 'Undercover bei Klimawandel-Leugnern', ZDF Frontal, 4 February 2020, Video footage min. 5, Online: https://www.zdf.de/politik/frontal/undercover-bei-klimawandel-leugnern-100.html.
150. Statista, 'Where Climate Change Deniers Live', Online: https://www.statista.com/chart/19449/countries-with-biggest-share-of-climate-change-deniers/.
151. William J. Ripple, Christopher Wolf, Thomas M. Newsome, Jillian W. Gregg, Timothy M. Lenton, Ignacio Palomo, Jasper A. J Eikelboom, Beverly E. Law, Saleemul Huq, Philip B. Duffy, Johan Rockström, 'World Scientists' Warning of a Climate Emergency 2021', *BioScience*, 2021, biab079, https://doi.org/10.1093/biosci/biab079.
152. Eliza Macintosh et al., 'World leaders meet for "last chance" COP26 climate talks in Glasgow', CNN, 1 November 2021, Online: https://edition.cnn.com/world/Lve-news/cop26-climate-summit-intl-11-01-21/index.html.
153. See https://www.greenpeace.org/usa/fighting-climate-chaos/climate-deniers/koch-industries/.
154. Matthew Taylor and Jonathan Watts, 'Revealed: the 20 firms behind a third of all carbon emissions', the *Guardian*, 9 October 2019, Online: https://www.theguardian.com/environment/2019/oct/09/revealed-20-firms-third-carbon-emissions.
155. 'behindert' in the German original.
156. Quarks Science Cops, 'Der Fall EIKE: So dreist tricksen Klimawandel-Leugner:innen', *Quarks*, 13 November 2021, Online Podcast: https://www.quarks.de/podcast/quarks-science-cops-der-fall-eike-so-dreist-tricksen-klimawandel-verharmloser/.
157. Aylin Woodward, 'As denying climate change becomes impossible, fossil-fuel interests pivot to 'carbon shaming'', *Business Insider*, 28 August 2021, Online: https://www.businessinsider.com/fossil-fuel-interests-target-climate-advocates-personally-2021-8.
158. Avaaz, 'How youth climate anxiety is linked to government inaction', 14 September 2021, Online: https://secure.avaaz.org/campaign/en/climate_anxiety_panel/.
159. Alice Echtermann, 'Gesucht: Influencer*in, jung, rechts', Correctiv, 21 February 2020, online: https://correctiv.org/faktencheck/hintergrund/2020/02/21/gesucht-influencerin-jung-rechts/

160. See original Facebook post by AfD: https://www.facebook.com/jungealternativerlp/posts/2511328659094706.
161. See for example: https://www.youtube.com/watch?v=v8dXpe1Pp6Q.
162. David Smith, '"Anti-Greta" teen activist to speak at biggest US conservatives conference', the *Guardian*, 25 February 2020, Online: https://www.theguardian.com/us-news/2020/feb/25/anti-greta-teen-activist-cpac-conference-climate-sceptic.
163. Christian Esser, Manka Heise, Katarina Huth and Jean Petersm 'Undercover bei Klimawandel-Leugnern', ZDF Frontal, 4 February 2020, Video footage min. 5, Online: https://www.zdf.de/politik/frontal/undercover-bei-klimawandel-leugnern-100.html; and Desmond Butler and Juliet Eilperin, 'The anti-Greta: A conservative think tank takes on the global phenomenon', *The Washington Post*, 23 February 2020, online: https://www.washingtonpost.com/climate-environment/2020/02/23/meet-anti-greta-young-youtuber-campaigning-against-climate-alarmism/.
164. Pu Yan, Ralph Schroeder & Sebastian Stier (2021) 'Is there a link between climate change scepticism and populism? An analysis of web tracking and survey data from Europe and the US', *Information, Communication & Society*, DOI: 10.1080/1369118X.2020.1864005.
165. 'Thüringen: AfD gewinnt vier Bundestags-Wahlkreise und wird stärkste Partei', MDR Thüringen, 27 September 2021, Online: https://www.mdr.de/nachrichten/deutschland/wahlen/bundestagswahl/thueringen-endergebnis-afd-ullrich-maassen-100.html.
166. NASA Climate Change, 'What is the difference between weather and climate?', 27 September 2019, Online: https://www.youtube.com/watch?v=vH298zSCQzY.
167. Cf. NASA's website explanation: https://climate.nasa.gov/causes/.
168. Ibid.
169. Max Falkenberg, Alessandro Galeazzi, et al., 'Growing polarization around climate change on social media', *Nature Climate Change* 12, November 2022, pp. 1114–1121.
170. See Benjamin Toff, Sumitra Badrinathan, Camila Mont'Alverne, Amy R. Arguedas, Richard Fletcher and Rasmus Kleis Nielsen, 'Depth and breadth: How news organisations navigate trade-offs around building trust in news', Reuters Institute for the Study of Journalism, Oxford University, 2 December 2021, Online: https://reutersinstitute.politics.ox.ac.uk/depth-and-breadth-how-news-organisations-navigate-trade-offs-around-building-trust-news.

171. Megan Brenan, 'Americans' Trust in Media Dips to Second Lowest on Record', Gallup, 7 October 2021, Online: https://news.gallup.com/poll/355526/americans-trust-media-dips-second-lowest-record.aspx.
172. Nic Newman with Richard Fletcher, Craig T. Robertson, Kirsten Eddy, and Rasmus Kleis Nielsen, 'Reuters Institute Digital News Report', Reuters Institute, June 2022, online:
173. 'Australians trust of the media and journalists is on the way down: Edelman', Radio Info, 24 February 2022, online: https://radioinfo.com.au/news/australians-trust-of-the-media-and-journalists-is-on-the-way-down-edelman/.
174. Nicole Hemmer, 'History shows we ignore Tucker Carlson at our peril', CCN, 15 April 2021, Online: https://edition.cnn.com/2021/04/15/opinions/tucker-carlson-replacement-theory-peter-brimelow-republican-party-hemmer/index.html.
175. Nicolas Confessore, 'What to Know About Tucker Carlson's Rise', *The New York Times*, 2022, 30 April 2022, Online: https://www.nytimes.com/2022/04/30/business/media/tucker-carlson-fox-news-takeaways.html.
176. Eric Deggans, 'I have a name for what fueled Joe Rogan's new scandal: Bigotry Denial Syndrome', NPR, 9 February 2022, Online: https://www.npr.org/2022/02/09/1079271255/joe-rogan-spotify-racism-controversy.
177. 'Kyrie Irving refuses to directly answer question about his beliefs on Jewish people', the *Guardian*, 3 November 2022, Online: https://www.theguardian.com/sport/2022/nov/03/kyrie-irving-admits-link-to-antisemitic-work-had-negative-impact-on-jews.
178. Sarah Polus, 'Ye, Candace Owens wear "White Lives Matter" shirts at Paris Fashion week', *The Hill*, 3 October 2022, Online: https://thehill.com/blogs/in-the-know/3672606-ye-candace-owens-wear-white-lives-matter-shirts-at-paris-fashion-week/.
179. Benjamin Lee and Ben Beaumont-Thomas, 'Kanye West on slavery: "For 400 Years? That sounds like a choice"', the *Guardian*, 2 May 2018, online: https://www.theguardian.com/music/2018/may/01/kanye-west-on-slavery-for-400-years-that-sounds-like-a-choice.
180. Center on Extremism, 'Unpacking Kanye West's Antisemitic Remarks', Anti-Defamation League, 14 October 2022, Online: https://www.adl.org/resources/blog/unpacking-kanye-wests-antisemitic-remarks; Dani Anguiano, 'Chorus of outrage against Kanye West grows . . .', the *Guardian*, Online: https://www.theguardian.com/us-news/2022/oct/24/

los-angeles-leaders-condemn-kanye-wests-antisemitic-comments; and Melissa Dellatto and Carlie Porterfield, 'Kanye West's Antisemitic, Troubling Behavior . . .', Forbes, Online: https://www.forbes.com/sites/marisadellatto/2022/11/04/kanye-wests-anti-semitic-troubling-behavior-heres-everything-hes-said-in-recent-weeks/?sh=7c679f975e8f

181. Chloe Melas, 'Exclusive: Kanye West has a disturbing history of admiring Hitler, sources tell CNN', CNN, 27 October 2022, Online: https://edition.cnn.com/2022/10/27/entertainment/kanye-west-hitler-album/index.html?utm_source=twCNNi&utm_medium=social&utm_content=2022-10-27T16%3A27%3A02&utm_term=link.

182. Dani Anguiano, 'Chorus of outrage against Kanye West grows as anti-Semitic incidents rattle LA', the *Guardian*, 25 October 2022, online: https://www.theguardian.com/us-news/2022/oct/24/los-angeles-leaders-condemn-kanye-wests-antisemitic-comments.

183. Brandy Zadrozny, 'Elon Musk's "amnesty" pledge brings back QAnon, far-right Twitter accounts', NBC News, 2 December 2022, Online: https://www.nbcnews.com/tech/internet/elon-musks-twitter-beginning-take-shape-rcna58940.

184. Link to Musk's original tweet: https://twitter.com/elonmusk/status/1602278477234728960.

185. Sophie Zeldin-O'Neill, 'Jeremy Clarkson condemned over Meghan column in the Sun', the *Guardian*, 18 December 2022, Online: https://www.theguardian.com/media/2022/dec/18/jeremy-clarkson-condemned-meghan-column-the-sun.

186. Cynthia Miller-Idriss, *The Extreme Gone Mainstream: Commercialization and Far-Right Youth Culture in Germany* (N.Y.: Princeton University Press, 2018).

187. Julia Ebner, *Going Dark: The Secret Social Lives of Extremists* (London: Bloomsbury, 2020).

188. Anita Snow, '1 in 3 fears immigrants influence US elections: AP-NORC Poll', Associated Press, 10 May 2022, Online: https://apnews.com/article/immigration-2022-midterm-elections-covid-health-media-2ebbd3849ca35ec76f0f91120639d9d4.

189. See Black Lives Matter global website: https://blacklivesmatter.com/.

190. Armed Conflict Location & Event Data Project (ACLED), Demonstrations and Political Violence in America: New Data for Summer 2020, September 2020, Online: https://acleddata.com/2020/09/03/demonstrations-political-violence-in-america-new-data-for-summer-2020/.

191. William Allchorn, 'Turning Back to Biologised Racism: A Content Analysis of Patriotic Alternative UK's Online Discourse', Global Network on Extremism and Technology, 22 February 2021, Online: https://gnet-research.org/2021/02/22/turning-back-to-biologised-racism-a-content-analysis-of-patriotic-alternative-uks-online-discourse/).
192. Jon Stone, 'Black Lives Matter is "not force for good" says Tory MP Sajid Javid', *Independent*, 5 October 2020, Online: https://www.independent.co.uk/news/uk/politics/sajid-javid-black-live-matter-blm-racism-tory-mp-b806336.html.
193. Arj Singh, 'Britons are more likely to view Black Lives Matter as a force for good than ill, data shows', *i* News, 25 July 2021, Online: https://inews.co.uk/news/politics/black-lives-matter-britain-take-knee-popularity-1118702.
194. Robert Booth, 'Black Lives Matter has increased racial tension, 55% say in UK poll', the *Guardian*, 27 November 2020, Online: https://www.theguardian.com/world/2020/nov/27/black-lives-matter-has-increased-racial-tension-55-say-in-uk-poll.
195. Simon Murdoch, 'Patriotic Alternative: Uniting the Fascist Right?', Hope not Hate, August 2020, Online: https://www.hopenothate.org.uk/wp-content/uploads/2020/08/HnH_Patriotic-Alternative-report_2020-08-v3.pdf.
196. Sarah Haylock et al., 'Risk factors associated with knife-crime in United Kingdom among young people aged 10–24 years: a systematic review', *BMC Public Health*, Vol 20 (1451), 2020, Online: https://bmcpublichealth.biomedcentral.com/articles/10.1186/s12889-020-09498-4.
197. Cf. Patriotic Alternative Website: https://www.patrioticalternative.org.uk/.
198. See 'The Enemy Within the Far-Right', Channel 4 *News Dispatches*, May 2022, Online: https://www.channel4.com/programmes/the-enemy-within-the-far-right-dispatches/on-demand/71213-001.
199. Ibid.
200. William Allchorn, 'Turning Back to Biologised Racism: A Content Analysis of Patriotic Alternative UK's Online Discourse', Global Network on Extremism & Technology, 22 February 2021, Online: https://gnet-research.org/2021/02/22/turning-back-to-biologised-racism-a-content-analysis-of-patriotic-alternative-uks-online-discourse/.
201. Milo Comerford, Tim Squirrell, David Leenstra and Jakob Guhl, 'What the UK Migrant Centre Attack Tells Us About Contemporary Extremism

Trends', ISD, digital dispatches, 14 November 2022, online: https://www.isdglobal.org/digital_dispatches/what-the-uk-migrant-centre-attack-tells-us-about-contemporary-extremism-trends/.

202. Stephanie Finnegan, 'Leeds neo-Nazi Mark Collet behind far-right group Patriotic Alternative pushing "hateful" home schooling with racist songs', Leeds Live, 21 February 2021, Online: https://www.leeds-live.co.uk/news/leeds-news/leeds-neo-nazi-mark-collet-19882854.
203. Stephanie Finnegan, 'Leeds neo-Nazi Mark Collet behind far-right group Patriotic Alternative pushing 'hateful' home schooling with racist songs', Leeds Live, 21 February 2021, Online: https://www.leeds-live.co.uk/news/leeds-news/leeds-neo-nazi-mark-collet-19882854.
204. 'England FA condemn racist abuse aimed at Marcus Rashford, Bukayo Saka, Jadon Sancho after Euro 2020 shootout loss', ESPN, 12 July 2021, Online: https://www.espn.com/soccer/england-eng/story/4431389/england-fa-condemn-racist-abuse-aimed-at-rashfordsakasancho-after-euro-shootout-loss.
205. 'Non-white footballers played better when stadiums were empty during the pandemic', *The Economist*, 10 June 2021, Online: https://www.economist.com/graphic-detail/2021/06/10/non-white-footballers-played-better-when-stadiums-were-empty-during-the-pandemic.
206. Rebecca Shabad, 'Where does the phrase "When the looting starts, the shooting starts" come from?', NBC News, 29 May 2020, Online: https://www.nbcnews.com/politics/congress/where-does-phrase-when-looting-starts-shooting-starts-come-n1217676.
207. Jamila Lyiscott, *Black Appetite, White Food*, (London: Routledge, 2019), p.23.
208. Stephen Menendian, Samir Gambhir and Arthur Gailes, 'The Roots of Structural Racism Project', Othering and Belonging Institute, 21 June 2021, Online: https://belonging.berkeley.edu/roots-structural-racism.
209. Christopher Ingraham, 'Three quarters of whites don't have any non-white friends', *The Washington Post*, 27 November 2014, Online: https://www.washingtonpost.com/news/wonk/wp/2014/11/27/three-quarters-of-whites-dont-have-any-non-white-friends-2/.
210. Tanya Abraham, '84% of BAME Britons think the UK is still very or somewhat racist', YouGov, Jun2 2020, Online: https://yougov.co.uk/topics/politics/articles-reports/2020/06/26/nine-ten-bame-britons-think-racism-exists-same-lev.
211. Office for Statistics, 'Births and infant mortality by ethnicity in England and Wales: 2007 to 2019', Online: https://www.ons.gov.

uk/peoplepopulationandcommunity/healthandsocialcare/childhealth/articles/birthsandinfantmortalitybyethnicityinenglandandwales/2007to2019.
212. Emma Kasprzak, 'Why are black mothers at more risk of dying?', BBC, 12 April 2019, Online: https://www.bbc.co.uk/news/uk-england-47115305.
213. HM Government, 'Unemployment by ethnicity', January 2021, Online: https://www.ethnicity-facts-figures.service.gov.uk/work-pay-and-benefits/unemployment-and-economic-inactivity/unemployment/latest#by-ethnicity.
214. HM Government, 'Black Caribbean ethnic group: facts and figures', 27 June 2019, Online: https://www.ethnicity-facts-figures.service.gov.uk/summaries/black-caribbean-ethnic-group#stop-and-search.
215. Nazir Afzal, Black people dying in police custody should surprise no one', the Guardian, 11 June 2020, Online: https://www.theguardian.com/uk-news/2020/jun/11/black-deaths-in-police-custody-the-tip-of-an-iceberg-of-racist-treatment.
216. Angelika Schuster and Tristan Sindelgruber, 'Operation Spring', 2005, Online: http://dok.at/film/operation-spring/.
217. Jakobi Williams, '"don't know woman have to do nothing'she don't want to do": Gender, Activism, and the Illinois Black Panther Party', *Black Women, Gender + Families*. Vol. 6, No. 2 (Fall 2012), pp. 29–54, Online: https://www.jstor.org/stable/10.5406/blacwomegendfami.6.2.0029.
218. Ashley Roach-McFarlane, *The Forgotten Legacy of Claudia Jones: a Black Communist Radical Feminist*, (Verso Books, 22 March 2021), Online: https://www.versobooks.com/blogs/5030-the-forgotten-legacy-of-claudia-jones-a-black-communist-radical-feminist.
219. See 2020 US Census: https://www.census.gov/library/stories/2021/08/improved-race-ethnicity-measures-reveal-united-states-population-much-more-multiracial.html.
220. Amnesty International, 'Gun Violence – Key Facts', 2022, Online: https://www.amnesty.org/en/what-we-do/arms-control/gun-violence/.
221. HM Government, 'Official Statistics: Hate crime, England and Wales, 2021 to 2022', Home Office, 6 October 2022, Online: https://www.gov.uk/government/statistics/hate-crime-england-and-wales-2021-to-2022/hate-crime-england-and-wales-2021-to-2022.
222. Jakob Guhl and Jacob Davey, 'A Safe Space to Hate: White Supremacist Mobilisation on Telegram', ISD, June 2020, Online: https://www.

isdglobal.org/isd-publications/a-safe-space-to-hate-white-supremacist-mobilisation-on-telegram/.
223. Adam Gabbatt and Jason Wilson, 'Klan leader charged over driving car into Black Lives matter protesters', the *Guardian*, 8 June 2020, Online: https://www.theguardian.com/us-news/2020/jun/08/klan-leader-charged-harry-rogers-virginia.
224. Kenya Evelyn, 'Drivers target Black Lives Matter protesters in "horrifying" spate of attacks', the *Guardian*, 9 July 2020, Online: https://www.theguardian.com/world/2020/jul/09/black-lives-matter-drivers-target-protesters-spate-of-attacks.
225. Min. 23, first recording of the event.
226. Min. 17, third recording of event.
227. See for example https://antisemitism.adl.org/power/.
228. See https://encyclopedia.ushmm.org/content/en/article/protocols-of-the-elders-of-zion.
229. For more detailed analysis of anti-Semitic stereotypes and myths about 'the Zionist-Jewish owned media' see Matthias J. Becker and Dr Daniel Allington, 'Decoding Antisemitism: An AI-driven Study on Hate Speech and Imagery Online', Decoding Antisemitism Discourse Report, August 2021, p. 9, Online: https://kclpure.kcl.ac.uk/portal/files/157768985/TUB_Decoding_Antisemitism_EN_FIN.pdf.
230. Min. 9, third recording of event.
231. Min 3, third recording of the event.
232. David Spiegelhalter, 'Is 10 per cent of the population really gay?', the *Guardian*, 5 April 2015, Online: https://www.theguardian.com/society/2015/apr/05/10-per-cent-population-gay-alfred-kinsey-statistics.
233. UCLA Williams Institute, 'How Many Adults Identify as Transgender in the United States?', June 2016, Online: https://williamsinstitute.law.ucla.edu/publications/trans-adults-united-states/.
234. Estimates based on US survey numbers in Gallup survey: https://news.gallup.com/poll/389792/lgbt-identification-ticks-up.aspx.
235. Vikki Julian, 'New research on reporting trans issues shows 400% increase in coverage and varying perceptions on broader editorial standards', IPSO, 2 December 2020, Online: https://www.ipso.co.uk/news-press-releases/press-releases/new-research-on-reporting-of-trans-issues-shows-400-increase-in-coverage-and-varying-perceptions-on-broader-editorial-standards/.

236. Michelle Goldberg, 'The Right's Disney Freakout', *The New York Times*, 1 April 2022, Online: https://www.nytimes.com/2022/04/01/opinion/disney-dont-say-gay.html.
237. Laurel Powell, '2021 Becomes Deadliest Year on Record for Transgender and Non-Binary People', Human Rights Campaign, 9 November 2021, Online: https://www.hrc.org/press-releases/2021-becomes-deadliest-year-on-record-for-transgender-and-non-binary-people.
238. 'Transphobic hate crime reports have quadrupled over the past five years in the UK', BBC, 11 October 2020, Online: https://www.bbc.com/news/av/uk-54486122.
239. Galop, 'Transphobic Hate Crime Report 2020', Online: https://galop.org.uk/resource/transphobic-hate-crime-report-2020/.
240. Nick Lowles, Nick Ryan and Joe Mulhall, 'State of Hate 2022: On the March Again', Hope not Hate, March 2022, Online: https://hopenothate.org.uk/wp-content/uploads/2022/03/state-of-hate-2022-v1_17-March-update.pdf.
241. Sanchez Manning, 'Now even the word "maternity" is facing a ban at Britain's "wokest" university after diversity chiefs said the term was now "problematic" and "exclusionary"', *Daily Mail*, 23 January 2022, Online: https://www.dailymail.co.uk/news/article-10431337/Now-maternity-facing-ban-Britains-wokest-university-diversity-chiefs-ruling.html.
242. See https://www.mumsnet.com/Talk/womens_rights/3159058-Disgusted-by-all-the-transphobia-here?pg=13.
243. Harriet Williamson, 'Rosie Duffield's views on transgender people should have no place in the Labour party', the *Independent*, 20 September 2021, Online: https://uk.news.yahoo.com/rosie-duffield-views-transgender-people-125635733.html
244. Alana Mastrangelo, 'Exclusive – Sarah Palin on Trans Athletes: "He is a dude" beating women's swimming records', *Breitbart*, 27 December 2021, Online: https://www.breitbart.com/politics/2021/12/27/exclusive-sarah-palin-on-trans-athletes-he-is-a-dude-beating-womens-swimming-records/.
245. Samantha Schmidt, 'Conservatives find unlikely ally in fighting transgender rights: Radical Feminists', *The Washington Post*, 7 February 2020, Online: https://www.washingtonpost.com/dc-md-va/2020/02/07/radical-feminists-conservatives-transgender-rights/ and https://www.nbcnews.com/feature/nbc-out/conservative-group-hosts-anti-transgender-panel-feminists-left-n964246

246. Kashmira Gander, 'Trans Women are Parasites for "Occupying the Bodies of the Oppressed"', *Newsweek*, 15 March 20218, Online: https://www.newsweek.com/trans-women-are-parasites-occupying-bodies-oppressed-says-academic-846563.
247. 'Pride in London sorry after anti-trans protest', BBC, 6 July 2018, Online: https://www.bbc.com/news/uk-england-london-44757403.
248. See website: https://www.gettheloutuk.com/.
249. Trevor Phillips, 'Trans extremists are putting equality at risk', *The Times*, 22 October 2018, Online: https://www.thetimes.co.uk/article/trans-extremists-are-putting-equality-at-risk-fjv8skwz0.
250. Leo McKinstry, 'We must halt this transgender madness – it is hurting women and girls, blasts LEO McKINSTRY,' *Express*, 29 October 2020, Online: https://www.express.co.uk/comment/columnists/leo-mckinstry/903140/Transgenderism-harming-women-must-be-stopped.
251. Tim Newark, 'This transgender madness is now a danger to women, says Tim Newark', *Express*, 13 October 2018, Online: https://www.express.co.uk/comment/expresscomment/1030959/transgender-madness-danger-women-comment-tim-newark.
252. Darren Boyle, 'Trans rapist, 25, who groomed a 13-year-old girl asking her on text "do you mind if my hands wander?" days after being released from prison is jailed for 100 months', *Mail Online*, 3 February 2022, Online: https://www.dailymail.co.uk/news/article-10472547/Trans-rapist-25-groomed-13-year-old-girl-jailed-100-months.html.
253. Shawn Cohen, 'EXCLUSIVE: "We're uncomfortable in our own locker room." Lia Thomas' UPenn teammate tells how the trans swimmer doesn't always cover up her male genitals when changing and their concerns go ignored by their coach', *Daily Mail*, 27 January 2022, Online: https://www.dailymail.co.uk/news/article-10445679/Lia-Thomas-UPenn-teammate-says-trans-swimmer-doesnt-cover-genitals-locker-room.html.
254. Robert Coulter et al., 'Prevalence of Past-Year Sexual Assault Victimization Among Undergraduate Students: Exploring Differences by and Intersections of Gender Identity, Sexual Identity, and Race/Ethnicity', Society for Prevention Research, 2017. Online: https://vaw.msu.edu/wp-content/uploads/2016/03/2-Coulter-Prev-Sci-2017.pdf.
255. See for example RAINN, 'Perpetrators of Sexual Violence: Statistics, online: https://www.rainn.org/statistics/perpetrators-sexual-violence, Office for National Statistics, 'Nature of sexual assault by rape or penetration, England and Wales, year ending March 2020', Census 2021, Online: https://www.

ons.gov.uk/peoplepopulationandcommunity/crimeandjustice/articles/ natureofsexualassaultbyrapeorpenetrationenglandandwales/yearending-march2020#perpetrator-characteristics; and Devon Rape Crisis and Sexual Abuse Services, 'Myths, Facts and Statistics', 2022, Online: https://devon-rapecrisis.org.uk/about-us/myths-facts-and-statistics/.

256. National Center for Transgender Equality, 'The Report of the 2015 US Transgender Survey', December 2015, Online: https://transequality.org/sites/default/files/docs/usts/USTS-Executive-Summary-Dec17.pdf.

257. FRA – European Union Agency for Fundamental Rights, 'Being Trans in the European Union: Comparative analysis of EU LGBT survey data', 2014, Online: https://fra.europa.eu/sites/default/files/fra-2014-being-trans-eu-comparative-0_en.pdf.

258. Nazia Parveen, 'Karen White: how "manipulative" transgender inmate attacked again', the *Guardian*, 11 October 2018, Online: https://www.theguardian.com/society/2018/oct/11/karen-white-how-manipulative-and-controlling-offender-attacked-again-transgender-prison.

259. See original tweet: https://twitter.com/jk_rowling/status/1269382518362509313?lang=en.

260. Katelyn Burns, 'Is J.K. Rowling Transphobic?, A Trans Woman Investigates' *Them*, 28 March 2018, Online: https://www.them.us/story/is-jk-rowling-transphobic.

261. YouGov, 'How Brits Define a Transgender Woman', 2022 Tracker, Online: https://yougov.co.uk/topics/politics/trackers/how-brits-define-a-transgender-woman.

262. Katelyn Burns, 'The internet made trans people visible. It also left them more vulnerable', *Vox*, 27 December 2019, Online: https://www.vox.com/identities/2019/12/27/21028342/trans-visibility-backlash-internet-2010.

263. 'Bathroom Bill to Cost North Carolina $3.76B AP Analysis Finds', NBC News, 27 March 2017, Online: https://www.nbcnews.com/feature/nbc-out/bathroom-bill-cost-north-carolina-3-76b-ap-analysis-finds-n738866.

264. Simon Murphy and Libby Brooks, 'UK government drops gender self-identification plan for trans people', the *Guardian*, 22 September 2020, Online: https://www.theguardian.com/society/2020/sep/22/uk-government-drops-gender-self-identification-plan-for-trans-people.

265. See for example, Jean Linis-Dinco, 'Machines, Artificial Intelligence and rising global transphobia', Melbourne Law School, March 2021, Online: https://law.unimelb.edu.au/news/caide/machines,-artificial-

intelligence-and-the-rising-global-transphobia; and Daniel Laufer, 'Computers are binary, people are not: how AI undermines LGBTQ identity', Access Now, 6 April 2021, Online: https://www.accessnow.org/how-ai-systems-undermine-lgbtq-identity/.

266. Jennifer Bilek, 'The agenda behind gender ideology, Women's Declaration International (WDI), 7 December 2021, Online: https://www.youtube.com/watch?v=5DpRlp_3ZZQ.
267. See https://twitter.com/bjportraits/status/1197507155403952128.
268. See https://twitter.com/bjportraits/status/1171413732171419648.
269. Ibid.
270. Trystan Reese, *How We Do Family*, (NY: The Experiment, 2021), pp. 147–148.
271. GLAAD, 'Social Media Safety Index', May 2021, Online: https://www.glaad.org/sites/default/files/images/2021-05/GLAAD%20SOCIAL%20MEDIA%20SAFETY%20INDEX_0.pdf.
272. Ashley Stahl, 'Why Democrats Should Be Losing Sleep Over Generation Z', *Forbes*, 11 August 2017, Online: https://www.forbes.com/sites/ashleystahl/2017/08/11/why-democrats-should-be-losing-sleep-over-generation-z/?sh=162371f77878; and Andrew Ellison, 'Teenagers oppose gay marriage and shun tattoos', *The Sunday Times*, 15 September 2016, Online: http://www.thetimes.co.uk/article/teenagers-oppose-gay-marriage-and-shun-tattoos-f2rf0td0b.
273. John Gramlich, 'Young Americans are less trusting of other people – and key institutions – than their elders', Pew Research, 6 August 2019, Online: https://www.pewresearch.org/fact-tank/2019/08/06/young-americans-are-less-trusting-of-other-people-and-key-institutions-than-their-elders/.
274. See https://www.prageru.com.
275. Nellie Bowles, 'Right-Wing Views for Generation Z, Five Minutes at a Time', *The New York Times*, 4 January 2020, Online: https://www.nytimes.com/2020/01/04/us/politics/dennis-prager-university.html.
276. 'A Snapshot of Anti-Trans Hatred in Debates around Transgender Athletes', Institute for Strategic Dialogue, 20 January 2022, Online: https://www.isdglobal.org/digital_dispatches/anti-trans-hatred-against-athletes-highlights-policy-failures-facebook-twitter/?mc_cid=d3f575d23e&mc_eid=1dcda39307.
277. 'It's Intersex Awareness Day – here are 5 myths we need to shatter', Amnesty International, October 2018, Online: https://www.amnesty.org/en/latest/

news/2018/10/its-intersex-awareness-day-here-are-5-myths-we-need-to-shatter/#:~:text=Myth%202%3A%20Being%20intersex%20is,intersex%20people%20are%20massively%20underrepresented.

278. Kat Chow, '"Model Minority" Myth Again Used As A Racial Wedge Between Asians and Blacks', NPR, 19 April 2017, Online: https://www.npr.org/sections/codeswitch/2017/04/19/524571669/model-minority-myth-again-used-as-a-racial-wedge-between-asians-and-blacks.

279. Jo Yurcaba, 'Texas governor calls on citizens to report parents of transgender kids for abuse', NBC News, 23 February 2022, Online: https://www.nbcnews.com/nbc-out/out-politics-and-policy/texas-governor-calls-citizens-report-parents-transgender-kids-abuse-rcna17455.

280. German Lopez, 'Women are getting harassed in bathrooms because of anti-transgender hysteria', *Vox*, 18 May 2016, Online: https://www.vox.com/2016/5/18/11690234/women-bathrooms-harassment.

281. Sam Jones and Guy Chazan, '"Nein Danke": the resistance to Covid-19 vaccines in German-speaking Europe', *Financial Times*, 10 November 2021, Online: https://www.ft.com/content/f04ac67b-92e4-4bab-8c23-817cc0483df5.

282. Brian Kennedy, Alec Tyson and Cary Funk, 'Americans' Trust in Scientists, Other Groups Declines', Pew Research, February 2022, online: https://www.pewresearch.org/science/2022/02/15/americans-trust-in-scientists-other-groups-declines/.

283. See D. Reynolds, J. Garay, S. Deamond, M. Moran M, W. Gold, R. Styra, 'Understanding, compliance and psychological impact of the SARS quarantine experience', in *Epidemiol. Infect.* 136, 2008, 997–1007; and Lieberoth Andreas, Lin Shiang-Yi, et al., 'Stress and worry in the 2020 coronavirus pandemic: relationships to trust and compliance with preventive measures across 48 countries in the COVIDiSTRESS global survey', The Royal Society, February 2021, Online: https://royalsocietypublishing.org/doi/10.1098/rsos.200589.

284. Lieberoth Andreas, Lin Shiang-Yi, et al., 'Stress and worry in the 2020 coronavirus pandemic: relationships to trust and compliance with preventive measures across 48 countries in the COVIDiSTRESS global survey', The Royal Society, February 2021, Online: https://royalsocietypublishing.org/doi/10.1098/rsos.200589.

285. Bruce Y. Lee, 'Graphene Oxide In Pfizer Coivd-19 Vaccines? Here Are the Latest Unsupported Claims', *Forbes*, 10 July 2021, Online: https://www.forbes.com/

sites/brucelee/2021/07/10/graphene-oxide-in-pfizer-covid-19-vaccines-here-are-the-latest-unsupported-claims/?sh=7c01e64274d7; and Reuters Fact Check, 'Fact Check- COVID-19 vaccines do not contain graphene oxide', Reuters, 23 July 2021, Online: https://www.reuters.com/article/factcheck-grapheneoxide-vaccine-idUSL1N2OZ14F.

286. 'The Pfizer vaccine isn't 99% graphene oxide', Full Fact, 14 July 2021, Online: https://fullfact.org/online/graphene-oxide/; Reuters Fact Check, 'Fact Check- COVID-19 vaccines do not contain graphene oxide', Reuters, 23 July 2021, Online: https://www.reuters.com/article/factcheck-grapheneoxide-vaccine-idUSL1N2OZ14F.

287. Pablo Campra Madrid, 'Detección de Oxido de Grafeno En Suspensión Acuosa', Universidad de Almería, 28 June 2021, Online https://www.docdroid.net/rNgtxyh/microscopia-de-vial-corminaty-dr-campra-firma-e-1-fusionado-pdf#page=16.

288. 'Covid-19 vaccines do not make you magnetic', Full Fact, 14 May 2021, Online: https://fullfact.org/online/covid-vaccine-magnet/.

289. Samantha Tatro, '"pH Miracle" Author Robert O. Young Sentenced', NBC San Diego, 29 June 2017, Online: https://www.nbcsandiego.com/news/local/ph-miracle-author-robert-o-young-sentenced/19346/.

290. 'Germany: Man refusing COVID jab attacks health workers, demands certificate', Deutsche Welle, 5 September 2021, Online: https://www.dw.com/en/germany-man-refusing-covid-jab-attacks-health-workers-demands-certificate/a-59088281.

291. Sharon Pruitt-Young, '3 Tourists Allegedly Attacked A Hostess Who Asked For Vaccine Proof At A Restaurant', NPR, 17 September 2021, Online: https://www.npr.org/sections/coronavirus-live-updates/2021/09/17/1038392877/new-york-tourists-attack-hostess-restaurant-vaccine?t=1636114243829.

292. Graeme Massie, 'Apple store security guard stabbed multiple times over mask dispute, police say', the *Independent*, 9 October 2021, Online: https://www.independent.co.uk/news/world/americas/crime/apple-store-mask-stabbing-b1935476.html.

293. '1 dead, 2 injured after dispute over mask at Georgia grocery store, sheriff says', CNN, 15 June 2021, Online: https://abc17news.com/news/national-world/2021/06/15/1-dead-2-injured-after-dispute-over-mask-at-georgia-grocery-store-sheriff-says/.

294. Michal McGowan, 'How the wellness and influencer crowd serve conspiracies to the masses', the *Guardian*, 25 February 2021, Online: https://

www.theguardian.com/australia-news/2021/feb/25/how-the-wellness-and-influencer-crowd-served-conspiracies-to-the-masses.

295. Center for Countering Digital Hate, 'The Disinformation Dozen: Why platforms must act on twelve leading online anti-vaxxers', CCDH, March 2021, Online: https://counterhate.com/research/the-disinformation-dozen/.

296. Laura Garcia and Tommy Shane, 'A guide to prebunking: a promising way to inoculate against misinformation', First Draft, 29 June 2021, Online: https://firstdraftnews.org/articles/a-guide-to-prebunking-a-promising-way-to-inoculate-against-misinformation/.

297. Carlotta Dotto, Rory Smith and Chris Looft, 'The "broadcast" model no longer works in an era of disinformation', First Draft, 18 December 2020, Online: https://firstdraftnews.org/articles/the-broadcast-model-no-longer-works-in-an-era-of-disinformation/.

298. Soroush Vosoughi, Deb Roy and Sinan Aral, 'The spread of true and false news online', *Science*, Vol 359, No. 6380 (2018): 1146–1151, Online: https://www.science.org/doi/10.1126/science.aap9559.

299. J-W. Van Prooijen, K.M. Douglas, 'Belief in conspiracy theories: Basic principles of an emerging research domain', *European Journal of Social Psychology*, Vol 48(7), 2018, pp. 897–908, Online: https://www.ncbi.nlm.nih.gov/pmc/articles/PMC6282974/.

300. Serge Moscovici, 'The Conspiracy Mentality', In: C.F. Graumann and S Moscovici (eds), *Changing Conceptions of Conspiracy, Springer Series in Social Psychology*, (NY: Springer), pp. 151–169, Online: https://link.springer.com/chapter/10.1007/978-1-4612-4618-3_9.

301. 'Servus TV in Österreich: Ein Sender für Corona-Leugne?', *Tagesschau*, 20 December 2021, Online: https://www.tagesschau.de/ausland/europa/servus-tv-corona-101.html.

302. Hannah Winter, Lea Gerster, Joschua Helmer and Till Baaken, 'Überdosis Desinformation: Die Vertrauenskrise', ISD, 8 May 2021, Online: https://www.isdglobal.org/isd-publications/uberdosis-desinformation-die-vertrauenskrise-impfskepsis-und-impfgegnerschaft-in-der-covid-19-pandemie/.

303. See https://londonreal.tv/episodes/.

304. Zoe Tidman, 'Eight police officers hurt after bottles thrown at anti-lockdown protest in London', the *Independent*, 25 April 2021, Online: https://www.independent.co.uk/news/uk/crime/anti-lockdown-protests-london-arrests-police-b1836982.html.

305. Committee to Protect Journalists, 'BBC news crew threatened by COVID-19 protesters in UK', 14 September 2021, Online: https://cpj.org/2021/09/bbc-news-crew-threatened-by-covid-19-protesters-in-uk/.
306. 'Germany FM condemns anti-lockdown protesters' attack on journalists', Deutsche Welle, 7 May 2020, Online: https://www.dw.com/en/germanys-maas-condemns-anti-lockdown-protesters-attack-on-journalists/a-53359614.
307. Committee to Protect Journalists, 'Protesters against Slovenian COVID-19 response and vaccination storm headquarters of RTVS broadcaster', 9 September 2021, Online: https://cpj.org/2021/09/protesters-against-slovenian-covid-19-response-and-vaccination-storm-headquarters-of-rtvs-broadcaster/.
308. Committee to Protect Journalists, 'BBC news crew threatened by COVID-19 protesters in UK, 14 September 2021, Online: https://cpj.org/2021/09/bbc-news-crew-threatened-by-covid-19-protesters-in-uk/.
309. Wolfgang Vichtl, 'Dieser Hass muss endlich aufhören', *Tagesschau*, 1 August 2022, Online: https://www.tagesschau.de/ausland/europa/kellermayr-corona-aerztin-tot-103.html; Anna Tillack, 'Das ist nicht a bissl Shitstorm', ARD, 31 Januar 2022, Online: https://www.tagesschau.de/ausland/europa/oesterreich-impfgegner-101.html; and Colette M. Schmidt, 'Landärztin schließt nach Morddrohungen aus Impfgegnerszene Ordination', *Der Standard*, 28 Juni 2022, online: https://www.derstandard.de/consent/tcf/story/2000136994081/landaerztin-schliesst-nach-morddrohungen-aus-corona-massnahmen-und-impfgegner-szene.
310. Brian Friedberg, 'The Dark Virality of a Hollywood Blood-Harvesting Conspiracy', *Wired*, 31 July 2020, Online: https://www.wired.com/story/opinion-the-dark-virality-of-a-hollywood-blood-harvesting-conspiracy/.
311. Creede Newton, 'What is Qanon, the conspiracy theory spreading throughout the US', Al Jazeera, 8 October 2020, Online: https://www.aljazeera.com/news/2020/10/8/what-is-QAnon-the-conspiracy-theory-spreading-throughout-the-us.
312. https://www.theguardian.com/us-news/2020/aug/11/qanon-facebook-groups-growing-conspiracy-theory.
313. A study led by researchers from Oxford University showed that vaccinated people were less likely than unvaccinated people to spread the delta variant. Singaporean researchers who tracked viral loads found that vaccinated people with the Delta variant might remain infectious

for a shorter period of time. For more information see: Nidhi Subbaraman. 'How do vaccinated people spread Delta? What the science says', *Nature*, 12 August 2021, Online: https://www.nature.com/articles/d41586-021-02187-1.

314. Barney Davis, '"Covid denier" Gary Matthews dies from the virus alone day after testing positive', *Evening Standard*, 28 January 2021, Online: https://www.standard.co.uk/news/uk/covid-denier-gary-matthews-dies-b908310.html.

315. Steve Almasy, 'Man who dismissed Covid-19 and then survived it says he is an example for doubters', CNN, 13 October 2020, Online: https://edition.cnn.com/2020/10/12/health/texas-coronavirus-skeptic-turned-survivor-guilt/index.html.

316. Anders Anglesey, 'COVID-19 Deniers Event Leaves Host Dead, 12 Infected', *Newsweek*, 14 April 2021, Online: https://www.newsweek.com/covid-19-deniers-event-leaves-host-dead-12-infected-1583553.

317. Nick Lowles, Nick Ryan and Joe Mulhall, 'State of Hate 2022: On the March Again', Hope not Hate, March 2022, Online: https://hopenothate.org.uk/wp-content/uploads/2022/03/state-of-hate-2022-v1_17-March-update.pdf.

318. Michael Powell, 'Exposed: Leader of ex-Army group that's plotting mayhem as 200 members of a sinister anti-vax group meet in a Staffordshire park to practise smashing through police lines', *Daily Mail*, 9 January 2022, Online: https://www.dailymail.co.uk/news/article-10382723/Exposed-Leader-ex-Army-group-thats-plotting-mayhem.html; and Miles Dilworth, '"We need to target vaccine centres, schools, and councils": Inside the chilling anti-vax group where ex-soldiers are teaching hundreds to wage "war" on the government and preparing them for "direct action"', *Daily Mail*, 9 January 2022, Online: https://www.dailymail.co.uk/news/article-10384239/Alpha-Men-Assemble-Inside-anti-vax-group-members-taught-wage-war-government.html.

319. START, 'Qanon Offenders in the United States', START Research Brief. May 2021, Online: https://www.start.umd.edu/sites/default/files/publications/local_attachments/START%20QAnon%20Research%20Brief_5_26.pdf.

320. James Crowley, 'Artist Claims His Song Was Banned from Soundcloud for Qanon Similarities But Points Out That "F★★★ Tha Police" Is Still Available', *Newsweek*, 29 October 2020, Online: https://www.newsweek.com/artist-song-removed-soundcloud-QAnon-nwa-police-1543277.

321. Community Security Trust (CST), 'Coronavirus and the Plague of Antisemitism', CST Research Briefing, 2020, Online: https://cst.org.uk/data/file/d/9/Coronavirus%20and%20the%20plague%20of%20antisemitism.1586276450.pdf; and European Comission and ISD, 'The rise of antisemitism online during the pandemic', Publications Office of the European Union, 1 June 2021, Online: https://op.europa.eu/en/publication-detail/-/publication/d73c833f-c34c-11eb-a925-01aa75ed71a1/language-en.
322. CST, 'Antisemitic Incidents Report 2010', October 2010, Online: https://cst.org.uk/data/file/b/4/Incidents-Report-2010.1425052704.pdf.
323. CST, 'Antisemitic Incidents Report 2021', February 2022, Online: https://cst.org.uk/news/blog/2022/02/10/antisemitic-incidents-report-2021.
324. Anti-Defamation League (ADL), 'Financial Crisis Sparks Wave of Internet Anti-Semitism, ADL, October 2009, Online: https://www.adl.org/sites/default/files/documents/assets/pdf/anti-semitism/united-states/financial-crisis-sparks-internet-anti-semitism-2008-10-24.pdf.
325. For more details see: Jigsaw Research, 'News Consumption in the UK: 2022', Ofcom Report, 21 July 2022 online: https://www.ofcom.org.uk/__data/assets/pdf_file/0027/241947/News-Consumption-in-the-UK-2022-report.pdf.
326. Jeff Grabmeier, 'Fact-checking works across the globe to correct Misinformation', Phys Org, Ohio State University, 6 September 2021, Online: https://phys.org/news/2021-09-international-fact-significantly-belief-misinformation.html.
327. Amy Mackinnon, Robbie Gramer and Jack Detsch, 'Russia Planning Post-Invasion Arrest and Assassination Campaign in Ukraine, US Officials Say', *Foreign Affairs*, 18 February 2022, Online: https://foreignpolicy.com/2022/02/18/russia-ukraine-arrest-assassination-invasion/.
328. See Kharkiv Human Rights Protection Group: https://khpg.org/en/1412628810.
329. Lauren Fryer, 'Some LGBTQ Ukrainians are fleeing Russian occupation. Others are signing up to fight', NPR, 13 March 2022, Online: https://www.npr.org/2022/03/12/1086274340/ukraine-lgbtq?t=1649154629479.
330. Hélène Barthélemy, 'How the World Congress of Families serves Russian Orthodox political interests', Southern Poverty Law Center, 16 May 2018, Online: https://www.splcenter.org/hatewatch/2018/05/16/how-world-congress-families-serves-russian-orthodox-political-interests.

331. Amy Cheng, Putin slams "cancel culture" and trans rights, calling teaching gender fluidity a crime against humanity', *The Washington Post*, 22 October 2021, Online: https://www.washingtonpost.com/world/2021/10/22/putin-valdai-speech-trump-cancel-culture/.
332. Ezra Klein, 'The enemies of liberalism are showing us what it truly means', *The New York Times* International Edition, 5 April 2022, Online: https://www.nytimes.com/2022/04/03/opinion/putin-ukraine-liberalism.html.
333. Morgenpost, Live Blog on Ukraine, Update from Sunday 10 April, 1 p.m., Online: https://www.morgenpost.de/berlin/article234941541/berlin-ukraine-krieg-fluechtlinge-news-hauptbahnhof-aktuell-giffey.html; and Hubert Gude, 'Wie es zum, "Autokorso der Schande" kam', *Der Spiegel*, 5 April 2021. Online: https://www.spiegel.de/panorama/gesellschaft/berlin-wie-es-zum-autokorso-der-schande-kam-a-533f7b3f-bd87-49e3-b648-713bb7d4a6b4.
334. German original: 'Wann bist du aufgewacht?', 'Ich bin schon vor Covid aufgewacht' 'Mit der ganzen Scheiße und den Lügen, die uns erzählt wurden, hab ich schon geahnt dass irgendwas passieren wird', 'Ich hatte Delta. Mir ging's so schlecht. Ich hab geschworen, mich impfen zu lassen weil's so schlimm war. Ich wär fast draufgegangen. Zum Glück hatte ich sechs Monate Zeit, da hab ich erst gesehen was die Impfung wirklich ist.'
335. German original: 'Richtig geil, wir wachsen mehr und mehr', ' Seit ein paar Monaten. Wir haben noch andere Gruppen.'
336. See author's recording from min 18.50, German original: 'Das würde man nie bei einer Schwuchteln-Demo sehen.'
337. German original: 'Ich hoffe Russland wird ihre Bestreben umsetzen können. Ich hoffe auf einen russischen Sieg.'
338. German original: 'Lügenmärchen' and 'globale Ausführungseliten'.
339. Live footage of the conversation can be found at min. 52:30 in Anni and Martin's YouTube video: https://www.youtube.com/watch?v=zZfVZRTIykE.
340. German original: 'Darf ich Sie fragen wofür Sie heute demonstrieren?' 'Für die Meinungsfreiheit im weitesten Sinne. Denn die Berichterstattung über alle möglichen Themen wird in letzter Zeit immer einseitiger, besonders durch die homogenisierten Leitmedien. Damit mein ich nicht nur die öffentlich-rechtlichen, sondern auch die privaten. Bis auf ganz wenige Ausnahmen ist da die Richtung ähnlich.'
341. Cf. 'Mensch Putin!', ZDF documentary, February 2015. Online: https://www.zdf.de/dokumentation/zdfzeit/mensch-putin-100.html.

342. German original: 'Wer schlägt nicht seine Frau? Oder wie oft kommt das vor? Ist das jetzt ein Qualitätskriterium?' Live footage of the conversation can be found at min. 1:45 in Anni and Martin's YouTube video: https://www.youtube.com/watch?v=1CvlasK1_pg.
343. German original: 'Warum wollen Sie nicht vor der Kamera sprechen?', author's own audio files min 37.10.
344. Live footage from the conversation can be found at min. 01:01:02 in Anni and Martin's YouTube video: https://www.youtube.com/watch?v=zZfVZRTIykE, min 35.45. in author's own audio recordings. German original: 'Dann haben sie die Pandemie erfunden und den Krieg gegen das eigene Volk. Jetzt ist das eigene Volk aufgewacht und weil das eigene Volk aufgwacht ist brauchen sie eine weitere Krise.'
345. German original: 'ungespritzt'.
346. German original: 'Singles ungeimpft'.
347. German original: 'An alle Pädagogen, Politiker, Journalisten, Impfärzte, Polizisten und weitere Unterstützer die immer noch mitspielen. Fahrt zur Hölle.'
348. German original: 'Hey Gabriel, hier ist Mary (Maria) von der Demo heute. Würd mich freuen, wenn ich bei deiner Gruppe dabei sein darf.'
349. German original: 'Heyyyyy ☺' 'Na klar darfst du'. Zwinkersmiley.
350. 'DIESE WELT WIDERT MICH AN. ICH KANN MICH NICHT EINMAL DARAUF VERLASSEN WAS ICH ESSE, SEHE, TRINKE, HÖRE, ODER ATME. ALLES IST VOM SYSTEM VERGIFTET.'
351. ADL, 'New World Order', Glossary, 2022, Online: https://www.adl.org/resources/glossary-terms/new-world-order.
352. German original: 'Gestern reingestellt schon über 10.8K.'
353. German original: 'Putin ist von Anfang an gegen diese Satanisten NWO!' 'Weiter machen müssen wir sowieso, auch wenn wir gegen diese Impfpflicht etc. gewinnen. Es geht trotzdem noch weiter . . . Bis diese Satanisten ihre Verdiente Gerechte Strafe bekommen und es (hoffentlich) zu Neu Wahlen kommt mit AFD als Sieger.'
354. German original: 'Kein Grund aufzuhören! Dieses Terrorregime muss weg!'
355. 'Ukraine Krieg und Corona: 43 Prozent der Ungeimpften glauben an Ablenkung', NTV, 22 March 2022 https://amp.n-tv.de/panorama/43-Prozent-der-Ungeimpften-glauben-an-Ablenkung-article23214090.html, citing a study conducted by COSMO: https://projekte.uni-erfurt.de/cosmo2020/web/about/.

356. Pia Lamberty, Maheba Goedeke Tort and Corinne Heuer, 'Von der Krise zum Krieg: Verschörungserzählungen über den Angriffskrieg gegen die Ukraine in der Gesellschaft', CeMAS, 5 May 2022, Online https://cemas.io/publikationen/von-der-krise-zum-krieg-verschwoerungserzaehlungen-ueber-den-angriffskrieg-gegen-die-ukraine-in-der-gesellschaft/.
357. German original: 'WWG1WGA. Corona dient dazu alles zu hinterfragen, von der Maske bis hin zu unserer Geschichte. Mit Spielfilmen wurden wir darauf vorbereitet was jetzt auf uns zukommt. Wir bekommen über 6000 Patente freigegeben. Corona ist ein Intelligenz Test. Der Q-Plan next Level. Der Q-Plan. Das große Erwachen. Befreiung der Menschheit. Einführung von Nesara Gesara. Mit meiner Video Sammlung lernst Du den Q-Plan verstehen und kommst aus der Angst. Danke Dein Q74You.'
358. See for example Peter Pomerantsev, *This is Not Propaganda: Adventures in the War Against Reality* (London/N.Y.: Public Affairs, 2029) and Nina Jankowicz, *How to Lose the Information War: Russia, Fake News, and the Future of Conflict* (London/N.Y.: I.B. Tauris, 2020).
359. Alexander Laboda, '"Querdenker", Verschörungsideologien und der Krieg: "Ein Nährboden für faschistische Agitation", MDR Aktuell, 23 March 2022, Online: https://www.mdr.de/nachrichten/deutschland/politik/ukraine-krieg-querdenker-verschwoerungstheorien-100~amp.html.
360. Lars Wienand, 'Putins deutsche Infokriegerin', t-online, 19 April 2022, Online: https://www.t-online.de/nachrichten/ausland/id_91759336/alina-lipp-auf-telegramm-einst-bei-den-gruenen-jetzt-putins-infokriegerin-.html.
361. Julia Smirnova and Francesca Arcostanzo, 'German Language Disinformation About the Russian Invasion of Ukraine', ISD, March 2022. Online https://www.isdglobal.org/digital_dispatches/german-language-disinformation-about-the-russian-invasion-of-ukraine-on-facebook/.
362. Jason Paladino and Anya van Wagtendonk, 'Meet Patrick Lancaster: A U.S. Navy veteran from Missouri and Russia's favorite war propagandist', Grid, 18 April 2022, Online: https://www.grid.news/story/misinformation/2022/04/18/russias-favorite-war-propagandist-is-a-navy-veteran-from-missouri/.
363. German original: 'Impflicht gescheitert. Aber wer sind die überhaupt, das die über Menschen-Würde bestimmen dürfen . . . diese Satanisten. Die werden es NIEMALS schaffen bei den Nicht-Geimpfte, Gesunde Normaldenkende. Koste es was es wolle.'

364. German original: 'DIESE VERBRECHER WISSEN ES – und trotzdem wird das Gift weiter injiziert! Für mich sind Lauterbach und Konsorten MASSENMÖRDER.'
365. German original: 'Verbrecher Lauterbach' and 'MASKE = SKLAVEN MASKE! IMPFUNG = GIFT-TOT. CORONA = STARKE GRIPPE! NICHT MEHR NICHT WENIGER! WIEVIELE STERBEN AN NORMALE GRIPPE FRAU DOKTOR Vannila ?! Vergessen oder 0 Ahnung?! Hirn einschalten bitte! WIR SIND IM 3.WELTKRIEG! WERDEN NUR VERARACHT! RAFF ES ENDLICH!'
366. DPA/AFP, 'Entführung von Lauterbach gescheitert: Rechtsextremisten planten Anschlag', taz, 14 April 2022. Online: https://taz.de/Entfuehrung-von-Lauterbach-gescheitert/!5848838/.
367. M. Götschenberg, H. Schmidt and F. Bräutigam, 'Razzia wegen geplanten Staatsstreichs', Tagesschau, 7. December 2022, Online: https://www.tagesschau.de/investigativ/razzia-reichsbuerger-staatsstreich-101.html.
368. German original: 'Mein emotionales Vermögen reicht gar nicht für Hass gegen Russen im Moment.'
369. German original: 'Soziale Medien haben diesen krieg geprägt wie noch keinen anderen.'
370. German original: 'Wenn man sagen würde, es gibt in der Ukraine besonders viele Neonazis, ist das auf jeden Fall Propaganda.' 'In Russland gebe es nämlich viel mehr Neonazis als in der Ukraine'. See 'Extremismusforscher zu Putins Propaganda: In Russland gibt es viel mehr Neonazis als in der Ukraine', Deutschlandfunk, 11 March 2022. Online: https://www.deutschlandfunk.de/ritzmann-ukraine-rechtsexteme-asow-putin-propaganda-100.html.
371. The Soufan Center, 'White Supremacy Extremism: The Transnational Rise of the Violent White Supremacist Movement', September 2019, p.8., Online: https://thesoufancenter.org/research/white-supremacy-extremism-the-transnational-rise-of-the-violent-white-supremacist-movement/.
372. Tara John and Tim Lister, 'A far-right batallion has a key role in Ukraine's resistance. Its neo-Nazi history has been exploited by Putin', CNN, 30 March 2022, Online: https://edition.cnn.com/2022/03/29/europe/ukraine-azov-movement-far-right-intl-cmd/index.html.
373. 'Russia planning to deploy 1,000 Wagner mercenaries to eastern Ukraine, says UK's defence ministry', *Euronews* with AP, 29 March 2022, Online:

https://www.euronews.com/2022/03/29/russia-planning-to-deploy-1-000-wagner-mercenaries-to-eastern-ukraine-says-uk-s-defence-mi

374. Mark Townsend, 'Russian mercenaries in Ukraine linked to far-right extremists', the *Guardian*, 20 March 2022, Online: https://www.theguardian.com/world/2022/mar/20/russian-mercenaries-in-ukraine-linked-to-far-right-extremists.

375. Tom Ball, 'Rusich's neo-Nazi mercenaries head for Kharkiv', *The Times*, 7 April 2022, Online: https://www.thetimes.co.uk/article/rusichs-neo-nazi-mercenaries-head-for-kharkiv-prjndp9rl?utm_medium=Social&utm_source=Twitter#Echobox=1649340917.

376. Daniel De Simone, Andrei Soshnikov and Ali Winston, 'Neo-Nazi Rinaldo Nazzaro running US militant group The Base from Russia', BBC, 24 January 2020, Online: https://www.bbc.co.uk/news/world-51236915.

377. Mikhail Klimentov, 'Alleged Russian sting operation uncovers "The Sims 3", guns, grenade', *The Washington Post*, 26 April 2022, Online: https://www.washingtonpost.com/video-games/2022/04/26/russian-assassination-sims-3/.

378. Anne Applebaum, Peter Pomerantsev, Melanie Smith and Chloe Colliver, '"Make Germany Great Again": Kremlin, Alt-Right and International Influencers in the 2017 German Elections', ISD, December 2017, Online: https://www.isdglobal.org/wp-content/uploads/2017/12/Make-Germany-Great-Again-ENG-061217.pdf; and Chloe Colliver, Peter Pomerantsev, Anne Applebaum and Jonathan Birdwell, 'Smearing Sweden: International Influence Campaigns in the 2018 Swedish Election', ISD, October 2018, Online: https://www.isdglobal.org/isd-publications/smearing-sweden-international-influence-campaigns-in-the-2018-swedish-election/.

379. German original: 'Butscha – Wo sind die Beweise. Russland wird vorgeworfen, in der ukrainischen Stadt Butscha ca. 300 Zivilisten getötet zu haben. Doch Beweise gibt es dafür einfach mal gar keine.'

380. Pia Lamberty, Maheba Goedeke Tort and Corinne Heuer, 'Von der Krise zum Krieg: Verschörungserzählungen über den Angriffskrieg gegen die Ukraine in der Gesellschaft', CeMAS, 5 May 2022, Online https://cemas.io/publikationen/von-der-krise-zum-krieg-verschwoerungserzaehlungen-ueber-den-angriffskrieg-gegen-die-ukraine-in-der-gesellschaft/.

381. ADL, 'Unmasking "Clandestine", the Figure Behind the Viral "Ukrainian Biolab" Conspiracy Theory', ADL, 5 April 2022, Online:

https://www.adl.org/blog/unmasking-clandestine-the-figure-behind-the-viral-ukrainian-biolab-conspiracy-theory.
382. Elise Thomas, 'QAnon goes to China – via Russia', ISD Digital Dispatches, March 2022, Online: https://www.isdglobal.org/digital_dispatches/QAnon-goes-to-china-via-russia/.
383. 'Statistiken zur Akzeptanz von und zum Umgang mit Verschwörungstheorien in Deutschland', Statista, 10 March 2022, Online: https://de.statista.com/themen/7332/akzeptanz-von-und-umgang-mit-verschwoerungstheorien-in-deutschland/#dossierKeyfigures.
384. Joel Rose, 'Even If It's "Bonkers," Poll Finds Many Believe QAnon And Other Conspiracy Theories', NPR/Ipsos, 20 December 2020, Online: https://www.npr.org/2020/12/30/951095644/even-if-its-bonkers-poll-finds-many-believe-QAnon-andother-conspiracy-theories.
385. Nick Lowles, Nick Ryan and Joe Mulhall, 'State of Hate 2022: On the March Again', Hope not Hate, March 2022, Online: https://hopenothate.org.uk/wp-content/uploads/2022/03/state-of-hate-2022-v1_17-March-update.pdf.
386. Lynn Vandrasik, Robert Amour and Al Jones, 'White Hat, Black Hat, White Hat: QAnon Sentiment Towards Xi Jinping, March 2018-April 2022', Q Origins Project, April 2022, Online: https://qoriginsproject.org/white-hat-black-hat-white-hat-QAnon-sentiment-towards-xi-jinping-march-2018-to-april-2022/.
387. See original quote collected by The Q Origins Project: https://dchan.qorigins.org/qresearch/res/16168326.html#16168398
388. Sean Illing, '"Flood the zone with shit": How misinformation overwhelmed our democracy', *Vox*, 6 February 2020, Online: https://www.vox.com/policy-and-politics/2020/1/16/20991816/impeachment-trial-trump-bannon-misinformation.
389. Sergio Olmos, '"Key to white survival": how Putin has morphed into a far-right saviour', the *Guardian*, 5 March 2022, Online: https://www.theguardian.com/us-news/2022/mar/05/putin-ukraine-invasion-white-nationalists-far-right.
390. Ayesha Rascoe, 'Russian intellectual Aleksandr Dugin is also commonly known as "Putin's brain"', NPR, 27 March 2022, Online: https://www.npr.org/2022/03/27/1089047787/russian-intellectual-aleksandr-dugin-is-also-commonly-known-as-putins-brain.
391. Alexander Dugin, *The Great Awakening vs the Great Reset* (Arktos Media, 2021).

392. Ibid.
393. Tim Hume, 'How COVID "Truthers" Stirred Up a Culture War Over Drag Queen Readings', *VICE*, 31 August 2022, Online: https://www.vice.com/en/article/y3p38b/drag-queen-story-hour-covid.
394. Matthew Rose, *A World after Liberalism: Philosophers of the Radical Right* (N.Y.: Yale University Press, 2021).
395. Anne Applebaum, 'There Is No Liberal World Order', *The Atlantic*, 31 March 2022, Online: https://www.theatlantic.com/magazine/archive/2022/05/autocracy-could-destroy-democracy-russia-ukraine/629363/.
396. Ezra Klein, 'The Enemies of Liberalism Are Showing Us What It Really Means', *The New York Times*, 3 April 2022, Online: https://www.nytimes.com/2022/04/03/opinion/putin-ukraine-liberalism.html.
397. See https://twitter.com/AtlanticCouncil/status/1504095197185167368.
398. Cynthia Idriss-Miller, 'How Extremism Went Mainstream', Foreign Affairs, 3 January 2022, Online: https://www.foreignaffairs.com/articles/united-states/2022-01-03/how-extremism-went-mainstream?check_logged_in=1&utm_medium=promo_email&utm_source=lo_flows&utm_campaign=registered_user_welcome&utm_term=email_1&utm_content=20220124.
399. Milo Comerford and Sasha Havlicek, 'Mainstreamed Extremism and the Future', ISD, The Future of Extremism Series, Online https://www.isdglobal.org/wp-content/uploads/2021/10/ISD-Mainstreamed-Extremism-and-the-future-of-prevention-3.pdf.
400. Jacob Davey, 'Gamers Who Hate: An Introduction to ISD's Gaming and Extremism Series', ISD, September 2021, Online: https://www.isdglobal.org/isd-publications/gamers-who-hate-an-introduction-to-isds-gaming-and-extremism-series/.
401. Fernando H. Calderón et al., 'Linguistic Patterns for Code Word Resilient Hate Speech Identification', *Sensors* 21(23), December 2021: 7859, Online: https://www.ncbi.nlm.nih.gov/pmc/articles/PMC8659976/.
402. See Strong Cities Network: https://strongcitiesnetwork.org/en/.
403. Bond Benton and Daniela Peterka-Benton, 'Hating in plain sight: The hatejacking of brands by extremist groups', *Public Relations Inquiry*, Vol 9, No. 1 (2019): 7–26, Online: https://journals.sagepub.com/doi/10.1177/2046147X19863838.
404. Kevin McSpadden, 'You Now have a Shorter Attention Span Than a Goldfish', *TIME*, 14 May 2015, Online: https://time.com/3858309/attention-spans-goldfish/.

405. Philipp Lorenz-Spreen, Bjarke Morch Monsted, Philipp Hövel and Sune Lehmann, "Accelerating dynamics of collective attention", Nature Communications 10, No. 1759 (2019). BBC, "Busting the attention span myth", 10 March 2017, https://www.bbc.com/news/health-38896790.
406. See for example Moustafa Ayad, 'Islamogram: Salafism and Alt-Right Online Subcultures', 16 November 2021, Online: https://www.isdglobal.org/isd-publications/islamogram-salafism-and-alt-right-online-subcultures/; and Cristina Moreno-Almeida and Paolo Gerbaudo, 'Memes and the Moroccan Far-Right', *The International Journal of Press/Politics*, Vol. 26, No. 4 (2021): 882–906, Online: https://journals.sagepub.com/doi/pdf/10.1177/1940161221995083
407. Ala' Alrababa'h, William Marble, Salma Mousa and Alexandra A. Siegel, 'Can Exposure to Celebrities Reduce Prejudice? The Effect of Mohamed Salah on Islamophobic Behaviors and Attitudes', *American Political Science Review*, Vol. 115, No. 4 (2021), Online: https://www.cambridge.org/core/journals/american-political-science-review/article/can-exposure-to-celebrities-reduce-prejudice-the-effect-of-mohamed-salah-on-islamophobic-behaviors-and-attitudes/A1DA34F9F5BCE905850AC8FBAC78BE58.
408. See Facts for Friends website: https://www.factsforfriends.de/.
409. Pia Lamberty, Maheba Goedeke Tort and Corinne Heuer, 'Von der Krise zum Krieg: Verschwörungserzählungen über den Angriffskrieg gegen die Ukraine in der Gesellschaft', CeMAS, 5 May 2022, Online: https://cemas.io/publikationen/von-der-krise-zum-krieg-verschwoerungserzaehlungen-ueber-den-angriffskrieg-gegen-die-ukraine-in-der-gesellschaft/.
410. N. Grinberg, K. Joseph, L. Friedland, S. Swire-Thompson and D. Lazer, 'Fake news on Twitter during the 2016 US presidential election', *Science*, Vol. 363 (2019): 374–378, Online: https://www.science.org/doi/10.1126/science.aau2706.
411. A. Guess, J. Nagler, J. Tucker, 'Less than you think: Prevalence and predictors of fake news dissemination on Facebook', *Science Advances*, Vol. 5 (2019), Online: https://www.science.org/doi/10.1126/sciadv.aau4586.
412. Nadia M. Brashier and Daniel L. Schacter, 'Aging in an Era of Fake News', *Current Directions in Psychological Science*, Vol. 29, No. 3 (2020): 316–323, Online: https://journals.sagepub.com/doi/10.1177/0963721420915872.
413. Laura Garcia and Tommy Shane, 'A guide to prebunking: a promising way to inoculate against misinformation', First Draft, 29 June 2021,

Online: https://firstdraftnews.org/articles/a-guide-to-prebunking-a-promising-way-to-inoculate-against-misinformation/.
414. Jakob Guhl and Jacob Davey, 'Hosting the "Holohoax": A Snapshot of Holocaust Denial Across Social Media', ISD, 17 August 2020, Online: https://www.isdglobal.org/isd-publications/hosting-the-holohoax-a-snapshot-of-holocaust-denial-across-social-media/.
415. ISD, 'Bankrolling Bigotry: An Overview of the Online Funding Strategies of American Hate Groups', 27 October 2020, Online: https://www.isdglobal.org/isd-publications/bankrolling-bigotry/.
416. See DeepDAO.io.

Born in Vienna in 1991, Julia Ebner is a Senior Research Fellow at the Institute for Strategic Dialogue in London, where she leads projects on online extremism, disinformation and hate speech. She is the author of two previous books, the award-winning international bestsellers *Going Dark* and *The Rage*. She has given evidence to numerous governments and parliamentary working groups, and has acted as a consultant for the UN, NATO, and the World Bank. Her journalism has appeared in *The Guardian, Newsweek, Politico* and *Süddeutsche Zeitung*, among other publications, and she regularly contributes to broadcast news stories. Ebner holds a DPhil in Anthropology from the University of Oxford and is a Research Fellow at Oxford's Centre for the Study of Social Cohesion.